REPORT FROM PEKING

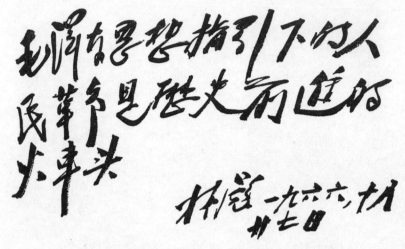

'Guided by Mao Tse-tung's thought, the people's revolution is the locomotive of historical progress' – Lin Piao, October 27, 1966 (reproduced in his own calligraphy).

REPORT FROM PEKING

Observations of a Western Diplomat on the Cultural Revolution

BY

D. W. FOKKEMA

MONTREAL
McGILL-QUEEN'S UNIVERSITY PRESS
1972

First published in Dutch, 1970, by
Uitgeverij de Arbeiderspers, Amsterdam, Netherlands
with the title *Standplaats Peking*

First published in the author's own English translation by
C. Hurst & Co. (Publishers) Ltd.
40a Royal Hill, Greenwich, London S.E.10

© 1971, by D. W. Fokkema

ISBN 0-7735-0146-0

Library of Congress Catalog Card No. 78-186299

Legal Deposit 1st quarter 1972

Printed in Great Britain by
Billing & Sons Limited, Guildford and London

FOREWORD

Between April 1966 and February 1968 I was working in the Office of the Netherlands Chargé d'Affaires in Peking, first as an Embassy Secretary, later as Chargé d'Affaires *ad interim*. When I left Peking, the Chinese authorities were aware of the fact that I had accepted a job in the academic world. A Chinese official urged me to inform the students about the Cultural Revolution.

I do not know whether this book, which I would have written without that encouragement, answers the Chinese expectations. However, I have tried to be fair. I am a convinced relativist and admit the partly arbitrary nature of my own presuppositions. I hope this will transpire from the text. But relativism does not necessarily mean renouncing one's own point of view. I saw no reason to revise my own hypotheses, convinced as I am that they provide at least as good a basis for social criticism and social reforms as does maoism.

If this may be a disappointment to the followers of Mao Tse-tung, it would have been more disappointing to them if I had remained silent and had joined those who prefer to ignore the People's Republic of China.

The book deals with the period 1966-69. It seemed natural to break off immediately after the Ninth Party Congress. Since then, I believe, nothing has happened that invalidates my conclusions. In fact, the communiqué of the recent session of the Central Committee, issued on September 6, 1970, confirms my view that China's belligerent terminology is often used in a metaphorical way; the Sino-Soviet border conflict developed along lines which also support that interpretation. One should distinguish clearly between China's actual foreign policy and her ideological proselytism which was greatly enhanced by the Cultural Revolution. Ideologically, China may become, or is already, an enormous challenge to European civilisation.

I should like to thank Mr. D. H. Landwehr of the Arbeiderspers, Amsterdam, for permitting an early English edition of the original Dutch book. I should also like to acknowledge my great debt to Mrs. Lucy Peters who kindly and patiently edited my English transla-

41800

tion. In other respects, too, this book is the result of a co-operative effort. I am very grateful for the straightforward and friendly exchanges of information that during the Cultural Revolution were customary among the few Chinese-reading diplomats in Peking.

University of Utrecht   DOUWE W. FOKKEMA
September 1970

CONTENTS

ILLUSTRATIONS

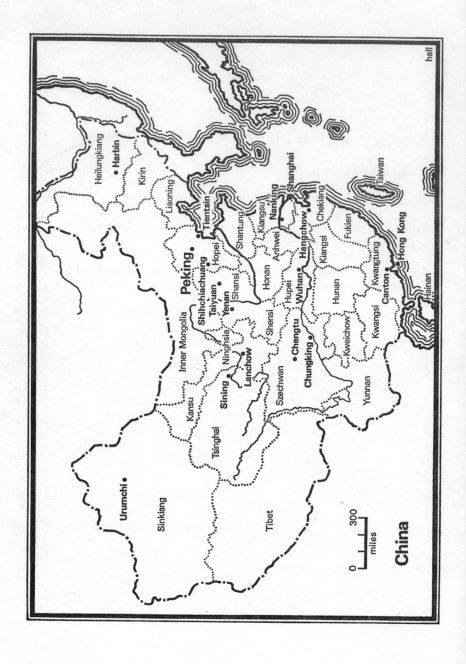

China

I

THE FIRST IMPRESSION:
SPRING 1966

The first impressions were largely sensory ones. I had never had a clear notion of the smells, the sounds and the colours of China.

In April we entered the People's Republic of China by the border at Shumchun, between Hong Kong and Canton. Our guide took care of the luggage. We walked over the railway bridge in no man's land behind a woman carrying her old lame mother on her back. The long cane of a cripple knocked against the railing of the bridge. Coolies passed us at the double. On the other side we were led first to the medical check-point. The Chinese asked me to act as interpreter for a French-speaking Algerian businessman on his way to the Spring Fair in Canton. In a spacious room, with chairs the covers of which had been washed a thousand times, we showed our vaccination certificates. The combination of the strange scent of an unknown brand of soap and the smell of lysol might have told a blind man that he was in China. 'Old China hands' have assured me that they are able to *smell* which shops in Hong Kong sell goods from the mainland.

Apart from the unknown scents, it is the space and tranquility that strike a traveller who has just left Hong Kong. The border formalities, although time-consuming, are carried out quietly and without fuss. There is no shouting or pushing at the counter where one changes money, as there is at the Polish-Russian border, and it is impossible to miss the train to Canton. The first-class passengers were led to deep armchairs (with crocheted antimacassars from grandmother's time on the white covers) and were offered extremely weak Chinese tea. A moment later the guide took us to the dining-room and, unsolicited, a Chinese lunch was served. We could choose between lemonade and beer. From the very first day I was intrigued by the Chinese attitude towards alcohol. Do Chinese citizens, as a rule, lack the money necessary for letting alcohol develop into a social evil? Or are the

Chinese communists perhaps less inclined by nature to puritanism? The positive appreciation of wine in the modern Peking opera *The Red Lantern* is rather curious. When the communist hero of this play knows he will be arrested, he gives himself dutch courage by drinking a cup of wine; at the same time this is a farewell ceremony. His mother and foster-daughter watch with approval.

In China it was an hour earlier than in Hong Kong. On the Chinese side of the border we felt as though we had time in abundance. In Hong Kong one anticipates the future. The skyscrapers in the centre of the city give an indication of what China may become, but for many people the development is too hurried. In Hong Kong past and future are curiously mixed. The Confucian scholar in his long gown goes to the supermarket. China seemed to be more orderly. Shumchun corresponded almost completely to the idyllic image of Chinese life that has been carefully built up by *China Pictorial*. The platform was clean, the tree trunks were painted white, the branches of the willows moved gently in the breeze, the customs staff in their trim, neat uniforms were lined up close to the train. They chatted with the train conductors and exchanged a few jokes. Then the music struck up, broad grins appeared on the faces and they began in a quiet and friendly way to wave good-bye. Slowly the train gathered speed. We passed some posters, card-playing workers, a gated level crossing, a village square and finally several clusters of banana trees and the luxuriantly green fields where rice was being cultivated.

In Canton we had three hours to spend before the Peking train was due to leave. I believe that the guide and the interpreter who waited for us would have loved to stow us away in one of the stuffy waiting-rooms which the larger Chinese railway stations seem to possess in abundance. I wonder who used these rooms in former times. An old-fashioned sideboard, a ewer and wash-basin are standard equipment, as are covers and crocheted antimacassars on the chairs. Of course, the waiting-room for the common people looks very different.

My wife and I were determined to see something of the town. A taxi which drove slowly and sounded its horn almost continuously drove us through the quiet outskirts of Canton to the Four Martyrs Memorial Park. After some consultations the girl who acted as our interpreter had been able to organise this for us. It was indeed a complicated affair. Her English was not at all fluent, and when our conversation flagged a charming wrinkle appeared on her forehead. Politically she seemed to be very loyal, but of what use can people be to the régime who are only loyal and not very bright? If the party is consistently to continue its anti-intellectual policies, it inevitably runs the risk of eventually being taken over by the few gifted people who will come forward from the proletariat. The leaders of the 'great proletarian cultural revolution' were probably fearing not so much a restoration of capitalism as a restoration of intellect.

The park, which was dedicated to the memory of four martyrs of the Kuomintang terror, is one of the less interesting sights of Canton. We had wanted to see the narrow streets in the old city, but we did not succeed. We passed the Sun Yat-sen Memorial Hall and the Fair, and finally drove back to the station along the Pearl River with its many sampans which often provide permanent living quarters.

Travelling by train at night is always fascinating. I usually wake up at every stop. German stations are distinguished by too much light and noise; the loudspeakers wake you up with their '*Umsteigen, bitte*' and '*Der Zug nach Basel fährt jetzt ab.*' In Russia one is awakened by long stops, or sirens, or the lights of blast furnaces and factories far away from the cities, which loom up mysteriously out of the darkness. The first stretch of the Canton-Peking journey which is through mountains, was covered during the night. I woke up when we stopped at a small station. A great many impatient Chinese were waiting behind a wooden gate and there seemed to be enough of them to push and shove, but there was no pushing or shoving. When the gate finally opened, they showed their tickets to the inspectors at both sides of the entrance. A young woman with a white mask over her mouth made certain that no one escaped the ticket inspection. The waiting-room was quickly empty, and in a great hurry but without confusion everyone tried to find a place for himself and his bundles of luggage in the carriages with the hard benches, or, as we would say, in the second-class. At this station, two thousand miles from the Soviet Union, there was a banner saying 'Long live the unity of the peoples of the countries of the socialist camp'.

The journey went fast. When we were between Hengyang and Chuchow the sun rose. The scenery south of the Yangtze was variegated, with hills, rivers, villages – sometimes consisting of no more than a few houses, small lakes and pools in which geese swam, and water-buffaloes up to their necks in water. We saw the things we had read about: the farmers who with forks and spades were levelling off a hill, long rows of wheelbarrows made from large bicycle-wheels, women with baskets loaded with soil or coal, ox-carts, and at times a lorry which drove over dusty gravel roads. New roads were being built, concrete piers could be seen rising from a river. The road was almost ready, but the bridge was still uncompleted. It seemed symbolic of China.

Sometimes our expectations far exceeded the reality. After having heard so much about the Yangtze River, it did not seem to be very wide when we saw it near Wuhan. The descriptions of China, which I had read in the Western press, on the whole appeared to give too pessimistic an impression. China was cleaner and less poor than I had thought it would be. On Sundays the people ate ice cream and drank fizzy lemonade, and in the intervals at football matches they would buy eggs, bread or apples. In the big cities before the Cultural Revolution there were traces of luxury. Sometimes a vice-minister of foreign affairs came to the International Club in Peking and danced a waltz or a tango. Another vice-minister frequented the tennis court of the International Club. In the train we met a small upper-class boy who wore seven sweaters and was playing with a toy gun. He seemed to be travelling to visit an aunt, accompanied by his father. For a while he made friends with my son, and the wooden gun was temporarily exchanged for an American-made toy dog.

North of the Yangtze the scenery changed fast. In the distance we saw mountains and closer were small hills intersected by sandy river beds that were usually completely dry. The next morning we awoke in the midst of an endless barren sand-coloured plain. Here and there groups of people were digging ditches. I wondered where they lived. The distances between the villages were large and sometimes no houses were visible. The grain, sown in long straight furrows, had just come up, and the branches of the trees were in bud. In the middle of this plain, where within a few weeks everything would be green, suddenly we were at Peking. There were friends who had come to welcome us, and the gigantic square in front of the station seemed suffused in a veiled light under a grey-beige sky that was still coloured by the dust and sand raised by a storm the day before.

Beginning of the Cultural Revolucion

Our arrival in Peking coincided with the launching of an ideological campaign. On the day before, April 19, 1966, a 'great socialist cultural revolution' was announced in an editorial in the *People's Daily*. The criticism of the historian and vice-mayor of Peking, Wu Han, which had assumed a biting tone since Yao Wen-yüan's critique of November 1965, became a political issue of the first order. As the author of the historical drama *The Dismissal of Hai Jui*, Wu Han was accused of having advocated a review of the case for the dismissal of the Minister of Defence, P'eng Te-huai, in 1959, who had been outspoken in his opposition to the Great Leap Forward and the people's communes and was under suspicion of being sympathetic towards Soviet policies. From the very beginning the shadow of P'eng Te-huai loomed large over the Cultural Revolution; also Teng T'o, one of the secretaries of the party committee of Peking, and Liao Mo-sha, both of whom, in co-operation with Wu Han, had published a great number of critical essays mainly in 1961 and 1962, were accused of revisionism. Soon more intellectuals were attacked, with criticism focused on the film industry. Even party ideologists of long standing were not immune from the seemingly genuine anger of the masses.

Initially the reason for the new campaign against every aspect of intellectualism was not at all clear. It seemed to do no more than continue from the repudiation of the philosopher Yang Hsien-chen, the critic Shao Ch'üan-lin and the art historian Chou Ku-ch'eng which had taken place in 1964 and 1965. It made use of old arguments dating from 1960 and even 1957, and revived maoist themes from 1942. However, when on June 3 the dismissal of P'eng Chen, First Secretary of the Party Committee of Peking, was announced, and on July 1 Chou Yang, Vice-Director of the Propaganda Department of the Communist Party and entrusted with supervising literary affairs, was attacked in the *People's Daily*, one had good reason to believe that in the higher regions of the party a power struggle had developed. This could explain the vehemence of the campaign, but not the campaign itself.[1]

On May the First we watched the fireworks, of which the Chinese are known to be masters, on the square in front of the Gate of Heavenly Peace. The first round amazed us, but as the 'bouquets of many-coloured chrysanthemums', 'butterflies on peonies', 'geese flying over the grain' followed each other endlessly, it became an effort to continue showing the admiration that was expected of one. There was no logical sequence, and no climax. In the same way we cannot expect that the Chinese authorities are drawing clear-cut conclusions from a rectification campaign aimed at intellectuals, or that those who participate in such a campaign reach the same logical conclusions as East European intellectuals in an analogous situation. In China the campaigns against the intelligentsia may be repeated again and again; they may be based on the same old patterns, and it is doubtful whether in 1966 many people wondered why the 'anti-socialist' publications of five years earlier had not been conclusively exposed before. In China the opposition to 'the dictatorship of the proletariat' is completely different from resistance in the East European countries or the Soviet Union. It is often comparable to the bamboo that bends in the storm and raises itself again when the wind has subsided.

During the first weeks we did not take much notice of the Cultural Revolution and looked at remnants of the old China. We visited a Lama temple in the north-eastern quarter of Peking, where a middle-aged monk in a wine-red robe showed us around. At a distance we were followed by an old Tibetan in a grey-black habit. Here it was completely quiet. The temple precinct was shaded by old pine-trees, and bells tinkled in the wind, but apart from the twittering birds and our two guides no living soul was to be seen. The other monks were working on a farm in the country, and the buddhist statues and offerings were covered with a thick layer of dust. We also visited the mosque on Northern Tung-szu Avenue where we were received by an imam, who had made the pilgrimage to Mecca. There were two big mosques in Peking, in which prayers were being said more or less regularly. Arabic could be studied at Peking University, and the 'Islamic Association' organised courses in the knowledge of the Koran for future religious leaders. The imam recited several quotations from it which were painted in Arabic orthography on the whitewashed walls. Here too the yard was quiet. Near the entrance we saw a washroom in which there were several old Chinese men who were wearing skull caps; they seemed to have found a restful meeting-place.

Special permission was required to visit the Lama temple and the mosque. But we could go freely to the Temple of Heaven in the southern part of the town, or to the temples at the foot of the 'Western Hills', the tombs of the Ming emperors and even the Great Wall. In the Western Hills we were allowed to follow the narrow footpaths between the temples. One of the most beautiful of these is the eighteenth-century Indian-style Diamond Throne Pagoda in the Temple of the Azure Clouds. Here and elsewhere in the Western Hills you could encounter a solitary walker who had fled from the bustle of the city, and as you climbed some steep trail, you might unexpectedly hear a nostalgic tune from an old Chinese opera. The

Chinese habit of seeking solitude among cliffs and pine-trees did not seem to have changed.

In early June the newspapers were filled with criticism of Lu P'ing, President of Peking University. The University has always been a centre of progressive ideas and unrest, even under the communist régime, and notably in 1957. The students, who publicised their grievances in big-character posters, complained that too few lectures were devoted to the thoughts of Chairman Mao, and that the professors who should have dealt with Mao Tse-tung's works had no respect for the maoist ideology. Apart from this substantial grievance, there was a problem of authority. Different orders were given through parallel hierarchical channels, and with hindsight it is possible to conclude that the action and conteraction in the University in May 1966 was fed by a power struggle between two political groups: the supporters of the Minister of Defence Lin Piao, Ch'en Po-ta and K'ang Sheng on the one hand, and those of Liu Shao-ch'i, P'eng Chen, Teng T'o and Chou Yang on the other. Rumour had it that six instructors, led by Nieh Yüan-tzu, a lecturer in philosophy, had prepared a poster which decried the University authorities for having failed to support the Cultural Revolution, but when they put up their poster on the wall of the dining hall, others interfered and tore it up shouting: 'This is not the party line!'

Perhaps it was not yet the party line at that particular moment, but as soon as the First Secretary of the Party Committee of Peking, P'eng Chen, was dismissed and the wall newspaper of Nieh Yüan-tzu on the special instructions of Mao Tse-tung had been published in the *People's Daily* of June 2, the writing of big-character posters became in fact the party line. The criticism of Lu P'ing, according to the *People's Daily*, boiled down to accusations that he had banned big-character posters from the campus, and that he had wanted to organise only closed discussion groups under the guidance of the Cultural Revolution teams that had been sent by P'eng Chen and no large public meetings; in short, that he had wanted to stifle the Cultural Revolution.

Of course, there is an essential difference between arguments in big characters which inevitably convey little more than slogans, and statements in normal-size writing or print. It is the same difference that exists between shouting and speaking, or between emotion and reason. Big-character posters are the weapons of the emotionalised masses – of people who have learned their letters but who cannot write an essay.

On June 3, towards the end of the afternoon, I happened to pass the People's University of Peking, an institution which takes care of the ideological education of cadres and promising workers. The students at this University are usually somewhat older than the average student. Imitating the students of Peking University they were pasting on the walls pink posters, printed with big black characters. Half an hour later I learned that the news had been broadcast that P'eng Chen had lost his position as First Secretary of the Party Committee of Peking, or, to be more precise, it had only been announced that Li Hsüeh-feng had been appointed First Secretary. For the time being there was no word about P'eng Chen. The next day the newspapers announced that 'the Central Committee of the Chinese Communist Party had decided to change the composition of the party committee of Peking'. This news was the signal that started mass demonstrations in support of the wise decision of the Central Committee and in honour of Chairman Mao and the Communist Party.

In no other world capital would one take the car to have a look at such demonstrations. One would drive one's car into the garage as fast as possible, stay at home and lock the door. In those days demonstrations were still quite orderly in Peking. The International Club, with its swimming pool and tennis courts, was situated in front of the headquarters of the Peking party organisation. By the end of the afternoon the Austins, Chevrolets and Citroëns were driving to and fro. They had to park just in front of the flight of steps where the new party committee stood and listened to vociferous expressions of loyalty. The traffic police often had to break up the long rows of demonstrators in order to enable a foreign diplomat to arrive or leave. In this, the police were politeness itself, and no one seemed disturbed by the incongruity of this civility and the meaning of the slogans that were chanted to the deafening accompaniment of drums and cymbals. The active young organisers even made arrangements for foreigners who wanted to take pictures. They were willing to halt a procession, and told the demonstrators to straighten their backs and to raise higher the framed portrait of Chairman Mao, carried in front of each of the groups.

The demonstrators varied from schoolchildren to workers of differing ages. The girls of primary school age had their cheeks painted red, and not only the schoolchildren, but also adults did not appear to consider having to demonstrate a burden. After all, it meant having a morning or afternoon free from their routine work. Moreover, the weather was beautiful, and not yet too hot. Those who had been appointed to play the cymbals and drums did it with great energy and sounded their beat through the streets, sometimes drowned out by larger groups who were going in the opposite direction or temporarily deafened by a lorry that carried passengers who produced a louder rhythm. The others, chatting and laughing, followed the music. The episode in front of the party building seemed no more than an interlude of no great importance. The chanting was punctuated by the raising of fists, but there seemed to be little enthusiasm.

Although there were continuous shouts of 'Long live Chairman Mao', 'Long live the Communist Party', 'Long live the new party committee', 'Down with the counter-revolutionary revisionists', apparently many did not understand why they were demonstrating. Peking was not yet inclined to take the demonstrations seriously.

Permanent Demonstrations and a Mass Trial

This lack of seriousness was noticed not only by us foreigners, but also by the party leaders. They took two measures to convince the indifferent masses of the gravity of the situation. They decided that the demonstrations, which were mainly carried out by young people, were to continue also during the night with the exception of a short interval between four and six o'clock in the morning. From then on, one could see boys and girls hurrying on bicycles to the rallying points at any time of the night, often carrying a friend holding a red flag on the back.

More effective was the dramatically staged conviction of the nine-teen-year-old Yang Kuo-ching, a 'counter-revolutionary', who on April 29 had stabbed two foreigners. According to the official Chinese view, he had hoped to create a diplomatic incident which would embarrass the Chinese government. On June 13 the verdict and judicial considerations were proclaimed in the Workers' Stadium on the Northern Kung-jen-t'i-yü-ch'ang Road in the presence of about 13,000 people. The meeting, fragments of which were televised, recalled the mass trials shortly after the communist take-over. The defendant was led before the crowd escorted by three policemen, and repeated close-ups on the television screen showed how strong the hands were that rested on the shoulders of the young man. The latter bowed his head and, seemingly without emotion, submitted to the judicial anger and to the fury of the masses. He seemed to represent weakness, in contradiction to his guards and the endless rows of fists raised at every slogan shouted in support of the speech of the President of the Supreme People's Court Yang Hsiu-feng. The latter emphasised that the crime of the counter-revolutionary criminal Yang Kuo-ching was no isolated case, but a result of the class struggle. The television commentator again and again repeated the word 'counter-revolutionary' and thereby put heavy emphasis on the political aspect of the trial.

The slogans that were chanted in chorus, such as 'Never forget the class struggle' and 'Down with the counter-revolutionaries', frightened the public, who themselves then participated in producing further terror. After the death sentence had been pronounced, the accused was led away and immediately executed. The effect of this mass trial was not only terror, but also the complicity of the spectators. Rumour has it that several months later the President of the Supreme People's Court committed suicide.

This mass trial completely changed the atmosphere among the demonstrators. As it was expressed in the *Red Flag* of June 8, the new ideological campaign was to be considered a life and death struggle.

Several days later we were invited to a large dinner in the restaurant at the Summer Palace, half an hour's journey outside Peking. The park was almost completely deserted and we could imagine ourselves being the heirs of the age-old Chinese art of living. Two boats waited for us and, as in the late light of the setting sun two boatmen rowed us over the lake, we toasted the farewell of a colleague. A rare bird called, crickets chirped. On the landing pier several old men were sitting quietly and day-dreaming. For us, that night meant a boisterous dance near the former apartments of the Empress-Dowager Tz'u Hsi. The Chinese servants were amused by the eccentric movements of the foreigners. Inevitably the idea forced itself on us, that it was not they but we who were behaving strangely.

When leaving around midnight, we walked through the seemingly endless gallery near the shore of the lake. All was deathly quiet. When we passed a house, someone moved the curtain and looked to see who was still out so late at night. We were glad the gates of the park were still open.

On our way home we drove through the centre of the city. The drums sounded from afar. Open lorries which were decorated with slogans and packed with demonstrators drove up and down. Spotlights illuminated the party building and the shouting crowd that had gathered in front of it. Even with the aid of the police, it was difficult to make one's way through the demonstrators who were joined again and again by new groups. It appeared to be serious now. We saw the unscrupulous manipulation, which aims at the realisation of the communist ideal and almost never reaches farther than continuous revolution.

During the beginning of the Cultural Revolution one could hardly take the accusations seriously. What were called revisionist misconceptions, often appeared to be expressions of common sense. For example, the criticism of Teng T'o did not have a strong ideological basis. How could a sincere communist be opposed to Teng T'o's exhortation not to be satisfied with copying quotations from the works of Chairman Mao, but to try to understand the meaning of Mao Tse-tung's words within their original historical context? Teng T'o gave this advice in a speech to young writers on January 12, 1966. On this occasion he also advised ignoring a suggestion to limit one's writing to subject-matter with official blessing. (According to his critics this suggestion originated with Lin Piao.) 'Do not trust the authority of the leaders blindly,' Teng T'o reportedly said. His opponents resented this position and caused it to boomerang against him. In the campaign against the old party committee of Peking, warnings not to trust the authority of cadres and professors were heard over and over again. It went without saying that the distrust should apply only in the case of the less orthodox authorities, that is the opponents of the Cultural Revolution.

If the actual disagreements among China's élite appear to be rather unimportant, we may wonder why so much energy was expended in the rectification campaign that made up the Cultural Revolution, and also whether the suffering that it caused to so many Chinese was worthwhile. Perhaps an answer may be found in a letter of Lin Piao which was printed in the Chinese press on June 19. Lin Piao pointed out that the great socialist China with its 700 million inhabitants should be of one soul and one mind: 'It needs unified thinking, revolutionary thinking, correct thinking.' And the only ideology to fit the need was the thought of Chairman Mao. When formulating this thesis, Lin Piao was probably guided by an exaggerated fear of opposition, of erosion of the people's loyalty and, in the last instance, of an erosion of the great Chinese empire. We would call this fear exaggerated, but it must be interpreted against the background of the Chinese past.

Indeed, initially the Cultural Revolution appeared to be a repetition of earlier rectification campaigns and it had certain imperfections in common with the other campaigns. Not everything was perfectly arranged and co-ordinated. In early June it was still possible to buy texts of the speeches of P'eng Chen who had been dismissed in May. Films which were criticised in the press continued to be shown in the cinemas. The Chinese people accepted the new leaders and were prepared to pay them homage, as was apparent from the demonstrations in Peking in June 1966. Apart from this, life went on. The street-vendors sold their ice cream, policemen regulated the traffic, and as always the people sauntered through Wang-fu-ching, the shopping street of Peking. The peasants went about their reaping, threshing and winnowing, and if someone was reading the works of Chairman Mao to them, they must have considered it a curiosity. Precisely as in all the past years, they spread grain on the road and let the carts, lorries and buses drive over it, which saved them some of the work of threshing.

However, a rectification campaign is not a natural phenomenon to be accepted as a matter of course. It is also not the result of perpetual motion that rotates in isolation on its axis. Present-day China is a reaction to a long history of contact with the West. In origin a product of the West, communism in China is an answer to Western politics and the Western way of life. We may find the Chinese reaction irrational and exaggerated, but we should not forget that in the past Western and Japanese activities in China were often marked by irrational exaggeration, and that the Chinese leaders remember too well a period that is a bygone age to us. Their *current* politics are attuned to our *past*.

REFERENCE

1. On May 16, 1966, the Central Committee of the Chinese Communist Party, in a circular letter to all regional, provincial and municipal party committees, accused P'eng Chen of high-handedness as a member of the 'group of five in charge of the Cultural Revolution'. In particular, P'eng Chen's mistake had been not to have consulted K'ang Sheng, who also was a member of the 'group of five', on important matters concerning an 'Outline Report on the Current Academic Discussion' of February 12, 1966. Apart from this, the circular letter criticised P'eng Chen's attempt to launch a 'rectification campaign' against the extreme Left. The circular letter was published by the official Chinese News Agency Hsinhua only on May 16, 1967.

2

RISE OF THE RED GUARD:
SUMMER 1966

There were English lessons on television: *Before liberation, very few children attended school; Hainan is the second largest Chinese island* (Formosa is bigger); *When morning came, the brave scouts found themselves deep behind enemy lines*. The construction of two nouns in succession as in *enemy lines* was explained with some more examples such as *party member, U.S. imperialism, paper tiger, army discipline*. The teacher was a friendly, somewhat slow young man who repeated the sentences three times. Sometimes he was relieved by a bespectacled girl with pigtails who, in contrast to the girl announcers, was certainly no beauty. The lesson usually took one hour or more, and since it lacked any variation, I regarded it as free from bourgeois taint. However, the principles of teaching a foreign language were soon to be re-evaluated, and during August the English lessons disappeared from the television programmes. Behind this was a purely political decision.

Chauvinism

The chauvinistic aspects of the Chinese revolution have always been important, but in July and August 1966 they became more evident. The campaign for the promotion of the art of swimming, which was highly stimulated by the personal example of Chairman Mao, aimed not only at the physical training of the Chinese people, but also at overcoming a natural fear of water and a sense of shame. Individual swimming, which amounts to unimpeded movement through water, instills a feeling of liberty which promotes self-consciousness. One might assume that collective swimming enhances the national self-consciousness. Whether or not it is true that, as reported in the *People's Daily* of July 25, the seventy-two-year-old Mao Tse-tung swam for sixty-five minutes in the Yangtze and covered fifteen kilometres, is of secondary importance. In fact I am inclined to believe it, since he was swimming downstream. What is important is that in imitation of the Chairman the campaign for swimming immediately assumed enormous proportions. On July 31 eight thousand people (the press said *healthy people*) swam across the lake at the Summer Palace. They took large boards with political slogans and portraits of Mao Tse-tung with them on rafts. Soldiers swam in uniform with tree branches for camouflage around their heads. They were pushing machine guns on floats and raised their fists while shouting slogans.

The very same day Mao Tse-tung, who had stayed in Shanghai and Hangchow for many months, visited a reception for the participants of an International Physics Congress in Peking. His presence had the effect of an electric shock. The words *Mao chu-hsi lai le* (Here comes Chairman Mao) were pronounced by the television commentator with the same exaltation as *Christ has risen* would be said during an Orthodox Easter celebration.

From August 1 to 12 Mao Tse-tung attended a meeting of the Central Committee which, after an interval of four years, had been finally convened. This was the eleventh session since 1956. It appeared from television transmissions that he played an important role at this session, and the final communiqué indicated that he had presided over the meeting. On the television screen one saw Mao Tse-tung as an old man in a rattan chair who addressed the audience in a friendly way. There was no gavel, no desk, no papers in his hand, and no direct transmission of his speech. Only a few people in Peking understand his Hunanese dialect, but this is not the only disadvantage of the simultaneous transmission of picture and sound. As a contrast, Lin Piao appeared on the screen, bespectacled and bald-headed, as he read a report. The audience was hardly shown. It is thought that almost half the members of the Central Committee were absent for one reason or another. Chou En-lai and Liu Shao-ch'i were present. In November, notably in Canton, wall newspapers appeared which suggested that Chairman Mao, Lin Piao and their supporters had been in the minority at the eleventh session, but in the calculation of the voting the absentees were probably counted as opponents of Mao. On the basis of later revelations we know that at the eleventh session Liu Shao-ch'i was criticised, Lin Piao was designated as the future successor of Mao Tse-tung, and a standing committee of the Politburo was elected.

On August 9 and 13 the results of the consultations of the Central Committee were proclaimed in, respectively, a resolution of 'sixteen points' and a final communiqué. These caused great excitement in diplomatic circles. The resolution seemed to call for moderation in the Cultural Revolution. It appealed to the intellectuals and technicians to serve the fatherland, to do 'positive' work, and not to oppose the party and socialism – in that order. The intelligentsia should abstain from 'illicit relations with foreign countries' in order to keep nearer to an ideal of intellectual autarchy. In exchange for their loyalty the intellectuals were assured that 'those who would provide a positive contribution would be protected'. They would be helped to change their world outlook gradually.

It sounded like moderation, and the only diplomats in Peking who warned against optimism were the Eastern Europeans. They recognised the element of xenophobia, which reminded them of the Zhdanovian cultural policies in stalinist Russia. 'In fact nothing has changed,' they said. 'The Chinese leaders are only trying to prevent the economy from being jeopardised by the Cultural Revolution.'

The critical reader will wonder who these leaders were. Thanks to Mao Tse-tung, Lin Piao had been raised to the number-two position in China. They probably persuaded Premier Chou En-lai to side with them, after promising that the Cultural Revolution was to have no serious effects on the nation's economy or foreign policy.

The impression that the Central Committee had decided in favour of a moderate economic policy was confirmed by the final communiqué, which emphasised a certain continuity. It said that the people's communes had been further developed and consolidated, and it recalled the Great Leap Forward of 1958–60 by predicting 'a new all-round leap forward' which, however, was not called 'great'. That for the time being foreign policy too was to be left alone, appeared from the modest ambitions in this field, in the description of which one could hear a vague echo of Stalin's 'socialism on one country'; 'We must do a good job of building socialist China, which has a quarter of the world's population, and make it an impregnable state of the proletariat that will never change its colour.' Of course, the ambition of exporting the maoist system was not sacrificed, but the Central Committee seemed to acquiesce in a temporisation of the foreign aspirations. The natural counterpart of this attitude was a tendency towards chauvinism.

On August 10 Chairman Mao addressed the young people who had come to the office of the Central Committee in order to express their support for the 'Sixteen Points'. On that occasion he spoke the now famous words: 'You must concern yourselves with state affairs and carry the great proletarian cultural revolution through to the end.' Here, too, the order is important. Several days earlier, the *People's Daily* was even more outspoken: 'We are not ashamed that our people are a great people, that our country is a great country, and that our army is a great army.' Later it appeared from wall newspapers that Lin Piao, in a speech, had touched on the question of China's sense of inferiority. 'We have no reason to feel inferior,' he is reported to have said, 'for we have our great teacher, leader, commander and helmsman, Chairman Mao.'

The propaganda media launched the idea that Mao Tse-tung was to be the saviour not only of China but of humanity as a whole. In a televised propaganda show, the portrait of Chairman Mao, surrounded by a halo of moving rays of light and enlarged to superhuman proportions, was projected over a chorus of several hundred people. The red handkerchiefs, which the girl dancers used to hold in their hands, had been replaced by extraordinary large dummies of the selected works of the Chairman. Mao was considered the contemporary Lenin, or 'the greatest genius of the present era', and the word 'maoism' (Chinese: *Mao-tse-tung-chu-i*), which was used in several posters but not in the official press, raised the thought of Mao Tse-tung to the same level as marxism and leninism. Extremely popular was a coloured poster that showed the proletariat, with representatives of the various continents in the front rank, marching onwards under the inspiring guidance of Mao Tse-tung.

First Appearance of the Red Guard

Even before the eleventh session of the Central Committee, Lin Piao and Mao Tse-tung had achieved a number of political successes. In collaboration with Ch'en Po-ta and K'ang Sheng, they arranged the replacement of Chou Yang and his boss Lu Ting-i, Director of the Propaganda Department of the Central Committee. On July 9 it was announced that T'ao Chu, First Secretary of the Central-South Bureau of the Central Committee, had succeeded Lu Ting-i. Three weeks later it appeared that the latter, who since early 1965 was also Minister of Culture, had been forced to abandon this function as well. Moreover, Lin Piao managed to dismiss the Chief of Staff Lo Jui-ch'ing in July, or earlier. The name of his successor, Yang Ch'eng-wu (who was to fall into disgrace in 1968), was casually mentioned in the *People's Daily* of August 1. However strong Lin Piao's position may have been, as a result of these sudden changes he must also have made additional enemies. If in August the decisions of the Central Committee were the result of some compromise, Lin Piao and Mao were forced to accept them for tactical reasons. But they did not appear to have any intention of resigning themselves to this compromise.

It is not known whether Lin Piao or Mao Tse-tung told the meeting of the Central Committee of the formation of the Red Guard, which appeared in public for the first time on August 18. Even if they did, few people will have suspected the role the Red Guard was to play. Since the younger generation had shown little interest in the former ideals of the communist establishment, it was only natural that the older leaders were worried. Lin Piao and Mao Tse-tung wanted to interest the young people in revolution by letting them participate in one. Perhaps they were insufficiently aware of the fact that they could give them only an *ersatz* revolution, since the Cultural Revolution was unleashed by the people in power.

On August 18, in the Square of Heavenly Peace, a demonstration was held of one million, mainly young, people. Loudly shouting their slogans they marched past Mao Tse-tung and Lin Piao, who were for the first time decorated with red armbands on which were written the characters *hung-wei-ping* (member of the Red Guard). Young people whose fathers and grandfathers had been full-blooded proletarians were immediately allowed to wear such an armband. These people were the future of the revolution and stood firmly on the side of Mao Tse-tung. Their task was to wipe out all bourgeois remnants, to destroy bureaucracy and to struggle against vested interests. Their first actions were iconoclastic.

One of the more harmless aspects of this iconoclasm was the changing of street names. The remnants of a feudal and religious past had to be destroyed. Street names which recalled the existence of a town gate or temple were changed into *Revolutionary rebellion* or *The red heart devoted to the party*, and the like. The road, on which the North Vietnamese Embassy (as well as the Office of the British Chargé d'Affaires) was situated, was renamed *Support Vietnam Road*. The name of the road to the Soviet Embassy was christened *Anti-revisionism Road*. Complications arose when it appeared that, after the unco-ordinated action of the Red Guards in the course of the weekend of August 20 and 21, several streets had been named *Anti-imperialist* or *Anti-revisionist*. For a long time the new name of the road to the Soviet Embassy was the only one that received official approval.

Somewhat less harmless were the activities of the Red Guards who aimed at wiping out bourgeois phenomena in the shops. In Peking they concentrated their efforts on Wang-fu-ching, soon renamed *Revolution Street*, and later again *People's Street*. Several shops were closed and plastered with big placards. 'We are the critics of the old world!' the characters shouted. 'We support the revolutionary Red Guard movement! You are rotten eggs! Before the liberation you were eating our flesh and drinking our blood!' The answer to the accusations usually was a sober announcement attached to the front door: 'Closed for redecoration.'

The only building in Peking that showed any influence of modern architecture (it has a corrugated roof and glass walls) was one of the first targets of the Red Guards. It was situated on the corner of Wang-fu-ching and Ch'ang-an Avenue, and served as a kind of snackbar. It was not long before all the windows had been covered with placards and the doors had been sealed with paper strips on which the redecorating was announced.

The antique shops in Liu-li-ch'ang were all closed and only opened months later. The arts and crafts shop in Wang-fu-ching was plastered with posters which put such questions as: 'How many hours do you actually work? And how many hours do the farmers work? And for whom do you work?' The restaurant Kwangtung, which was renowned for a touch of luxury and where on their free Sunday afternoons many people went to admire a miniature rock-garden, attracted the attention of the Red Guards. Furthermore, various barbers ran into trouble since they were supposed to be asking too high prices. At some places a 'revolutionary barber' pitched a tent on the sidewalk, and passers-by, who had not had sufficiently martial hair-cuts, were helped free of charge with the aid of Red Guards. It recalled the revolution of 1911, when the men shaved off their pigtails, or were forced to do so. Among Red Guards there was certainly a tendency towards conformism and egalitarianism, notably in these first weeks. For Chinese it was dangerous to wear jewellery or to dress in Western style. The 'Hong Kong style' was officially disapproved of in the press. If one did not want to conform voluntarily to the wishes of the masses, a violent confrontation was inevitable.

The Red Guards demanded that the small amount of advertising in neon lights in Peking should disappear. With long sticks the owners managed to smash the neon lights which had been acquired with great effort. For days the pavements of the shopping streets were strewn with broken glass. The beautiful façades of old houses also fell prey to vandalism. Ornaments were considered a redundant luxury and the stone lions on top of the house fronts were demolished with hammers. The doors and window-frames, and in places the whole fronts of the houses, were painted red. In the course of just a few days the appearance of Peking changed.

It was not always simple to wipe out the remnants of the so-called feudal past. The large stone lions at the entrances of the various parks and official buildings offered stout resistance to the untrained hands of the self-styled demolitionists. The lions in front of the Ministry of Foreign Affairs were removed by break-down lorries and probably transported to a safe place. The bronze lions near the gate of the Fragrant Hills (Chinese: *Hsiang shan*), west of Peking and known among foreigners as the 'Hunting Park', remained untouched.

However, worry about easier targets for the iconoclasm was justified. This uneasiness was shared by the Chinese authorities, who closed the gates of the Forbidden City. Although Red Guards were admitted to various rooms of the old imperial palace, which could serve as dormitories, nothing was destroyed here. However, the Summer Palace was damaged. The paintings in the extensive galleries, where they represented scenes from the bourgeois and feudal past, were covered with pink or white paint. There are different opinions as to whether or not this paint can be removed without damage to the original pictures. The circumspection with which the Chinese may operate under such circumstances can be illuminated by the following detail. If in the Hunting Park one follows the southern road, one reaches the ruins of the old villa *Shuang-ch'ing*. Only a pool and a small pavilion remain surrounded by tall leafy trees. The foundations of the original house are still visible, but, apart from this, only the garden reminds one of the fact that people once lived here. There is a fountain and behind it a small sandstone Buddha, standing in a niche in the northern wall. In early September 1966, paper strips had been plastered over the inscriptions on both sides of the niche. The face of the statue was covered with clay and on the wall was written: 'Destroy superstition.' That the paper strips were not going to last long was clear from the very beginning, and, when several weeks later we returned to this deserted place, the clay had been removed and the statue restored to its original glory. A year later, however, we saw that the statue had been irreparably damaged.

Usually short work was made of the destruction. The wooden

statues from several temples in the Western Hills were reportedly burnt. In many places the heads of stone turtles which bear memorial tablets were knocked off, as one could see for oneself if one visited the immediate surroundings of Peking.

The iconoclasm that swept the Northern Netherlands in 1566 constitutes a black page in my country's history. A similar judgement must be passed on the Chinese iconoclasm of 1966. The Chinese leaders understood this immediately, but, if they had the power to check it, they refrained from doing so for fear of extinguishing the revolutionary fire that had just been lit. Cultural loss was the price that had to be paid for the revolution. In the beginning, the authorities did not interfere either, when psychological or physical sufferings were inflicted on innocent people. The initial behaviour of the Red Guards can be compared only with the first years of the communist régime. The excesses that accompanied the land reform and the movement for the suppression of counter-revolutionaries claimed hundreds of thousands of lives. The total number of victims of the Cultural Revolution, of which a high percentage died through suicide, cannot yet be estimated.

Initially most of the Red Guards were no older than twelve to seventeen or eighteen years of age. Assisted by even younger children, they did not leave even a single house in their search for supposed revisionism. They smashed the gates, or climbed over the walls that give the Chinese houses their typical individual character, and destroyed or seized everything that was the expression of a personal preference: works of art, porcelain, foreign gramophone records, old books, musical instruments, jewellery. 'Bourgeois' furniture was seized. This included linen cupboards and armchairs. Lorries, loaded with these things, drove to and fro through the city. The goods that had been seized were brought to central check-points or to second-hand shops, where they were sold in aid of the Red Guards who indeed needed money. The Red Guards struck or spat upon elderly people, and forced them to charge themselves with crimes they could not have committed. In the centre of Peking one could see groups of pushing and kicking children, who had exposed old people as members of the 'Black Clique' and forced them to carry boards on which the accusations were written.

The Red Guards were also active in San-li-tun, the neighbourhood where we lived. They 'helped' with the burning of papers and books. The red glow of fires that flared up again and again illuminated the grey walls of the houses and unpaved roads. We saw that our neighbours were selecting their family papers in the weak light of an electric bulb, that was suspended from the ceiling with a simple cord. They hesitated before tearing up photographs and they hung a portrait of Chairman Mao on the wall. Children's voices shouted. It was their day and the older generation had to accept their dictatorship with bowed heads. Pottery was broken in bits, and loud-speakers called numbers of Red Guard groups who had to report to the check-points. The next day a meeting was organised at a near-by school playground. Hysterical voices shouted into the microphone. The accused were led to the platform and were not allowed to raise their heads.

Sometimes the Red Guards had lorries at their disposal, which they used for their raids. As a rule, their prisoners were fettered. Boards, on which was written 'I am a representative of modern revisionism' or 'I am a bourgeois' hung by a rope around their necks. And if some prisoner dared look around, there was usually a Red Guard who could not resist the sadistic temptation of hitting him in the face with a leather belt. This happened in broad daylight, in the centre of the capital, and was observed by numerous foreigners. Outside Peking the Red Guards' activities were not checked by any scruples. In the countryside victims were fettered and dragged behind bicycles with an iron chain around their necks. Or they were forced by children to kneel again and again in front of a portrait of Chairman Mao.

The Red Guards, or their superiors, had arranged that all savings of over one thousand yüan (about four hundred American dollars) should be confiscated. All private houses were also seized. In practice this meant that the owner had to hand over his title deed to the police, who informed him then whether he was allowed to stay in the house or not. If he was lucky he was permitted to stay and assigned one room for every person in the household. The 'rooms' of a Chinese house are in general smaller than in Western Europe. Moreover they do not need to be separated by a wall, but a visible beam may serve as the partition between two rooms. In such a case we would speak of one room.

Almost every citizen was summoned to write a self-criticism, in which not much could be suppressed. However, one man was cleverer than another, and the street committees differed from each other in dealing with the criticism and self-criticism. Hypocrisy and trickery were rewarded. The few people who, in all naïvety, told the truth, or who had become the envy of their neighbours because they were slightly brighter or occupied a somewhat better position, were almost certainly lost.

Little is known of the suffering and injustice caused by the Cultural Revolution. The history of the Franciscan nuns of the Sacred Heart, who were in charge of an international school in Peking, has been widely reported. They were humiliated, handcuffed and hit. Several days after the Red Guards had occupied the school, the foreign nuns were allowed to leave the country. One of them, Sister Eamon, died a few hours after she had crossed the frontier between China and Hong Kong. Of about twenty Chinese nuns at least four died. The others were reportedly sent back to their 'places of origin'. It will probably never be known how these nuns who were mostly elderly were treated in their birthplace.

Islam suffered as much as the remnants of Roman Catholicism. The imam of the mosque on the Niu Street was reportedly murdered. The mosque remained closed for two months and was decorated with portraits of Chairman Mao when it reopened.

Resistance to the Red Guard

Not everyone submitted to the terror. There were street committees who resisted the wild charges of the politically and otherwise inexperienced Red Guards. For instance, in a stencilled wall newspaper of early September two street committees defended the Geological Institute of Peking which, according to a Red Guard group, was a centre of the Black Clique. 'If the Red Guards pretend to know this, they have to mention names and to furnish evidence', the pamphlet read. In those days Peking buzzed with rumours of violent resistance to the Red Guards. A pamphlet of late August mentioned that since the 23rd of that month, a member of the Red Guard was missing and that eight Red Guards and one pioneer were seriously wounded in a fight near the Northern Tung-tan Avenue. According to another poster, in the same neighbourhood on the night of August 27–28 four people were killed. When two Red Guards attacked an elderly woman, her husband came to her assistance and fatally wounded the two boys with a knife. Thereupon the couple committed suicide.

More forceful resistance originated with the workers. Whereas many scuffles between workers and Red Guards also took place in Peking, the friction between the two was more serious where particularistic sentiments played a role. The main incidents occurred in the provinces, and the Red Guards from the big cities who were involved usually felt compelled to report on these fights. There was a serious clash in Lanchow, where students vented their criticism of the party committee of Kansu province. The party committee refused to accept the charges and mobilised workers from the oil refinery of Lanchow and the railways to teach the students a lesson. According to some pamphlets five thousand workers surrounded the University and clashed with the students. However, the students got their way. Their criticism was accepted by higher authorities as reasonable, and the result of their action seems to have been that two secretaries of the provincial party committee were dismissed.

In such incidents local chauvinism often made its influence felt. This appeared from reports from Tientsin and Shanghai which, as well as the news of the Lanchow incident, dated from early September. Red Guards from Peking committed an irreparable mistake in man-handling a party secretary of the pedicab-riders in Tientsin. The unfortunate party secretary, who according to the most recent party view had an impeccable record, died from the consequences of this rough treatment, which enraged the whole Tientsin. As a result, placards were posted in Tientsin reading 'Peking dogs, go home.'

I shall deal somewhat more elaborately with an incident that occurred in Shanghai on August 31. The immediate cause was a differ-ence of opinion as to how the Cultural Revolution should be put into practice. Although politically the incident was of little relevance, it was important as a symptom of how the Red Guards and the local party cadres were fighting each other. Both posed as supporters of the Cultural Revolution. The party apparatus had sent out Cutural Revolution teams in order to remove certain people from the political stage (and to spare those who were loyal to the Liu Shao-ch'i faction). In most cases the Red Guards were the rivals of the Cultural Revolu-tion teams, which in the Chinese press were usually indicated as 'work teams'. The Red Guards were controlled directly by the Central Committee and had no relations with the lower party organisations which they considered infected by revisionism. Apart from being a clash between local party cadres and Red Guards, the incident of August 31 was one between Peking and Shanghai.

The incident was reported in a printed pamphlet of September 9, signed by students of a high school in Peking. It was posted up on the walls of a shop in Wang-fu-ching and contained about four thousand characters. The contents were, in short, as follows: Red Guards who had travelled from Peking to Shanghai were amazed to find there little enthusiasm for the Cultural Revolution. They wondered why

B

the party committee of Shanghai had issued 'ten rules for the destruction of old ideas, culture, customs and habits'. Was it as if to say that the struggle against the feudal past should be subjected to rules? Moreover the Peking Red Guards demanded an explanation of the slogan: 'Defend the party committee of Shanghai.'

'Initially', the Red Guards reported, 'we called on the lower party organisations in Shanghai, but when these could not produce conclusive answers, we decided to apply for an interview with the party committee of Shanghai. For us this is a normal procedure, because when we were still in Peking, we were often received by members of the Central Committee, even at short notice. In the evening of August 30 we telephoned a member of the Shanghai party committee, and told him that we wished to see him the next morning. But when we arrived at the office of the party committee with about thirty people, there was a group of so-called Red Guards from Shanghai waiting for us, who did not want to let us pass. They asked what made us come and we said: "We come to destroy revisionism and to inquire about the Cultural Revolution in Shanghai." They answered: "If you want to fight revisionism, you should go to Peking!" After some consultations, we decided to send two representatives to the entrance of the building, but these too were turned away. In the meantime several revolutionary students from Shanghai had joined us and they started pushing from the back, so that we almost reached the entrance. The so-called Red Guards from Shanghai began pushing back, which led to tough fighting. Three girls managed to enter the building. But once inside, they were hit, kicked and knocked down. Their clothes were torn from their bodies! Such a thing should not be possible in a socialist state!'

'Of course,' the pamphlet continued, 'this behaviour filled us all with indignation and we tried our hardest to come to their assistance. We succeeded in entering the building, but we then had to fight against heavy odds. We were separated and surrounded. Fascist methods were used against us! Nevertheless, mindful of Mao's words, we stood firm as a rock. We continued to shout for an interview with the party committee. Gradually more and more revolutionary young people from Shanghai came to support us and our combined action resulted in an interview with Vice-Mayor Sung Chi-wen. Immediately we asked him: "Is our action justified? Is the slogan 'Defend the party committee of Shanghai' correct? Did the party committee of Shanghai give orders to stop us by force?" The first question he answered in the affirmative, the second in the negative, and to the last he replied: "We will have to investigate that matter."

'Thereupon a meeting was held, which, however, immediately went wrong. Sung said that the revolutionaries from Shanghai should be silent, since the grievances of the Red Guards from Peking were to be dealt with. This was completely in contravention of the Sixteen Points which were formulated under the personal guidance of Chairman Mao. The Sixteen Points say that the masses should not fight between themselves and that one is not allowed to play different groups of students off against each other. Sung tried to do precisely that. Apart from this, he could not give a satisfactory answer to our questions, and after some time he left. When finally yet another member of the Shanghai party committee who attended the meeting had disappeared without having made us much wiser, we decided to leave the building. It was not easy to do so, because there was an enormous crowd. Everywhere one fought and pushed, and we were allowed to leave only when the rumour spread that all the three thousand Peking Red Guards who stayed in Shanghai were on their way to liberate us. Near the entrance we were met by more than two hundred revolutionaries.

'We strongly protest against this outrageous treatment by the Shanghai party committee! Long live Chairman Mao! Long live the Great Cultural Revolution!'

A footnote mentioned particulars about the 'losses': 'Some figures in relation to the incident in Shanghai. Thirty-one Peking Red Guards managed to enter the office of the Shanghai party committee. Thirty of them were severely struck. The clothes of nine Red Guards were torn to pieces (unimportant damage has not been taken into account). The red armband was ripped from two Red Guards and those were the same armbands that they had worn when they were received by Chairman Mao on August 18!'

The Red Guards did not fight only the bourgeoisie, but also each other, even if they originated from the same city. The rivalry resulted from deficient organisation. During October it was made known that the Red Guards, in fact, dated from May 1966, when a group of students of the high school attached to Tsinghua University in Peking joined in order to defend the Central Committee, Chairman Mao and the dictatorship of the proletariat. But the movement had not been sufficiently prepared before it was launched officially on August 18. Hence in Peking in September and October, various organisations came into existence which operated independently. Soon one could distinguish the 'Red Guard', 'Flame Red Guard', 'Red Guard of the Thought of Mao Tse-tung', 'Red Guard of the Red Flag', '*Chingkang-shan*' (name of an historic place in the history of communist guerrilla warfare), and several other units. They considered Chairman Mao their highest leader, and, with the exception of the Central Committee, recognised no other authority. Discipline was plainly bad. Very few heeded the 'three main rules of discipline or eight points of attention', which boiled down to a prohibition of hitting, swearing, stealing, ill-treating captives, and taking liberties with women.

Degradation of President Liu Shao-ch'i

Perhaps the Red Guard entered the political battlefield earlier than Lin Piao had expected. Undoubtedly its function was to impress his opponents and indeed it played an important part in the display of power that accompanied the degradation of Liu Shao-ch'i.

The mass parade that was reviewed by Mao Tse-tung on August 18 was not only important as a manifestation of the Red Guard, but also because it created an opportunity to publish the new hierarchy of the Chinese leaders. The position of Lin Piao as Mao's 'close comrade in-arms' was officially confirmed. Chou En-lai maintained his position as number three. However, T'ao Chu, an influential man in Southern China, surprisingly had risen to the fourth position, and Ch'en Po-ta, Editor-in-Chief of the *Red Flag*, to the fifth. Teng Hsiao-p'ing, General Secretary of the Communist Party, occupied the sixth position. Instead of the aged Vice-President Tung Pi-wu, K'ang Sheng, who is closely associated with the secret police, was mentioned as number seven. The head of state, Liu Shao-ch'i, had been degraded from the second to the eighth position. In this way the top leadership had been rejuvenated. It was also new that Mrs. Mao Tse-tung, also called Chiang Ch'ing, was mentioned in the list of officials. She had been nominated first vice-chairman of the Cultural Revolution group (a committee that was established by the Central Committee) and was mentioned as number twenty-five. She was the first collaborator of Ch'en Po-ta, chairman of the Cultural Revolution group, but, unlike him, not a member of the Central Committee or alternate member.

Apart from the question whether the Red Guard started their political activities in too great a hurry, the fact is that many people believed that in their revolutionary zeal they went too far. Lin Piao probably was no exception. Before the end of August, the Chinese leaders were trying hard to reinforce their grip on the movement. A controlling organisation was set up and its members wore special red armbands. Chou En-lai was among those who were seen with such an armband, on which were the characters *chiu-ch'a-tui* (inspection brigade). Gradually more adults were added to the ranks of the Red Guard. In a later stage military men were seen commanding groups of Red Guards. The whole history of the Red Guard in the second half of 1966 may be described as an attempt to encapsulate a semi-spontaneous youth movement by the army, and forebodings of this encapsulation were visible already by the end of August. Although the *People's Daily* of August 23 was still exhorting the workers, peasants and soldiers to support the Red Guard, five days later the same newspaper mentioned that the young revolutionaries should take their cue from the army.

With reference to clashes between workers and students, the *People's Daily* of September 11 wrote that under no condition could it be allowed that 'workers and peasants were incited to fight students'. This warning was not only addressed to the workers and peasants, but was also a hint that the revolutionary young people should not antagonise the actual proletariat. On September 15 a million 'Red Guards, revolutionary students and teachers' participated in a mass rally, at which everyone brandished the red booklet of quotations from Mao's works in probably unfeigned enthusiasm. On that occasion Lin Piao warned the demonstrators again, without appearing in any way as a symbol of gentleness. In imitation of Mao Tse-tung, he exhorted the Red Guards to 'bombard the headquarters and to bombard the handful of people in power who are taking the capitalist road', but at the same time he pointed out that the power of the red guards was limited: 'The workers, peasants and soldiers always have been the main force of our revolution. Also now, they are the main force of our socialist revolution and socialist construction, and at the same time the main force of our great proletarian cultural revolution.' The Red Guards should follow the example of the workers, peasants and soldiers and learn from their high sense of organisation and discipline. So far Lin Piao.

At the same rally Chou En-lai elaborated on this theme. He warned the Red Guards not to interfere with industrial and agricultural production. In the communes the revolution should be continued on the basis of the Four Clean-ups Campaign, which had been launched in

1963, and the Red Guard did not need to bother about it.[1] 'Unlike the schools,' Chou En-lai said, 'the factories and farms cannot be closed and stop production because of the revolution. The revolutionary students must respect the masses of the workers and peasants, trust them and be assured that they are fully capable of completing the revolution by relying on their own force.'

It could hardly have been said more clearly, and the warnings, which were published only in the *People's Daily* and not in the English bulletin of Hsinhua News Agency, must have been motivated by serious anxiety. An additional reason for advocating moderation was the approaching National Day, on which occasion many visitors, foreigners and overseas Chinese, were to pay a visit to Peking. It was impossible to confront them with the anarchy of late August and early September, when the Red Guards were masters of the streets and, armed with sticks, tried to stop every car in order to force the 'bourgeois' passengers to continue their journey on foot.

The Chinese leaders found a temporary solution by mobilising groups of Red Guards for assistance in the harvest. Singing revolutionary songs, carrying red flags and framed portraits of Chairman Mao, the young revolutionaries took up their new assignment. In the area surrounding Peking, they helped with the harvest of maize, sorghum and aubergines. The youngest boys were assigned to collect garbage, or to dig ditches or to do similar work where they could cause no damage.

But not all by far went to the countryside. The Square of Heavenly Peace remained an important meeting place. There, coupons for meals were distributed to Red Guards who formed queues hundreds of yards long. On the square were parked great numbers of lorries and buses, which had transported Red Guards from other cities to Peking. In the shade of the cars, exhausted revolutionaries lay sleeping, undisturbed by the carpentering and other labour of workmen who were giving the finishing touches to the festive illumination and the display of portraits and slogans. The portraits were the same as the year before: Marx, Engels, Lenin, Stalin, Mao Tse-tung. Also the portrait of Sun Yat-sen, the founder of the Kuomintang, was erected, although Hong Kong newspapers had reported that in Shanghai the house of his widow, who was a Vice-President of the People's Republic of China, had been ransacked by Red Guards.

The end of September was overshadowed by October the First, and the Red Guards were to play a considerable role in its celebration.

The approaching National Day brought some relaxation as well. The worst terror seemed to have passed. After the First of October a new stage in the Red Guard movement began.

Cultural Criticism

One should not make the mistake of equating the objectives of the Red Guards with the objectives of the Cultural Revolution. Lin Piao mobilised the Red Guards in order to carry out political plans of limited range. The Red Guard movement played a role within the province of the Cultural Revolution, but was not destined to give that revolution its cultural dimension.

In short, the Red Guards and the cultural criticism each had their own function in the political upheaval. The cultural criticism, which since 1964 had been characterised by a certain continuity, received added significance in April 1966, since it could be used as a weapon against those who resisted the policies of Mao Tse-tung and Lin Piao. The very few intellectuals who had sided with Mao and Lin Piao launched a relentless struggle against the group of P'eng Chen and Chou Yang by attacking their cultural and ideological theories. The maoists did not hesitate to pronounce accusations which were largely unfounded and for the rest almost entirely of political significance only.

After Wu Han, Teng T'o and Liao Mo-sha, many others, such as Ch'in Mu, Ouyang Shan and Lin Mo-han were added to the list of revisionists. Li Fan accused Chou Yang of being an advocate of a 'literature of the whole people,' a concept that bordered upon Khrushchevian heresy. Several prominent historians were charged with collaboration with Wu Han. The actors wore red armbands on the stage or disappeared, and later all cinemas and theatres were closed and used for lodging the Red Guards who flocked to Peking. The destruction of art treasures by the Red Guard evoked resistance among most intellectuals. Many became victims of ransacking, and psychological and physical torture. The schools and universities were closed. Many professors committed suicide. Only very few intellectuals such as Kuo Mo-jo, who in April 1966 – even before the Cultural Revolution was officially launched – had made an early self-criticism, were considered immune from bourgeois taints and rewarded by being invited to the rostrum of the Gate of Heavenly Peace each time a mammoth rally of Red Guards was held.

The case of the famous writer Lao She, who committed suicide after having been interrogated by the Red Guards, became widely known. He drowned himself in one of the lakes in the centre of Peking, and it was rumoured that he carried a copy of the works of Mao Tse-tung in his own calligraphy with him as a symbol of his loyalty to the Chairman. Against the walls of his house in the Nai-tse-fu-feng-sheng Street I saw posters which questioned: 'Since you have eaten the bread of the people, what did you do in return?' On this no discussion was possible. Like Mao Tun and Pa Chin, who are of the same generation, Lao She had tried to combine artistic integrity and political loyalty; of course, with varying success. He was attacked repeatedly for political reasons, and from a literary point of view his post-1949 work, mainly drama, is not of a high quality. For many years Lao She had been lame; he had developed a talent for cultivating chrysanthemums. He was sixty-eight years old when he died.

August and September were months that were characterised by an urge towards self-destruction. Much that happened then would have been impossible or improbable, or anyway unnecessary a few weeks later. But the irreparable could not be repaired, and the gamut of unnecessary sufferings will never be known precisely. Again the Chinese people had paid their tribute to fate.

REFERENCE

1. The Four Clean-ups (*szu-ch'ing*) Campaign, or Socialist Education Movement, aimed to clean up 1, accounts; 2, granaries; 3, properties; and 4, work points. In late 1964 the emphasis shifted and the movement focused on reforms in the field of 1, politics; 2, economics; 3, ideology; and 4, organisation. See Richard Baum and Frederick C. Teiwes, *Ssu-ch'ing: The Socialist Education Movement of 1962–1966*, Berkeley, Calif.: Center for Chinese Studies, 1968.

3

THE CHAIRMAN AND THE MASSES: AUTUMN 1966

The Red Guard, at least in Peking, appeared to have shot their bolt soon, and the fireworks, which they produced, served as a terrifying décor that suited the liquidation of a number of political figures, but had no other function. The relative meaninglessness of the movement appeared from the stereotyped character of its principal activities: copying posters and waiting for an opportunity to see Chairman Mao. Soon the Red Guard became a political and economic problem of enormous proportions. This was the result of confusion to which the movement itself contributed.

On the night of September 30–October 1 the necessary arrangements were made in order to enable one and a half million people to participate in a parade celebrating the seventeenth anniversary of the People's Republic. In the newspapers, the times were announced when the approaches to the Square of Heavenly Peace were to be closed. In doing so, the old street names were referred to, because the new names had not yet been confirmed. On the eve of October the First, those taking part in the parade gathered in the streets in the centre of the town, ready to march the next morning under military command past Chairman Mao.

Actually, 'marching' is not the right word. When several columns of soldiers carrying a gigantic white statue of Mao Tse-tung and enormous figures, which represented the years 1949–66, had passed the Gate of Heavenly Peace, hordes of young people followed. As their only contribution to the festivities, they carried a great number of red flags. The carnival element, which in previous years had played a considerable role but now was considered bourgeois, was absent. The demonstrators, mainly 'Red Guards and revolutionary young people', were driven on, often at the double. First aid posts were busy dealing with people who had been overcome by heat.

During the parade several speeches were made. When the last sounds of the national anthem had faded away, which for lack of drums of a sufficient calibre was punctuated by gunshots, Lin Piao made the first speech. His slender, ascetic stature, his penetrating look and his fanatic way of speaking, which easily switches from a long drawl to clipped words, contributed to the impression of a real demagogue who apparently was able to do whatever he liked with the, at one and the same time, disciplined and bewildered Chinese people. However, the Hupei dialect which he speaks restricts the scope of his oratory.

The Chairman was present and shouts of 'Long live Chairman Mao' sounded continuously through the square. He was silent, but waved back. Chiang Ch'ing started making nervous movements on the rostrum. She introduced the Chinese leaders to foreign or unexpected guests. Chou En-lai and others hardly appreciated her sociability. Almost everyone who was invited to watch the parade from the rostrum carried the red booklet. Only Liu Shao-ch'i did not. He received a copy from Chou En-lai.

The newspapers wrote: 'Which sun is the reddest? The sun on the Square of Heavenly Peace. Which is the highest happiness? To see Chairman Mao.' This happiness was seemingly inexhaustible. On October 18 arrangements were made again for meeting Chairman Mao. On that day the Chairman and a number of his collaborators went for a drive and were cheered by hundreds of thousands of Red Guards, holding banners with slogans such as: 'Protect Chairman Mao' and 'Protect the Central Committee that is guided by Chairman Mao.'

Was Mao Tse-tung in danger? The Chinese also wondered at these slogans. The next day I read a poster, which under the title of 'Why is this all necessary?' asked the awkward question whether Chairman Mao needed protection. The author had very much enjoyed the opportunity of seeing his beloved Chairman Mao, and he believed that everyone was of a similar opinion. 'But who is behind these slogans that appeal to the people to protect him?' he wondered.

It was a natural question to ask. Indeed, in early October it transpired indirectly from wall newspapers that Mao Tse-tung and Lin Piao had been criticised. Also, during the height of the Red Guard terror. the complaint was heard that Mao wanted everyone to be poor, except himself; this, in its simplicity, was a devastating criticism, and it passed from mouth to mouth. What the people did know about Mao's way of life was that he smoked cigars, loved to sit in red plush armchairs and wore leather shoes. That was enough to make him alien to the actual Chinese proletariat. Such criticism, however, was too general to become a factor of political significance. Therefore, it is hard to believe that Mao Tse-tung really needed protection. The idea was probably launched with the aim of fanning the hunt for revisionists and causing confusion in the enemy camp as well as among the maoists, in order to force every individual to take sides.

The confusion grew when in mid-October the Red Guards were urged to struggle against 'the reactionary elements among the leaders of the Red Guards of Peking'. Apparently one could not trust even those in one's own ranks, and with great zeal one began looking for scapegoats – both inside and outside the Red Guard.

The Hunt for Revisionists

Red Guards of Tsinghua University impeached Wang Kuang-mei, the wife of Liu Shao-ch'i, who during the first stage of the Cultural Revolution had played a role in their University as a member of a work team. They demanded that she appear at a meeting to answer for her political standpoint, and notified Chou En-lai of their plans. But, as it appeared from a poster of mid-October, Chou ordered his secretary to reply that the case of Mrs. Liu Shao-ch'i was to be investigated by a commission of the Central Committee and that the Red Guards did not need bother about her. However, the students persisted, and in January 1967 managed to kidnap her. They informed Wang Kuang-mei by telephone that her daughter was in hospital. When Wang Kuang-mei went to visit her, she was intercepted by students and brought to Tsinghua University, where she was subjected to extensive interrogations.

The Minister of Foreign Affairs, Ch'en Yi, was also attacked. On the walls of the former compound of the Netherlands diplomatic mission, now belonging to the Ministry of Foreign Affairs, was written in large characters: 'Destroy the party committee of the Ministry of Foreign Affairs and burn Ch'en Yi.' Initially, the minister seemed not to be very much impressed; anyway, he had enough courage left to allow his charming wife to wear a 'bourgeois' Shanghai silk blouse at functions although, for safety's sake, he himself preferred an army uniform. After October 1966, however, Mrs. Ch'en Yi was not seen any more in public. Of Ch'en Yi we shall hear more in the next chapter.

The criticism of Li Hsüeh-feng, First Secretary of the Peking party committee since May, was a great surprise. For it now appeared that the choice of a successor to P'eng Chen had been wrong. The first criticism appeared by the end of September. He was accused of 'right opportunism'. In a Red Guard newspaper of October 17, twenty crimes of Li Hsüeh-feng were listed. His main mistake had been his resistance to Mao Tse-tung and the Central Committee, and his collaboration with Teng T'o. A poster of October 16 questioned why he had refused to address a Red Guard meeting on August 2, and why he had suggested that Liu Shao-ch'i should replace him.[1] 'What are actually your contacts with Liu Shao-ch'i?' another question read, as though the very association with the President of the People's Republic was something ominous. By mid-October the criticism of Li Hsüeh-feng and Liu Shao-ch'i was still in an early phase. It could not prevent their participation in Mao's drive on the 18th of that month.

In late October Po I-po, Chairman of the State Economic Commission, was attacked. His arrest followed soon. An important element in the criticism of Po I-po was that he had let slip his opinion that the Cultural Revolution had begun without sufficient ideological preparation. Po must have been impressed by the effect of the Red Guard activities on the economy. He must have agreed with Chou En-lai, who, also in October, called it impermissible that the Red Guards blocked about 20 per cent of all means of transportation. Because of his position Po I-po felt obliged to warn against the growing confusion and waste. But he forgot that Mao Tse-tung and Lin Piao in fact needed a certain amount of chaos in order to carry out their plans. *Tsao-fan yu li!* (rebellion is justified) was and remained the main propaganda theme.

Also in late October serious criticism of Liu Shao-ch'i and Teng Hsiao-p'ing began. Liu Shao-ch'i made a substantial self-criticism on October 23, 1966, in which he confessed to having committed serious mistakes in the form of rightist opportunism.[2] However, Mao Tse-tung, Lin Piao and Ch'en Po-ta did not consider this enough and continued to air their objections to Liu and Teng at a Central Committee working session, whereupon it was again Nieh Yüan-tzu, lecturer in philosophy at the University of Peking, who shouldered the responsibility of popularising their slashing judgment. On November 8, she called

Liu an admirer of Soviet revisionism and the principal leader of the capitalist faction in the party. The President of the People's Republic of China had allegedly been aiming at a restoration of capitalism and of the class-ridden society. She charged Teng Hsiao-p'ing too with revisionist leanings and sympathy for the decisions of the Twentieth Congress of the Communist Party of the Soviet Union of 1956. His admiration for revisionism had appeared from his report on the revision of the constitution of the Chinese Communist Party in September 1956. In this report Teng Hsiao-p'ing had warned against the danger of the personality cult, which Nieh Yüan-tzu interpreted as a criticism of Chairman Mao. In her statement she did not take the historical conditions of that year into account and completely neglected the fact that in 1956 some liberalisation was also necessary in China. Mao Tse-tung himself seemed to have been well aware of this when he announced his Hundred Flowers policy. Nieh Yüan-tzu further accused Teng of resistance to the Socialist Education Movement[3] in the University of Peking. Teng was believed to have instigated P'eng Chen, the former First Secretary of the Peking party committee, to boycott the movement.

Ideological Justification of the Cultural Revolution

In early November T'ao Chu, since August number four in the Chinese hierarchy, was also criticised in wall newspapers, and the simultaneous criticism of so many important party leaders gave rise to the suspicion that the campaign of Lin Piao and Mao Tse-tung was more or less directed against the party as such. In order to reform the party, the old structure should be destroyed. In a speech during a rally of Red Guards on the Square of Heavenly Peace on November 3, Lin Piao tried to give this policy an ideological basis. He certainly did so in agreement with Chairman Mao. Lin Piao emphasised the democratic aspects of the Cultural Revolution and urged the practice of 'extensive democracy' along the principles of the Paris Commune, which distinguished itself by abolishing the existing administrative apparatus and replacing it with a body of elected officials.

In his day, Marx had reservations about the Paris Commune, because the role of the marxists in the Commune was small indeed. An article on the Paris Commune in the *Red Flag* of March 24, 1966, recalled that the Commune had not been guided by a marxist political party. Lin Piao must have been aware of this, but it is typical of the leaders of the Cultural Revolution that they wished, nevertheless, to follow the example of the Paris Commune. However, the term 'extensive democracy' should not be misunderstood. It meant something completely different from the so-called bourgeois 'ultra-democracy'. Extensive democracy implied that one was allowed to criticise the party leadership, with the significant exceptions of Mao Tse-tung and Lin Piao. In advertising extensive democracy, the green light was given to a large-scale attack on the party structure. Lin Piao was not so injudicious as to fail to build up another power apparatus at the same time; moreover, if necessary, he always could fall back on the army.

The Paris Commune reminds us more of barricades than of democracy, and Lin Piao certainly did not want to avoid that association. According to him, there was a need for more fighting spirit. The commemoration of the thirtieth anniversary of the death of Lu Hsün was to serve this end. The way in which Lu Hsün was commemorated in 1966 differed widely from the commemoration in 1956. In that year the literary reviews devoted special issues to the great Chinese writer. Kuo Mo-jo, Mao Tun and many other writers gave speeches at commemorative meetings. The Soviet Writers' Union was represented by the novelist Boris Polevoi. Apart from a number of political discourses, serious attention was paid to Lu Hsün's works.

In 1966, however, Mao Tun remained silent, whereas Kuo Mo-jo in a short speech defended the view that Lu Hsün, although he had never been a member of the communist party, should still be called a communist. In the summer of 1966 the publication of the well-known literary reviews was suspended with the exception of *Literature and Art of the Liberation Army*, which, however, had not much to say on the literary works of Lu Hsün either.

An article by Lu Hsün's widow Hsü Kuang-p'ing in the *People's Daily* of November 1 was largely devoted to criticism of Chou Yang, who, as a vice-director of the propaganda department, had falsified the history of his quarrel with Lu Hsün in order that he himself would not be put in too unfavourable a light. According to the Chinese press, at the commemorative meetings in Shanghai, Lu Hsün's birthplace Shaohsing, and elsewhere, apart from Kuo Mo-jo, only one author had spoken, namely the well-known 'worker-writer' Hu Wan-ch'un. For the rest, Red Guards and other revolutionary young people made the commemorative speeches.

Why, actually, was Lu Hsün commemorated? According to the *People's Daily*, he believed in 'beating the wild dog even though it is already in the water' and advised 'once you start beating it, to beat it to death'. Lu Hsün was elevated to the position of spiritual father of the Red Guards. This was possible only on the basis of a strained interpretation of his works. An editorial in the *Red Flag* of November 1 argued that Lu Hsün had greatly despised all that was old, whether it was legends, bronzes, jade Buddhas or traditional medicine. He was depicted as an extremely courageous man, who in his isolated position had shown great intrepidity. The isolation of Lu Hsün should console the warriors of the Cultural Revolution, who gradually were isolated as well. Isolation, encirclement and persecution were to temper the Red Guards and to steel their will to complete their anarchist programme. The same editorial described that programme as: 'destruction first, and construction in the course of destruction'. It was a simple formula, but it remained an open question what the young revolutionaries in fact could do, besides joining the endless rallies and copying posters that had been written by the chosen few.

Interior Monologue

If one believes that one must try to run away from the falsehood of ideologies, Peking probably is one of the last places to go to. If one wants to experience the isolation in which nobody may justify the existence of someone else, Peking seems to provide the ideal setting. It is an excellent place for an experience of complete loneliness. Here one will find not even *ersatz* understanding, or the soothing quasi-security of coffee-house or cinema. A Westerner does not exchange exploring looks with Chinese girls for the simple reason that his glances will never be returned. Here there is no trace of comfortable luxury as in the cafés on the Boulevard St.-Germain in Paris, or at the bar of the Rainbow Room, high above Rockefeller Plaza in New York. The only coffee-house which, if one is tired, might be visited, is *Ho-p'ing* (Peace) in the covered market. In earlier years, someone used to play the piano here. The benches with their white covers, which could have been borrowed from the waiting room of a Russian railway station, were usually unoccupied, whereas during 1956–7, the period of the Hundred Flowers, they had been crowded. Several African students and a rare tourist, who could be recognised by his camera and Basque beret, are among the few visitors.

Peking: an ideal post for the philosopher, since every-day contact with the environment will be greatly reduced. Usually he will not be able to talk to the Chinese, for either political or linguistic reasons. The world of every-day things is often alien to him, and the concepts that are propagated by the press, radio and television also seem to have unfamiliar meanings. He will be alone with the reminiscences of the tradition of his own country, as far as he manages to keep those reminiscences alive.

Alone, he will *not* be able to keep his own tradition alive, and soon everything will appear to be reduced to a strained effort to distinguish truth from falsehood. More than ever he will need a sharp and immediate intuition, and on the whole, from resistance to a not unimaginable brainwashing, his spontaneous judgement will rise more easily to the surface.

Unintentionally I was more annoyed in Peking to hear Yugoslav diplomats defend the official view that Mihajlov was an eccentric and swindler, than I ever would have been in Holland. Involuntarily the more than life-size plaster statue of Lenin in the Russian Embassy disturbed me more than if I had not seen a great number of similar busts of Mao Tse-tung. In modern Chinese propaganda paintings I recognised the famous themes of nazi art: the glorification of physical power, the facial expressions of unflinching resolution, the heroism, and the prefiguration of a victory which is beyond doubt.

A film show in the Hungarian Embassy evoked in me a whole series of mixed feelings. The entrance was romantic. Having passed the narrow gate, which was built more for the size of a small horse carriage than that of an American car, I drove through an old, European-style garden to a building that had once housed the legation of the Austro-Hungarian monarchy. The rottenness and injustice of the way of life in the Danube monarchy were crowned with the fall of the Habsburg dynasty. In Hungary Horthy was appointed regent and gradually developed into a dictator. The film which was shown, and which was of recent date, dealt with Hungarian fascism, militarism under Hungarian officers and the rise of bolshevism before and during the Second World War. But in the criticism of the Horthy régime, and in the description of the defeat of the Hungarian army on the Eastern front and the rise of the new, communist forces, truth was, to say the least, one-sidedly represented. After the victory of the communist ideology in Hungary, the 1956 uprising took place. In the film this was passed over in silence. After the film show my colleagues, out of politeness, did not raise the subject. And outside, in the severe cold, the Chinese demonstrators banged their drums and shouted slogans in criticism of that same ideology which in 1945 had been full of promise to a great number of Eastern Europeans.

It had all happened within one lifetime: the fall of the Austro-Hungarian monarchy, Horthy's regency, the rise of fascism, and then communism which in its Eastern European realisation was rejected by the Chinese as revisionism. That night half a century of history passed by.

As I left the Embassy, the demonstrators could not be avoided. Their drums sounded through the night and were followed by endless columns of people with white face masks over their mouths because of the cold. Therefore, no expression could be identified on their faces. I was tempted to jump out of my car and to tell them that so many people had already paid their tribute to this kind of quixotism, and that the ideology of Mao Tse-tung would not be the last. I drove home, knowing that my convictions were fanatically negated by millions of individuals around me.

I do not want to leave the impression that these lines were written by an incorrigible pessimist. There were also gayer evenings. Social intercourse in the Western-oriented diplomatic circles in Peking can be compared to that on an ocean liner. But this diplomatic atmosphere has as little to do with China as the entertainment on board a ship has to do with the sea, and is therefore irrelevant here.

Journey to Tientsin

Of course, the impression which one got in Peking of the Cultural Revolution was not representative of the whole country. In the other larger towns the fact that the Red Guard movement was not achieving anything positive was probably even harder to conceal than in Peking. The Red Guards who had come to Peking had at least one clear aim: to see Chairman Mao. To reach that goal they travelled hundreds, or even thousands of miles. That they also wished to see what a large Chinese town had to offer was of secondary, but not negligible importance.

The Gate of Heavenly Peace, or T'ien-an-men, is represented in the Chinese coat of arms, and appears on every coin. Participating in a rally on the square in front of that gate is officially the highest happiness. But what was the purpose of the Red Guards in Canton, Shanghai, or Wuhan? There, too, were 'revolutionary young people', who had come from far and near. In Canton, Red Guards from Urumchi, Peking and the North-east had been seen, but they complained that they were not able to contribute to the Cultural Revolution, because they could not make themselves understood. Many Red Guards flocked to Shanghai, but as a result of the inadequate identification of their task, there, too, apart from reading Mao Tse-tung's works, their activities were of limited range. An additional frustrating factor was that relations between the local Red Guards and those who had come from elsewhere were often strained. The latter group was met with distrust. They did not know the local conditions and could hardly be considered qualified to judge someone's political reliability. They had to base their opinion on outward appearances: clothes, hair-styles, the kind and origin of one's means of transportation. Naturally their elbow-room was curtailed. Finally little was left with which the Red Guards were allowed to interfere, and the Chinese leaders were compelled to find an outlet for the superfluous energy of the young revolutionaries. The walks which they undertook in imitation of the famous Long March of 1934-5 provided a way out.

From the press one could get very little impression as to what extent the idea of making walking tours had materialised. When in early November a colleague and I travelled by car to Tientsin and from there to the port of Hsinkang, it appeared that many groups of Red Guards were on the road, moving in both directions, but predominantly towards Peking. Gaily marching and brandishing the red booklet, they devoted themselves to their new revolutionary assignment which was to strengthen both body and spirit. Usually they flew a red flag. Everyone took care of his own luggage, which usually consisted of a folded winter coat and bedding neatly tied round with rope and carried on the back, and attached to it a pair of plimsolls or straw sandals. Then a small bag containing toilet articles, a towel and perhaps an electric torch was carried, and sometimes provisions in a separate plastic bag.

Along the road there was the atmosphere of a sports event. At places cabins had been built from rush mats, where people could rest. Here the hikers could warm themselves at a fire and were offered a bowl of hot water. Older people, who wore yellow armbands with characters indicating that their business was traffic control, arranged arrivals and departures. The next day I asked someone who would know, what exactly the function of these *chiao-t'ung-chien* was. He called them tax officials in charge of the inspection of freight traffic.

When a lorry driver regularly covers the same route, he usually pays a fixed amount of money on a yearly basis. If not, then at certain check-points he must pay road tax. The inspectors look whether the character '*chien*' (inspection) has been painted on the windscreen, which signifies that one pays tax on a yearly basis. If that character is missing, the inspectors stop the lorry – and thereby create an ideal opportunity for hitch-hiking.

The supervision of the walking Red Guards probably had become an additional task of the inspectors. As reliable revolutionaries, they must have wanted to meet the Red Guards' wishes. By the end of the afternoon the walks were changed into hitch-hiking. And if the Red Guards were unsuccessful at the tax check-points, they began walking in the middle of the road, making it difficult for cars to pass. If they had not reached their destination before darkness, they hooked arms across the road and, like strikers in more heroic times, they forced the lorries to stop.

Imperturbably the mules and donkeys pass the young revolutionaries. No passengers can be transported on top of the high cart-loads of pressed cotton, the bales of raw wool in vague purple or brown colours, the Chinese cabbage, the concrete irrigation pipes, or the flattened loads of coal. If there is a seat left, it is for the driver, who in his sheepskin coat lies sleeping or leans on one elbow, staring with a fixed look at the horizon. His face is weather-beaten or, as it is called in Chinese stories, black. Dust, sand, wind and sunshine have made it deeply lined. He laughs, or is it a grimace? The cart-drivers with their fur caps with widely projecting ear-flaps, deeply hidden in dirty, shaggy fleece, whip in hand and seemingly completely passive, are probably the most independent souls of China. They do their work, look after their animals and passively accept their fate.

It goes without saying that in China driving a car is not without its dangers. Apart from the road to Tientsin, foreigners are not allowed to drive by car outside the immediate surroundings of Peking. We were glad to arrive in Tientsin after more than two hours' drive.

The remnants of European influence are clearer in Tientsin than in Peking. The western outskirts of Tientsin look like a badly maintained French provincial town, whereas in the centre British styles are dominant. The town party committee is housed in a hybrid building, whose architect must have seen pictures of the Tower of London. It has crenellations and is flanked by two towers which one might date as medieval English if one did not know better. The entrance was guarded by soldiers with rifles with fixed bayonets, but that seems to have been the case in normal times as well. The park in front of the party office was temporarily closed. Barbed-wire entanglements obstructed the entrances, and rush mats prevented one from seeing what happened inside.

We had lunch in the Great Tientsin Hotel on the Northern Liberation Road, which is famous for its cooking. The name of the road was apparently new. Inside we saw an Eastern European ambassador and several other foreigners, but no Chinese guests. When we left the restaurant, we heard that on the first floor a meeting was being held where one recited in chorus from the red book. In front of the hotel four cars were parked: a Ford (ours), a Chevrolet (the ambassador's) and two cars of an East European make on which the characters *fan-hsiu* (anti-revisionism) had been painted. These four passenger cars were practically the only ones we saw in Tientsin. The streets were dominated by people on foot, bicycle riders, pedicabs, tramways and buses. Draught animals seemed to avoid the centre of the city. The traffic was extremely quiet, which was unexpected in a town with large department stores in imperial style, fitted with domes and colonnades – in short, a town which, although much less developed, evoked reminiscences of Hong Kong or San Francisco.

The passers-by seemed to move more slowly than in Peking. It was rather chilly, but the sun shone and the cold was no reason for the Chinese in their padded coats to quicken their pace. One street, with big-character posters on both sides, was full of young people. An important local personality, Liu Tzu-hou, alternate member of the Central Committee and since September First Secretary of the provincial party committee of Hopei, was being attacked on the grounds of his cultural policies. He was charged with revisionism, but it was unclear why. Unlike Peking, almost nobody wore a red armband. Had the Red Guards all gone to Peking, or was that red armband still pinned to the sleeve of a jacket that was at home? Perhaps here they did not regard these armbands as important. However, the various armbands that we saw were marked by an official stamp of the town party committee, as they were in Peking.

It is a well-known fact that in August 1966 Red Guard behaviour in Tientsin had been much more active than in Peking, and now again Tientsin seemed to be ahead. It seemed as though here a next stage of the Cultural Revolution had been reached, and soon the resumption of teaching and a return to normalcy was to be expected. Later, how-

ever, it appeared that in Tientsin it took longer before the disturbances subsided than in Peking.

The nearer we came that day to our destination (a Dutch ship), the
more the Cultural Revolution seemed to lose its ominous features.
The scenery changed, as it changes between Belgian Brabant and the
north coast of Holland. The rivers with their sandy banks, on which
grew poplars that shed their yellow leaves, gave way to shallow pools
and alluvial land. The colour of the clay of which the houses were
built became darker. Between Tientsin and Hsinkang we did not see
Red Guards, but road-menders who were assisted by soldiers. A barren,
treeless landscape. Houses near ditches, hens on the road, and finally
the sea, which here, as elsewhere, conveyed a sense of freedom.

Departure of the Red Guards

I bought a Chinese fur cap and buttoned a fur lining into my winter
coat. In general the Red Guards who had come to Peking to see
Chairman Mao were not less well protected against the cold. In
addition to the Red Guards, workers and peasants from the provinces
crowded into the streets of Peking. They came to hand over a petition
to the Central Committee, and made use of the opportunity to do
some sight-seeing. The railways were in confusion. There were days
during which the main station in Peking was almost completely
reserved for special trains that were to take Red Guards and other
visitors back to their homes.

When, late one evening in mid-November, I went to have a look at
the crowds at the main station, the enormous square in front of it was
completely occupied by young people who, in their heavy padded or
fur-lined blue coats, were lying on the ground and trying to sleep,
leaning against each other or their luggage. If necessary, they made
room for someone who wanted to pass. Some were awake and were
bending over a trophy of the Cultural Revolution: a looted toy car.
There were children of eight or nine years old, pale and exhausted as
at the end of a tiring school outing, amazed to see foreign cars and
Europeans. There was the atmosphere of concluding a world jamboree.
The girls appeared tireless and gay. Clear eyes and flushed apple-round
cheeks, as on the pictures in *China Pictorial*. The number of people that
were packed together there must have been between ten and twenty
thousand. They lay and sat waiting for the trains that were to take them
home. Some of them would have to wait for two or three days.

Normal travellers could not leave from the main station, but had to go to a goods station near a gate in the north-west quarter of the town (Hsi-chih-men). Curiosity made me go there. Here too a great number of people had gathered, but they were of various types. The travellers had formed long queues which covered the street for hundreds of yards, and prepared themselves for the night: elderly people travelling to their children, young families on the way to the parental house in the countryside, armed military men in full marching-order going to their posts, merchants with rush mats, hens in rattan cages, and an enormous amount of bundles of clothes and cotton material, sacks of grain, earthenware pots, pans, thermos flasks and washbasins. It was dark. Many people slept on the pavement or had their bedding spread on the ground. There was no confusion at all, nor was there any crowding. Everyone seemed prepared to wait quietly and see whether the train that was to leave the next morning could take them all. Naturally there was a hot water vendor who attracted a great many customers.

Near this station a proclamation of the Central Committee and the State Council had been posted. It concerned a decision of the party and the government that the revolutionary young people who had come from the provinces had to leave Peking at once. The printed announcement was peremptorily worded and dated November 16. (Similar proclamations had been published earlier.) The government was realistic enough to understand that, although many of the young revolutionaries had arrived on foot, they could not be expected to be willing to leave Peking that way. The text of the proclamation was roughly as follows: 'The Central Committee and the State Council have decided that from November 21 onwards the Red Guards and other revolutionary young people cannot be allowed to make use of trains, ships and buses, since all means of transportation are needed, if we want to reach the targets of the first year of the Third Five Year Plan. It is no small thing that since August 18 a total of nine million Red Guards have visited Peking. This influx must end. Free tickets for public means of transportation will be given to Red Guards and other revolutionary young people only if they return home. They are not allowed to break their journey. All those who have not yet had a chance of seeing Chairman Mao must be patient until April. When the warm spring weather begins, they may come to Peking. The winter months must be used for preparing the walking tours which have been organised in imitation of the Long March. In his speech of November 3, comrade Lin Piao rightly indicated that this way of travelling in order to exchange revolutionary experiences must be well prepared and organised.'

The purpose of the proclamation was clear. The leaders were fed up with the wandering Red Guards. Mao Tse-tung indeed had said that in this way the young people could get acquainted with all aspects of society, but he too had not foreseen all the consequences. The plan to have the young people 'exchange revolutionary experiences' reportedly originated with T'ao Chu, then propaganda chief. A Red Guard newspaper disclosed that he had boasted of having suggested to Chairman Mao the idea of walking tours in imitation of the Long March. It is conceivable that T'ao Chu, who by the end of 1966 was being seriously criticised and in January 1967 was dismissed as director of the propaganda department, was not acting in good faith. The confusion, which resulted from the displacement of millions of young people, was tremendous. The economic burden weighed heavily. The leaders in Peking were not pleased to see the Red Guards arrive, but the opponents of the Cultural Revolution in the provinces liked to see them depart. The borders of several provinces, such as Szechwan and Tibet, were temporarily closed to Red Guards who came from other parts. The larger groups were usually commanded by a teacher or by a military man; not so the smaller groups, of which the participants were having the time of their lives. For the first time since 1949 they were allowed to move freely through China, without needing to bother about travel permits or the exchange of food ration coupons. This greatly stimulated the Red Guards' enthusiasm, who were happy to carry a framed portrait of Chairman Mao, if they could thereby gain the freedom of movement that had been denied them for so long. The question of whose interests the Red Guards were serving in these months must be answered with the sobering observation that the Red Guard movement, notably in its spontaneous aspects, was largely motivated by self-interest.

Revoking the freedom that had been given to the young people was no simple matter. The promise that in the spring of 1967 they could resume the pilgrimage to Peking was never redeemed. It was difficult enough to convince the non-Pekinese in Peking, who often numbered over a million at a time, to leave the town. The orders of the Central Committee and the State Council were largely ignored. The time limit within which one was permitted to travel free of charge was repeatedly extended, as far as I know, at least towards late December.

There were more indications that attempts were being made to curtail the excesses of the revolution. The destruction of cultural monuments was officially disapproved of. For as long as I stayed in China the paintings in the galleries of the Summer Palace had not been restored to their original state, but works of art that had so far remained untouched were taken under protection. The bronze birds and lions in the park of the Summer Palace had strips of paper attached that admonished the young people to leave the cultural objects alone, by appealing to them to 'Respect and protect the antiquities!'

Goods which in late August and early September had been confiscated by the Red Guards were returned, but a number of practical difficulties were involved, since in the meantime much had been sold through second-hand shops. And the authorities to whom one could complain about the confiscation of an armchair or a violin used to parry the claim by asking: 'Do you happen to have a receipt?' The answer of the claimant was usually in the negative, whereupon he was chided: 'But how can you have forgotten to ask for a receipt? Red Guards are honest and disciplined people. You don't believe that they would not have wanted to hand over a receipt, do you?' Which is a typical example of Chinese revolutionary logic.

The Fall of T'ao Chu, Head of Propaganda

Something more should be said about T'ao Chu. This powerful man from the South, a trained marxist of the first order, a poet and inspiring administrator, seemed pre-destined to reach a very high position in the party hierarchy. In his function of propaganda chief, which he had held since June 1966, he made the impression of being on the one hand a loyal supporter of the Cultural Revolution, whereas on the other he tried to create a more or less independent position for himself. His loyalty – whether pretended or not – is shown in the following anecdote. In September Red Guards were angry that a party secretary of the province of Kirin had not attended a party meeting 'because it was raining too hard'. They telephoned T'ao Chu and asked whether they were allowed to dismiss the lax official. With faultless feeling for the political situation of the moment, T'ao Chu replied: 'Do as you wish, you are the masses.'

On the other hand, T'ao Chu often boasted of belonging to the four top leaders. He used to say: 'Mao, Lin [Piao], Chou [En-lai] and I have decided to . . . ' His endeavour to maintain himself in his high position possibly resulted in a fraudulent attempt to confirm his image as number four by means of a picture in the national press media. Red Guard publications, which unlike the official *People's Daily* and other newspapers and magazines available in the post offices should be called 'unofficial', revealed that an accomplice of T'ao Chu published a fake picture in the *People's Daily* of November 6, 1966. A picture, which originally represented Mao, Lin Piao, Chou En-lai and Ch'en Po-ta on the rostrum of the Gate of Heavenly Peace, had a portrait of T'ao Chu placed between Chou En-lai and Ch'en Po-ta. Indeed, the picture looks rather unnatural. T'ao Chu seems to be standing too close to Chou En-lai and, unlike the others, does not have his hands placed on the balustrade of the rostrum.

Undoubtedly T'ao Chu had his reservations about the Cultural Revolution. Apart from his opposition to extending the Cultural Revolution to industry, the countryside and the government offices, it was the criticism of Liu Shao-ch'i and Teng Hsiao-p'ing that made him hesitate. This hesitation was the end of his career. Only by December 13 was he prepared to charge in public the President of the People's Republic of China and the General Secretary of the Communist Party with betrayal of the interests of the people. But by then it was too late. Mass meetings for the criticism of T'ao Chu were convened in early January, and in the same month Wang Li took over his job as head of propaganda.

Although one might have expected from the director of the propaganda department that he would provide the Cultural Revolution with a theoretical basis, T'ao Chu failed to do so. When on November 28, 1966, a mass meeting of 20,000 'militant revolutionaries' was devoted to the *cultural* ends of the Cultural Revolution, it was not T'ao Chu, but Chiang Ch'ing (Mrs. Mao Tse-tung) who made the main speech. At this meeting Liu Shao-ch'i and Teng Hsiao-p'ing were conspicuously absent. The literary world was represented by Kuo Mo-jo, Li Ying-ju, Chin Ching-mai and Ch'en Ya-ting. At least, no other writers' names were mentioned in the official press.

Chiang Ch'ing defines the Cultural Policy

Who actually was Chiang Ch'ing? After a period of study and library work in Shantung, where she was born, she went to Shanghai in the 'thirties to launch herself as a film actress under the name of Lan P'ing.

It was probably not before 1939 that she arrived in Yenan, where she became the third wife of Mao Tse-tung, who had separated from his second wife in order to marry her.[4] Mao's colleagues were not at all happy with the affair, and Chiang Ch'ing had great difficulty in having herself accepted, first as Mao's wife, and secondly as a political worker in her own right. For many years it was, in fact, Wang Kuang-mei (Mrs. Liu Shao-ch'i) who was considered as the first lady.

It is, of course, nonsense to attach much significance to rumours of an old feud between Chiang Ch'ing and Wang Kuang-mei, but the relationship between the two had never been friendly. And the fall of Wang Kuang-mei ran parallel with the rise of Chiang Ch'ing. With all her energy the latter plunged into the Cultural Revolution and was undoubtedly carried away by the tide of events. She did not recognise her own limitations. She felt young with the young and was still young enough to be a teen-age idol. The way in which she moved among the masses, with short, waved hair, walking erect and surrounded by fanatical adorers, brought to mind her earlier life as an actress. She emanated a magnetic power, which cannot have been derived only from talks with her husband but also from her own monomaniac emotionalism. She was famous for her demagogic way of speaking. She used to interrupt her speeches with questions such as: 'Am I right?' or 'Will you follow me?', which were always answered by stormy cries of 'Yes!'

One of Chiang Ch'ing's difficulties was that she hardly possessed an official function, apart from being a vice-chairman of the Cultural Revolution group. Lin Piao helped her in this by appointing her as Adviser on Cultural Work to the People's Liberation Army. This provided her with a uniform and also ended an old quarrel with the First Peking Opera Company of Peking, which on many occasions she had pressed to accept her advice. At the same time the Opera Company was incorporated into the army, and so a completely different relationship between Chiang Ch'ing and the actors came into existence. In addition to the First Peking Opera Company, the National Peking Opera Theatre, the Central Philharmonic Society, the ballet troupe and the orchestra of the Central Song and Dance Ensemble were taken over by the army. It could only mean that persuasion had failed, with the result that the leaders of the Cultural Revolution took refuge in military discipline.

Against the background of these measures, Chiang Ch'ing gave her important speech. It is understandable that nobody with greater authority in cultural affairs was prepared to explain the cultural principles of the Cultural Revolution. Her position was as extreme or more extreme than that of Zhdanov when he defined the stalinist cultural policies. As far as I know, no Chinese authority has ever spoken so disparagingly of Western culture yet with so little understanding of it. 'Capitalism has a history of several centuries,' Chiang Ch'ing said, 'nevertheless, it has only a pitiful number of "classics".' Some works modelled after the "classics" have been created, but these are stereotyped and no longer appeal to the people . . . On the other hand, there are some things that really flood the market, such as rock-'n'-roll, jazz, striptease, impressionism, symbolism, abstractionism, fauvism, modernism – there is no end to them – all of which are intended to poison and paralyse the minds of the people. In short, there is decadence and obscenity to poison and paralyse the minds of the people.'

In previous years, numerous discussions had taken place on the question of whether ghosts and gods should figure on the stage. This was one of the points on which Chiang Ch'ing had differed from the First Peking Opera Company. Now she indicated that the supernatural element had to be banned completely. This caused great alarm in intellectual circles, for, if a ban was put on the representation of supernatural beings, this was not only an attack on religion (with which they were on the whole prepared to agree), but also an attempt to disparage almost the whole of the Chinese and part of the Western cultural heritage. Among Chinese intellectuals the counter-argument was heard, that in this way the ties with the past were cut, whereas it was useful to know how the people had thought and lived in earlier ages. Of course, it was wrong to believe in ghosts, but one should know that superstition had existed. Progress in modern society could be measured only in comparison with the past. Several people were worried that the prohibition of ghosts implied the prohibition of playing Hamlet. They aired their admiration for Japan, which had modernised but was keeping certain old customs and traditions alive at the same time. So argued Chiang Ch'ing's opponents but at this juncture they got little publicity.

Chiang Ching's speech also provoked Russian reactions. Her ideas could hardly be called marxist. Marx and Engels had a completely different conception of European literature and admired Dante, Cervantes, Shakespeare, Schiller and Balzac. Assimilating this admiration, the Russian communists have made a positive valuation of part of the cultural heritage of the bourgeois past theoretically possible, and, therefore, could in no way agree with the new Chinese cultural policy.

The official Chinese press, of course, highly praised the new approach. Chou En-lai, who also spoke at the meeting of November 28, extolled Chiang Ch'ing to the skies. He confessed humbly that he knew nothing at all about culture and hoped to learn much from her in the field of music and drama. His speech was, in fact, a self-criticism, the necessity of which was evident, since Chou En-lai is known as an admirer and protector of the old Peking Opera. His homage to Chiang Ch'ing was rewarded. At the end of the meeting, after a mass recitation from the red book, he was asked to conduct the chorus of twenty thousand people in singing a maoist song.

The speech of Chiang Ch'ing meant that the revolution was to continue its extreme course. The last resistance to public criticism of Liu Shao-ch'i and Teng Hsiao-p'ing disappeared. The army was to take control of the arts. In early December the former First Secretary of the Peking party committee, P'eng Chen, and the writers Wu Han, Liao Mo-sha, Teng T'o and T'ien Han were arrested. Ch'en Po-ta said on January 3, 1967, that in 1966 four hundred thousand 'enemies of the people' had been moved from the cities to the countryside. One question was not yet answered, namely, how the workers should react to the Cultural Revolution. In September, Chou En-lai had warned against interference with industry. Would he be able to maintain this position? The stormy developments of January 1967 would answer that question.

REFERENCES

1. On August 2, 1966, Liu Shao-ch'i indeed said, in a talk to the Peking Institute of Construction Engineering, that he was replacing Li Hsüeh-feng. See Liu Shao-ch'i *Collected Works*, Kowloon: Union Research Institute, 1968, p. 331.

2. *Ibid.*, pp. 357–65.

3. See note 1 to Chapter 2.

4. See the somewhat romanticised biography of Chiang Ch'ing: Chung Hua-min and Arthur C. Miller, *Madame Mao: A Profile of Chiang Ch'ing*, Kowloon: Union Research Institute, 1968.

4

THE JANUARY REVOLUTION
AND ITS CONSEQUENCES:
WINTER AND SPRING 1967

During December 1966 Mao Tse-tung, Lin Piao and the Cultural
Revolution group realised that the Red Guards alone could not win
the battle against Liu Shao-ch'i, Teng Hsiao-p'ing and their followers.
Heavier guns were needed for 'bombarding the headquarters' of the
enemy. The workers had to provide these heavier guns.

Whether it was wise to involve the workers in the Cultural Revolution seems to have been the topic of a series of high-level discussions.
In September Chou En-lai had expressed the view that the workers
should be left alone. It was disclosed in the unofficial press that T'ao
Chu was also against it. It became known that the Central Committee
had its reservations. On December 26 the official press appealed to the
workers to carry the Cultural Revolution through into industry. The
new policy line was based on a decision of the Central Committee (in
fact, an enlarged Politburo meeting) of December 9, but the way in
which the decision was interpreted differed considerably from the
purport of the original text. The Central Committee had made the
conditions that industrial production would not be jeopardised, that
the eight-hour day would be respected, and that the exchanges of
revolutionary experiences would take place in the evening. These and
other restrictions were *not* mentioned in the *People's Daily* of December 26. Therefore, the intentions of the leaders remained unclear. The
article caused great confusion and quarrels in the industrial centres, and
led to measures restricting the disturbances, the description of which
could easily fill a book. I shall have to confine myself mainly to trying
to convey the atmosphere in which the developments of January 1967
took place.

Boxing Day – or the birthday of Mao Tse-tung which also falls on December 26 – was about the coldest day we had in Peking. But the cold

did not seem to affect revolutionary activities. Groups of Red Guards posted new pamphlets; pedicabs and small tricycle lorries delivered the Red Guard newspapers at news-stands. In spite of a temperature of fifteen degrees below zero and an icy wind, quite a lot of people were reading the wall newspapers. Seldom was any comment heard. Never was a look of mutual understanding exchanged with me. That day there happened to be a great number of new slogans and posters. The criticisms of the President of the People's Republic of China Liu Shao-ch'i, the General Secretary of the Communist Party Teng Hsiao-p'ing and the propaganda chief T'ao Chu were revived. Others were also attacked, such as Wang Jen-chung, who had succeeded T'ao Chu as First Secretary of the Central-South Bureau and was to play a key role in the Wuhan rebellion six months later. Lorries drove through the streets on which representatives of the Black Clique were shown to the people. They wore dunce's caps and carried boards on which their crimes were written.

The renewed criticism of President Liu seemed inevitable. The leaders of the All-China Federation of Trade Unions had their reservations about the decision of the Politburo to involve industry in the Cultural Revolution; they were also hesitant in accepting the objections of the Cultural Revolution group to the contract labour system, which had reportedly been introduced at the instigation of Liu Shao-ch'i. This system regulated temporary assignments, at the end of which dismissal followed. It was branded as part of a system of exploitation.[1] The Federation of Trade Unions was punished by being disbanded on December 27, and its president was accused of being a henchman of Liu Shao-ch'i. Whether the latter charge had some foundation or not is hard to prove, but it can be explained on historical grounds. Liu Shao-ch'i had a large following among the workers. Precisely because of his trade union work and the organisation of successful strikes, Liu Shao-ch'i had made his career in the Chinese Communist Party. In the 'twenties and 'thirties he had won his spurs in this field, and many Chinese workers must have known, for instance, that strikes organised by Liu Shao-ch'i forced the British in 1927 to give up their concession in Hankow.

Disturbances in Shanghai

The new policy of the central government in Peking provoked protests and fights in Shanghai, the largest industrial town of China.

During the first days of the new year rumours to that effect reached Peking. During January it appeared from both the official and the unofficial press that large-scale disturbances had occurred which caused Mao Tse-tung and Lin Piao to moderate their plans. The *People's Daily* reported that in Shanghai two irreconcilable parties had been formed. Resistance to the Cultural Revolution was stimulated by a group which carried the misleading name of 'Red Workers' Brigade for the Protection of the Thought of Mao Tse-tung' and similar organisations. On January 9, the *People's Daily* published an open letter by several Red Guard and other maoist organisations to the citizens of Shanghai, in which they admitted that, at the instigation of the Red Workers' Brigade for the Protection of the Thought of Mao Tse-tung, strikes had been organised in many factories and that 'a handful of reactionary elements' had tried to cut off water and electricity supplies and bring public transport to a standstill. The open letter of the Red Guards is one of the documents that formed the basis of what later in official terminology was proudly called the 'January Revolution'.

The success of the strikes is well known. The dock workers' strike was almost total and as their work could hardly be taken over by Red Guards or the military, it resulted in long delays in loading and unloading. Furthermore there were large-scale strikes in Shanghai's textile industry. Railway transportation was in great confusion as the combined result of strikes by railway staff and overcrowding.

The overcrowding of the trains was caused by a new phenomenon in the Cultural Revolution: the petitioning of the central government by wronged groups. This had occasionally occurred in the past, but now it grew to enormous proportions. Prompted by the Red Workers' Brigade, many Shanghai workers travelled to Peking to complain about the confusion and political insecurity. The first groups arrived in Peking in early January. Undoubtedly the journey was motivated by the wish to protest against the growing chaos. But a certain rivalry vis-à-vis the students also played a role. Why should only the students be allowed to travel through China at public expense? Was the working part of the population not entitled to its share of the cake? Within a couple of days the number of petitioners in Peking had risen to several tens of thousands.

The financial aspect of the strikes and the petitioning was of some interest. For almost twenty years there had been no strikes in China and the trade unions were ill-prepared for them. There were in fact funds for sick pay and pensions, but the status of these funds had become uncertain now that the Federation of Trade Unions had been disbanded. Part of these funds was used to enable workers to go to Peking and other towns to participate in the revolution. Industrial enterprises also shared in the costs. Those who performed the function of employer, or had otherwise risen above the position of untrained labourer, foresaw that, if the Cultural Revolution was to be carried through in industry, they could only expect to lose by it. Resistance to the Cultural Revolution was organised by the more competent workers and employees. The stakes were high. As a result of the new policy, which was detrimental to industrial production, they did not feel responsible any more for the performance of state enterprises. They took their fate into their own hands. In some cases they tried to continue production by offering the workers differentiated wages, extra allowances and premiums, on the condition that they would forget about the Cultural Revolution. In other factories the resistance was more overt: work was stopped and the labourers, provided with cash by the employers or trade unions, went to Peking in order to complain of the adverse effects of the Cultural Revolution.

That such was in fact the situation may be concluded from articles in the official press. On January 12, the *People's Daily* published an 'urgent notice' from over thirty maoist organisations in Shanghai, which appealed to the workers to remain at their posts on the assembly line. Those who had gone to other cities in order to 'exchange revolutionary experiences' were requested to return at once. The notice declared the certificates authorising the strikers to travel to other towns null and void, and ordered that the funds of all organisations and enterprises should be frozen, with the exception of expenditure for production, wages, and the Cultural Revolution. Readjustment of wages and payment of extra allowances were forbidden. It also stated that nobody was permitted to seize public buildings. The 'urgent notice' was recommended by the Central Committee, the State Council, the Military Commission of the Central Committee, and the Cultural Revolution group. Its publication in the *People's Daily* was ordered by Chairman Mao himself. This is what the press wanted us to believe, and, looking back, there is no reason to doubt it.

Economism

The attempts of a number of industrial enterprises to influence the workers by means of extra allowances was called 'economism', and was vehemently attacked by the central government. From the very first moment the struggle against economism had been one of the main motives of the Cultural Revolution. The long-standing practice that industrial workers were encouraged to greater efforts by means of material incentives was also looked upon as 'economistic'. It was not the material incentive but 'proletarian consciousness' that should be the main stimulus. The Cultural Revolution brought about a fierce criticism of the current economic theories. In early August 1966, during the eleventh session of the Central Committee, the official press attacked the ideas of the Western oriented economist Sun Yeh-fang. In order to prevent possible misunderstanding here, I must emphasise that both before and during the Cultural Revolution wages, at least in part, were based on the quantity and quality of the work performed. One could differ, however, on the way in which this principle of the 'socialist phase' should be worked out in practice. Sun Yeh-fang, who called himself a follower of Liberman and possibly counted President Liu Shao-ch'i among his admirers, believed that the *value* of the product should be taken as a basis for calculating the wages. If, for instance, a worker produced twice the norm, this should be clearly reflected in his salary. According to the Cultural Revolution group, this went much too far. Another reason why the theories of Sun Yeh-fang were rejected was that he attributed a key role to profit, which he wanted to use as a yardstick for judging the performance of individual enterprises and which was to play a role in national economic planning. In this way such planning would assume a more purely economic character. Sun's critics argued that, as a result of this, the authority of party and state in economic affairs would be greatly affected. Of course, Sun Yeh-fang was accused of revisionism.

It seems as if Mao Tse-tung, in launching the Cultural Revolution, harked back to ideals he nursed when introducing the people's communes, and that he wanted to lay the foundation of a wage system of a purely communist type; a system through which greater efforts would not be compensated by higher wages, but in which everyone would exert himself spontaneously to the benefit of the community, without expecting extra payment. The Cultural Revolution was intended to raise proletarian consciousness to a level where the introduction of the new remuneration system, based exclusively on everyone's need, would be possible. If this in fact has been the aim of Mao Tse-tung – an assumption which is supported in principle by the equal payment of all Red Guards, the confiscation of savings and other

C

egalitarian trends of the Cultural Revolution – little of it has materialised. During the Cultural Revolution the wage system hardly changed.
Depending on his age, number of children and his position, a trained
worker in the more developed parts of the country earned between 40
and 60 yüan a month (18 and 27 U.S. dollars). A cabinet minister
received a multiple of this, but not more than 400 yüan.

The reason why Mao Tse-tung believed he could not accept Sun
Yeh-fang's suggestions might be that Mao and his advisers thought
that China could not afford the luxury of powerful material incentives.
They may have argued that, if a Great Leap Forward in industrial
production brought about a considerable rise in wages, less money
could be reserved for investments, the result of which would be that
the Leap Forward was less great. Also for other, non-economic reasons, a liberalisation of the economy as in Yugoslavia or Czechoslovakia (under Dubcek) was out of the question. Material incentives, as
such, conflicted with Mao's efforts to play down the role of individual
property, which was to be made subordinate to the great collective
goal of achieving communism.

During the Cultural Revolution the idea of a new Great Leap
Forward, which was predicted by several Red Guard leaders, played
a certain part. The official press, almost exclusively, mentioned the
possibility of a 'Leap Forward', without the qualification 'Great'.
This signified that the party leaders believed that the people were
not mentally prepared to make extraordinary efforts without asking
for compensation. The reactions of the workers in Shanghai must have
further convinced Mao Tse-tung that the Cultural Revolution had not
yet worked.

The problems that confronted the Chinese leaders were many. And
there was no way back. They were restricted by the options of the
present situation and by the support of specific power groups. They
wished to restore order by means of practical compromises, but were
not prepared to sacrifice their economic and ideological principles.
Restoration of a minimum of order, and limitation of the economic
damage were high on the agenda. The confusion in the economic
field had assumed enormous proportions and in several large towns was
no different from total anarchy. The extent of the confusion appeared
from the announcement of a series of decisions by revolutionary
rebels in the financial and trade organisations, which were published
in the *People's Daily* of January 22. ('Revolutionary rebels' was a common denominator of workers, students and others who supported the

Cultural Revolution, or pretended to do so.) The decisions were aimed at opposing economism and bourgeois reactionaries. They boiled down to the following: taxes, which in the past had been collected in a legal way, should not be returned to those who had paid them. All taxes that had already been returned illegally should be collected back again. The increase of wages and payment for travel and other allowances for 'the exchange of revolutionary experiences' were prohibited. The officials who had been involved in unauthorised payments were made personally responsible for the repayment. The goods and funds that the Red Guard had confiscated in its struggle against old habits and old customs belonged to the public; if these goods and funds had been privately divided, they should be returned and handed over to the state. It was forbidden to besiege banks and to appropriate one's own savings. Immediate measures should be taken in order to solve the problem of stoppages in the ports. Anyone who incited dock workers to strike was to be punished as an 'active counter-revolutionary'. It was strictly forbidden to distribute state property. Finally there was a warning against black marketeers.

But who could watch the implementation of these decisions and supervise the administration of the returned money and goods? In Shanghai fights broke out between the Red Workers' Brigade and the revolutionary rebels. The Red Workers' Brigade had reportedly mobilised a hundred thousand people. Fifty persons were wounded and several killed. In other cities similar confrontations took place; incidents in Harbin, Nanking, Urumchi, Chengtu and Sining were extensively covered in the unofficial press. On top of this, the peasants, who make up over 80 per cent of the Chinese people, became involved. It was again the official press, notably the Shanghai newspaper *Wen-hui pao* of January 20, which reported that the old, revisionist party committee of Shanghai had encouraged the peasants from the countryside around Shanghai to leave their villages and march to the town in order to underline their demands for higher wages and better living conditions. The peasants demanded wages similar to those of the factory workers, but the Shanghai newspaper considered this premature: 'The present conditions are not ripe to eliminate the differences between town and countryside, between workers and peasants.' Furthermore the government was painfully surprised by the liquidation of collective property in the countryside. In late January the official press urged the peasants to return the distributed production funds and grain reserves.

Humiliation of the Revisionists; the Criticism
of Liu Shao-ch'i

The disturbances and contradictions were reflected in barbaric measures against the persons who were blamed for them. On January 11 the revolutionary rebels in Shanghai managed to arrest two people of the old local party committee and carried them, with the inevitable dunce's caps on their heads, on lorries through the streets of Shanghai. Among them was Sung Chi-wen, the vice-mayor who had been involved in the incident of August 31, 1966, which was described earlier. There were mass meetings in Shanghai, where revisionists were tortured in front of the crowd. Red Guard newspapers published pictures of this. One of these pictures shows the hand-cuffed vice-mayor of Shanghai, lying on the ground while a soldier stands with his shoes on his face. In Peking on January 4 and 5 the former mayor, P'eng Chen, and others were subjected to similar treatment. In the Red Guard press, pictures were published showing how the former director of the propaganda department Lu Ting-i, the former Chief of Staff Lo Jui-ch'ing and P'eng Chen are each held by two military men, who bend their arms backwards and up, and so force them to bow their heads; in Peking this uncomfortable position was called the 'jet-treatment', to which, later in the year, several diplomats were also exposed.

The meetings of January 4 and 5 were elaborately described in the unofficial press. More than twenty Red Guards and representatives of the revolutionary rebels made speeches in which they voiced their disapproval of the 'dirty attacks' that the defendants had launched on Chairman Mao, 'who, as the reddest red sun, shines in our hearts', and on his close comrade-in-arms Lin Piao. Popular fury was worked up to a point where 'the public started to stamp their feet, and their hands began itching for a sound thrashing'. The victims 'were as timid as rats, and, like dying pigs, broke into cold sweat'. During the pandemonium the revolutionary rebels who showed their victims to the masses could not resist the temptation of throwing them to the ground. Several posters added the significant detail that at that moment P'eng Chen, who had repeatedly refused to confess, tried to commit suicide in front of the crowd by striking his head against the stones. However, his guards stopped him in time.

The accusations varied considerably. It was held against the former propaganda chief, Lu Ting-i, that he had failed to publish a sufficient number of the works of Chairman Mao and that high quality paper had been used for editions of the speeches of Khrushchev and Tito. Lu had considered a circulation of ten million copies of the selected works of Mao Tse-tung as large enough. As a result of the Cultural Revolution, however, more than thirty million copies had been printed by the end of 1966 and plans were announced to increase this figure by fifty million in 1967, so that one out of every ten Chinese would possess a complete set of Mao's works. Early in 1969 a circulation figure had been reached which provided every Chinese household with the possibility of buying Mao's works. Lu Ting-i was further blamed for having incited his wife, who was subjected to the same struggle meetings of January 4 and 5, to write threatening letters to the fifteen-year-old daughter of Lin Piao, in which she had tried to prove that Yeh Ch'ün was not her real mother. Miss Lin was so upset by this that she had to be treated in hospital.

Families, children, wives: everyone was involved and nobody was spared, including the President of the People's Republic. On the Square of Heavenly Peace a collection of twenty or thirty posters, containing an elaborate analysis of Liu Shao-ch'i's past, were on display. In his booklet about education in communism, known in the Anglo-Saxon world by the title *How to Be a Good Communist*, he reportedly had not sufficiently emphasised the class struggle, particularly in the slightly revised edition of 1962. The Red Guards also drew attention to the fact that in this edition the name of Stalin occurred less often than in the earlier text of 1949, and that the author had once written 'Stalin' where the edition of 1949 had 'comrade Stalin'. The posters blamed Liu Shao-ch'i for having established too close relations with Khrushchev after Stalin's death. They further revealed that in 1946 he had been opposed to the military tactics which Lin Piao had advocated using in the fight against the Kuomintang. In the field of education Liu had been a protagonist of bourgeois concepts and had objected to introducing a system in which as much time would be devoted to work as to study. It was held against him that in 1964 he had addressed a letter to the provincial party committees, in which he warned against dogmatism. This was explained as indirect criticism of the ideas of Mao Tse-tung. It was especially distasteful that his children were forced to testify against him. Liu, who was married to Wang Kuang-mei, had a daughter from an earlier marriage named Liu T'ao, who contended that her own mother had disclosed a large amount of material which provided evidence of the incorrigibly bourgeois nature of Liu Shao-ch'i. Apart from Liu T'ao, two sons of Liu Shao-ch'i also testified against him and their stepmother, after having been urged by Chiang Ch'ing to do so. However, Liu T'ao and her brothers did not escape being criticised thus themselves. Again the old rivalry between Chiang Ch'ing and Wang Kuang-mei came into play.

The staff of the large government compound Chungnanhai could not afford to lag behind the general mood of criticism. On January 26, the revolutionary rebels among them organized a meeting at which Liu Shao-ch'i and Wang Kuang-mei, who lived in Chungnanhai, were called to account for their political activities and beliefs. The unofficial press published a touching report on that meeting, part of which I shall quote. 'The revolutionary masses demanded that Liu should recite the first paragraph of the first page of the red book of quotations from Chairman Mao. Wang Kuang-mei said: "He can certainly do that." However, the result was that Liu, stammering and hesitating, could not get any farther than "the force at the core leading our cause is . . .", and, while saying that, he still forgot the words "at the core". Wang Kuang-mei hurried to explain to her husband that he had forgotten "at the core". Again and again she tried to defend him. Because the attitude of Liu was not straightforward, the masses took his cap away. Thereupon Kuang-mei said: "You should not do that, for he might catch a cold and in that case it would not be possible to continue struggling against him." The masses asked Liu why he had resisted Chairman Mao, which he answered by saying that he had *not* resisted the Chairman. The masses then asked why he had outlined a reactionary policy. Liu replied: "In order to oppose the *thought* of Mao Tse-tung." When the masses were not content with these answers, Kuang-mei protected him and wanted him to leave. She proposed that the masses should wage their struggle against herself, but Liu feared that his wife would run into difficulties and did not want to leave. Then the masses pushed him out of the room. They told Wang Kuang-mei to stand on a bench and struggled further against her.'

In an important publication of the Red Guard of January 10, Liu Shao-ch'i was depicted as a 'counter-revolutionary revisionist'. Chou En-lai, who attended all mass meetings at which Liu, Teng Hsiao-p'ing and T'ao Chu were impeached (but at which they themselves were not present), advocated that in criticising the President one should differentiate between the person of Liu Shao-ch'i and his policies. What did this actually mean? Did Chou want to save Liu's policies, or his person? Because Chou (or Mao Tse-tung) has always until now prevented the humiliation of the President in front of the furious masses of the people, and so respected his person – and since Chou never completely dissociated himself from Liu's policies, notably his foreign policy – this question is hard to answer. His position remaining somewhat ambivalent, Chou played a dangerous game. In early January he too was attacked in big-character posters, which, however, were immediately removed. On January 8, Premier Chou En-lai explained his position to the Red Guards. He pointed out that all vice-premiers, except Lin Piao, had been criticised in posters and in the unofficial press. He said that five of them, although they had been properly exposed, now wanted to correct their mistakes and had to be left alone so that they could again devote themselves completely to their work. So the Red Guards should stop their accusations. The vice-premiers who were protected by Chou were: Ch'en Yi, Minister of Foreign Affairs, Li Fu-ch'un, Chairman of the State Planning Commission, Li Hsien-nien, Minister of Finance, T'an Chen-lin, Director of the Agricultural and Forestry Office of the State Council, and Hsieh Fu-chih, Minister of Public Security. With the exception of T'an Chen-lin, the Premier succeeded in helping his main deputies to survive the Cultural Revolution, although they often ran into serious trouble.

Nobody was completely secure from criticism. Even Mao Tse-tung was not. But in his case the criticism was not produced by the revolutionary rebels, but by those who resisted the Cultural Revolution – criticism which could hardly be openly vented and had recourse to satire and covert allusions, sometimes pretending to be printing errors in both the official and unofficial press.

Mao Tse-tung calls on the Army; the Criticism of General Lo Jui-ch'ing

The situation was grave. It was evident that a great part of the population would not agree with the criticism of President Liu Shao-ch'i, that many people close to Mao Tse-tung had their reservations about the attempts to involve the workers in the Cultural Revolution, and that almost no one knew any more how to settle the intentionally incited conflicts between students and labourers, or between revolutionary rebels and the more conservative workers. Moreover, as has been mentioned, the peasants spoke up. They had expressed demands which could not be complied with. Mao Tse-tung believed that order could be restored and a victory in the Cultural Revolution ensured if the army would side with the revolutionary rebels. As

appeared from a report in the unofficial press, Lin Piao warned that the
army could not be trusted in all respects. Looking back on it now,
one must conclude that Lin Piao's estimate of the army's morale was
more exact than that of Mao Tse-tung, who must be considered to
some extent alienated from everyday reality. Mao and Lin talked about
the problem on the night of January 22–23. Mao Tse-tung persisted
in his view, and the next day, in the name of the Central Committee,
the State Council, the Military Commission of the Central Committee
and the Cultural Revolution group, a decree was signed whereby the
armed forces were authorised to support the Left. In the introductory
text of the communiqué the observation was made that under the
guidance of Mao Tse-tung the great proletarian Cultural Revolution
had entered a new phase: 'The most important feature of this new
phase is that the proletarian revolutionaries are forming great alliances,
and seizing power from the handful of people within the party taking
the capitalist road and from the conservative elements who follow the
bourgeois reactionary line.' The communiqué pointed out that, if
'the truly proletarian Left' would request the armed forces to assist
them in the take-over, they should do so. The army was obliged to
take action against counter-revolutionary elements. If the latter were
to use weapons, the army had to launch a powerful counter-attack.
Finally the decree called for a campaign in all army units to demonstrate
the incompatibility of the proletarian revolutionary line represented
by Mao Tse-tung, and the bourgeois reactionary policy of Liu Shao-
ch'i and Teng Hsiao-p'ing.

The decree raised a number of questions. For instance, how could
the army unfailingly know who belonged to 'the truly proletarian
Left'? And how could the armed forces be united in their action if
they themselves were entangled in criticism of Liu Shao-ch'i and discussions on the Cultural Revolution? Not everyone in the army was
inclined to accept the criticism of Liu and Teng at face value. Lin Piao
was right when he counselled prudence. Moreover, the unreliability
of the armed forces, or at least of several generals, had already come to
light well before the decree of January 23 was published.

Earlier it was mentioned that the former Chief of Staff of the
People's Liberation Army, General Lo Jui-ch'ing, was subjected to
struggle meetings on January 4 and 5. Pictures show him sitting on a
chair with his left leg in bandages, while soldiers give him the 'jet-
treatment'. The rumour was that in an attempt to take his own life
Lo Jui-ch'ing had jumped out of a window and had broken one of his

legs. A Red Guard publication confirmed that Lo had tried to commit suicide 'fearing lest he be punished'. According to the Red Guards, Lo had been a time bomb in the party and the army for thirty years. After his exposure in the summer of 1966 he had allegedly continued his resistance to the policies of Mao Tse-tung. One of the speakers at the struggle meetings reported on a curious piece of conversation between the arch-enemies Lin Piao and Lo Jui-ch'ing: 'Vice-Chairman Lin said: "The thought of Mao Tse-tung is the highest and most living marxism–leninism of our time." Lo Jui-ch'ing answered slightingly: "You cannot say 'the highest'. Would there also be a 'less high' marxism–leninism? Or a 'higher' marxism–leninism? 'Highest and most living' is difficult to understand and for foreigners hard to translate." Vice-Chairman Lin then said: "The thought of Mao Tse-tung is the acme of marxism–leninism of our era." But this was also not acceptable for Lo Jui-ch'ing: "You cannot say that either. It does not make a good impression on foreigners." '

It appeared also from the rest of the accusations that Lo Jui-ch'ing considered that exaggerated propaganda for the thought of Mao Tse-tung was not a good advertisement. The foreigners, whose feelings he wished to consider, were the Russians. One of the speakers said this in so many words, and it may well have been true.

An analysis of the criticism of Lo Jui-ch'ing brings us closer to one of the origins of the Cultural Revolution. Lo was described as a faithful follower of Khrushchev. According to his critics, he adhered to the view that the class struggle would gradually die out, and propagated the theory of the abolition of the dictatorship of the proletariat. In this, Lo Jui-ch'ing and the arch-revisionist Khrushchev were reportedly as alike as two peas in a pod.

To what extent Lo Jui-ch'ing should in fact be considered guilty of Soviet revisionism is hard to say. The charges, which were heaped on the heads of the supposed followers of Liu Shao-ch'i and Teng Hsiao-p'ing, were often based on talks that were never recorded. The accusations often took possible intention for accomplished fact. The differences between Mao Tse-tung and Lo Jui-ch'ing on military matters probably provide more solid ground. According to revelations in the unofficial press, Lo was opposed to the maoist doctrine that ideological and political education were more important than military training. Lo had aimed primarily at a technical improvement of the equipment of the armed forces. He was charged with having sabotaged the formation and training of the people's militia, for which

C*

Mao Tse-tung had given explicit directives in 1960. One might infer that Lo had advocated normal relations with the Soviet Union, in order to receive from that country the modern equipment which the People's Liberation Army badly needed. Hence Lo had his reservations vis-à-vis the propaganda for the thought of Mao Tse-tung as the 'highest marxism–leninism'.

On the other hand, the objections of the maoists to a friendly relationship with the Soviet Union can easily be explained. Moscow was not inclined to share its advanced knowledge of rocket technique or nuclear weapons with Peking, and, if we may indulge in speculation, Moscow might have been willing to assist China in modernising her conventional arsenal on the condition that Peking would abandon its ambitious and extremely costly nuclear programme. If this condition was ever implicitly or explicitly expressed, it was rejected by Mao Tse-tung. One should not be misled by Chinese propaganda, which focuses on the ideological training of the soldier and emphasises his courage and morale, which are called more important than modern equipment. Mao did not so much want the modern conventional equipment that Lo Jui-ch'ing hoped to receive from the Soviet Union, but the very modern, super-armament of a nuclear power which China will now have to develop herself, since no country is willing to help her with it. One should not forget that a 'people's war' with primitive means can be a success only by the grace of a nuclear balance. Undoubtedly Mao Tse-tung is aware that the success of the people's war in the last instance depends on whether he possesses modern atomic weapons.[2]

The foremost slogan of the People's Liberation Army is: 'Politics first.' By the ideological training of the soldier, which is aimed at enhancing his fighting spirit without offering any compensation, and which prepares the military to combat 'economism' when they have left active service, the foundation is laid for additional efforts by the Chinese people without raising their standard of living. To a large extent the state revenues are being invested in the development of China's nuclear capability. Thus the Cultural Revolution and the Chinese nuclear tests go hand in hand. When on June 17, 1967, the first Chinese hydrogen bomb was exploded, this was rightly called 'a victory of the thought of Mao Tse-tung'.

Did the Revisionists plan a Coup d'Etat?

In 1965 and 1966 the differences between Mao Tse-tung and Lin Piao on the one hand, and their opponents P'eng Chen, Lo Jui-ch'ing and others on the other, reached a point at which the fear of a coup d'état to neutralise Mao's influence was not completely unfounded. The imagination of over-zealous Red Guards, however, has clouded the issue. In my opinion, they have not been able to produce evidence that the opponents of Mao Tse-tung had in fact plotted a coup. But they did throw suspicion of high treason on a number of unfortunate persons. We have to consider this, since otherwise the Chinese attitude towards the Soviet Union will remain obscure.

In the struggle meetings of January 4 and 5 a certain Yang Shang-k'un was involved, who for about twenty years had served as a staff official of the Central Committee, most recently as a deputy secretary of the Secretariat. It seems that he was permitted to enter Chairman Mao's study and was part of his immediate entourage. From the charges the following can be distilled. Like General Lo Jui-ch'ing, Yang was sceptical about the cult of Mao Tse-tung. 'This is called a victory for the thought of Mao Tse-tung, and that is called a victory for the thought of Mao Tse-tung', Yang once disparagingly said. 'If one plays ping-pong and one wins, it is a victory for the thought of Mao Tse-tung, but what should one say if one loses?' Yang was charged with treason. He had allegedly installed a listening device in the Chairman's study in order to record his talks with members of the Politburo. In this way party secrets leaked out to P'eng Chen and General Lo Jui-ch'ing, who, in connivance with President Liu Shao-ch'i and General Secretary Teng Hsiao-p'ing, were planning a coup d'état. In the years following the Great Leap Forward, Yang united with the class enemy inside and outside China. He became 'the messenger-boy and slave of Khrushchev' and gave crucial information to the Soviet revisionists.

Another more elaborate variation on the theme of a coup d'état appeared in posters which were displayed in mid-April. The coup, which was allegedly planned by President Liu Shao-ch'i and Teng Hsiao-p'ing, should have materialised in February 1966. Notably P'eng Chen had been involved in the plotting. The Liu-Teng clique had taken steps in moving troops and making logistical preparations. They intended liberating tens of thousands of political prisoners and concentrating loyal troops around Peking. They had wireless communications with 'a foreign country', in order to ask for 'foreign aid', if necessary. On an island in the Dragon Lake in the south of Peking they had ordered a fish pond to be built, intending to invite a number of important generals who were loyal supporters of Mao Tse-tung to come and fish there at the time the coup was to take place. They would, in fact, be held prisoners. In early 1966 Liu Shao-ch'i had travelled to see his friend Wang En-mao, the party secretary and military commander of Sinkiang, for secret talks. In the same period Teng Hsiao-p'ing visited Liu Lan-t'ao, First Secretary of the Northwest Bureau, to inform him. The posters which related this drew large groups of readers for several days. However, they were soon covered with other less sensational placards, probably by order of Chou En-lai or the Cultural Revolution group.

Why should the Chinese leaders have been opposed to the exposure of the plotters? One might consider the following possibilities: (a) the story was completely invented; (b) the story was based partly on facts, but suggested a rather massive resistance to Chairman Mao, and it was inopportune to create the impression that such were possible; (c) the story was largely based on truth, but compromised several influential party officials in the provinces who were not yet arrested (here I think, for instance, of Wang En-mao, the powerful man in Sinkiang, whom the Red Guards had charged with 'counter-revolutionary revisionism', but who for the time being was being spared by the central government for tactical reasons); (d) the posters demanded a public trial and capital punishment of the main plotters, including President Liu Shao-ch'i and General Secretary Teng Hsiao-p'ing. It is conceivable that in Mao's opinion this went too far, or was inopportune, since it could foment the internal dissensions. A public trial of Liu Shao-ch'i would contradict the trend towards moderation. In the months of February and March successful attempts had been made to slow down the pace of the Cultural Revolution and to promote co-operation between groups with different interests.

The Conspiracy of Marshal Ho Lung, the Committee for United Action, and other Resistance to the Cultural Revolution

Back to January 1967. The description of the confusion, the world of the Red Guard, the violence and hatred, slander and conspiracies is still far from complete.

In late December and early January a number of generals were arrested and accused of revisionism. Among them was Marshal P'eng Te-huai, but the reports differ as to exactly where and when he was captured. One report mentions Changsha in Hunan province, another

Chengtu, the capital of Szechwan, far in the interior, as the place of the arrest.[3] On January 11 the official press reported a shake-up of the recently established Cultural Revolution group of the army, which was evidently related to the arrest of the generals. On or about January 13 the Red Guards revealed the conspiracy of Marshal Ho Lung. It tells us much of Chinese family relations, but little about the military system. Marshal Ho Lung, who was close to P'eng Te-huai,[4] allegedly wanted to bring the armed forces on the side of Liu Shao-ch'i. He had been in league with the former Chief of Staff of the People's Liberation Army (General Lo Jui-ch'ing), a vice-commander of the air force, a political commissar of the navy, a vice-minister of defence who happened to be a nephew of Ho Lung, and a number of lieutenant-generals. The military commander of the province of Szechwan, who resided in Chengtu, played a key-role in the plot. In case fighting broke out, Ho Lung had planned to withdraw to Chengtu. He had ordered a bunker to be ready for him there. The Marshal was also supported by Li Ching-ch'üan, First Secretary of the South-west Bureau, to which the province of Szechwan belonged. The truth of the old Chinese saying seemed to be confirmed: 'When the whole country is in disorder, Szechwan is the first to be in disorder; when order is being restored, Szechwan is the last to be brought to order.' The inhabitants of Szechwan are known as hot-tempered people.

Several young people had their place in the conspiracy, and in that way the Red Guards had opponents of their own generation. Marshal Ho Lung communicated with the First Secretary of the South-west Bureau, Li Ching-ch'üan, through his own son. The latter, as well as the sons of Li Ching-ch'üan, studied at Tsinghua University. When the son of Ho Lung left Peking in order to 'exchange revolutionary experiences', like everyone did in the autumn of 1966, he reportedly stayed in Szechwan in the home of Li Ching-ch'üan. Ho Lung's son was moreover on friendly terms with Liu T'ao, the daughter of Liu Shao-ch'i. The son of Ho Lung, the sons of Li Ching-ch'üan and the daughter of Liu Shao-ch'i were charged with having obstructed the Cultural Revolution in Tsinghua University. In mid-January posters announced that in Peking one of the sons of Li Ching-ch'üan had been arrested by the police. In reaction to this and other arrests, students who did not wish to support the more extreme tendencies in the Cultural Revolution turned against the Ministry of Public Security. They formed the so-called 'Committee for United Action' and, armed with knives and stones, made several attempts to storm the ministry.

This was reported in the unofficial press, and foreigners also saw large groups of students in front of the gates of the ministry, which is on the south-east side of the Square of Heavenly Peace. The assaults on the ministry took place during the night. Posters revealed that the Committee for United Action numbered about five hundred followers, but in reality the influence of the Committee was believed to be much greater. It reportedly had contacts in several provinces, including Sinkiang. The policy of the Committee was tersely stated in the slogan: 'Fry Chiang Ch'ing, and overthrow Chou En-lai and Ch'en Po-ta.'

How should we rate these 'conspiracies'? Undoubtedly the maoists tried to give the Cultural Revolution a class struggle aspect. The privileged sons of the high party officials were all thrown together and branded as enemies of the revolution. A Red Guard newspaper reported that in the Western Hills, the Second Headquarters of the Red Guard, to which the 'Red Banner Combat Group of the Peking Aviation College' and affiliated organisations belonged, had built an underground hide-out for the rich people's sons. The sons of President Liu Shao-ch'i, of General Secretary Teng Hsiao-p'ing, of the Minister of Foreign Affairs Ch'en Yi, and of the chairman of the State Ecomonic Commission Po I-po, could, if necessary, go into hiding there. They all seemed to be bona fide Red Guards and were members of the Inspection Brigade of the Red Guard of the Western part of the town. During January it was made known that Liu Yün-jo (a son of Liu Shao-ch'i), Ch'en Yi's son and Ho Lung's son had been arrested. Although these students were opposed to the official policy of the régime vis-à-vis the Red Guard, it is hardly conceivable that they were a danger to the régime. However, by their arrests their fathers were put under pressure. Whether the blackmail had any success remains open to doubt. In the case of Li Ching-ch'üan, who, until his own arrest in Szechwan many months later quite effectively resisted the Cultural Revolution group, it may have been counter-productive.

On the basis of what we know now, which is not much, I do not believe that before the Cultural Revolution there existed a conspiracy of any significance against Mao Tse-tung. Perhaps several party leaders harboured the wish to push the Chairman to one side. The unofficial press repeatedly suggested that in December 1958 Mao Tse-tung was not acting of his own free will in announcing his resignation from the presidency of the People's Republic, which was subsequently taken over by Liu Shao-ch'i. In those days, however, it was said that Mao resigned because he wanted to devote himself more to theoretical work. This was acclaimed from all sides since he was difficult to deal with in practical matters. The impression that Chairman Mao was alienated from reality is confirmed by revelations of the Japanese communists, who, headed by Kenji Miyamoto, in March 1966 came to Peking for consultations and hesitated to accept the maoist policies that were thrust upon them. The Japanese refused to prepare themselves for an armed take-over, which in their view would inevitably result in failure, as in Indonesia. They managed to reach an agreement with their Chinese counterparts on a draft-communiqué, which was, in fact, a compromise between the Japanese and maoist views. Among the Chinese participants in these talks were Teng Hsiao-p'ing, P'eng Chen, Chou En-lai and K'ang Sheng. However, when the draft-communiqué was submitted to Mao Tse-tung, he resisted all compromise. The result was that Miyamoto was declared a revisionist and that Mao Tse-tung accelerated preparations for the Cultural Revolution, which was launched in mid-April 1966. This was done, in conformity with a universal law, at a moment when his greatest enemy Liu Shao-ch'i was abroad, paying a state visit to Pakistan and Burma. The combined action of Teng Hsiao-p'ing and P'eng Chen during these talks (from which K'ang Sheng and Chou En-lai may have dissociated themselves in varying degrees), might, of course, be interpreted as a conspiracy against the authority of Mao Tse-tung.

However, actual resistance to Mao, in my opinion, does not date from *before* the Cultural Revolution, but was born spontaneously *during* the Cultural Revolution. The resistance was primitive and badly organised, but sometimes assumed a massive appearance. On January 26 the official press reported a confrontation in Harbin between three hundred war veterans, armed with daggers and clubs, and the local garrison. A number of arrests were made. The veterans presumably had relations with the so-called Red Flag Army, which Chou En-lai in a speech on January 19 branded as a 'counter-revolutionary organisa-tion' with branches in several towns. The Premier also said that several commanders of the Red Flag Army and of another 'counter-revolu-tionary organisation', viz. the National Headquarters for a Take-over by Workers, Peasants and Soldiers, had been arrested in a medical institute in Peking. Initially the counter-revolutionaries had resisted their arrest, and disarmed and imprisoned the police who came to capture them, but when reinforcements arrived, who presented them with an ultimatum, they capitulated. Chou En-lai said that, among the counter-revolutionaries was a henchman of Li Ching-ch'üan, the rebellious First Secretary of the South-west Bureau. The speech of the Premier was reported in *Tung-fang-hung pao* of January 23, published by Red Guards of the Geological Institute.

At the same moment the Cultural Revolution was convulsing the armed forces, where, on the basis of the January 23 decree, a campaign was launched to draw a clear demarcation line between the policy of Liu Shao-ch'i and Chairman Mao. As everywhere else, the military combined this campaign with criticism of certain personalities. In Peking, generals with dunce's caps on their heads were driven through the streets in lorries. Naturally, this weakened military discipline at just the wrong moment, when high demands were being made upon the preparedness and loyalty of the armed forces. It was therefore no surprise when on January 28 the Military Commission of the Central Committee announced further regulations which, in effect, restricted the military support of the Left. One of these regulations read that, in carrying out the Cultural Revolution in the armed forces, it was inadmissible to apply corporal punishment or to force people to wear dunce's caps. This was a concession to the army officers, against whom, of course, the charges of revisionism and bourgeois leanings had been mainly directed. It appeared as though Lin Piao had gained the support of the commanding officers by promising them that ideological fault-finding would not be enforced by physical harassment. The decree of January 28 also contained a paragraph to the effect that fighting units and secret departments should not be interfered with. It requested the wandering students, workers, medical doctors, etc. to return home at once, and also prohibited strikes.

Thus the armed forces became the only power machinery which was not undermined by the Cultural Revolution. It gave reason to hope that order and peace in China could be restored. However, because the army was more or less exempt from going through a genuine Cultural Revolution, it prevented the extreme Left, for which it had little sympathy, from coming to power. Hence the Cultural Revolution was bound to end in a series of compromises. The alternative would have been complete confusion, civil war and possibly the end of maoism.

Conflict with the Soviet Union

The wave of internal tension had risen so high that it broke over the heads of the foreigners in Peking as well. Several Chinese leaders had been accused of collaboration with Soviet revisionism and, as the Cultural Revolution fomented an atmosphere of conspiracy and high treason, the popular fury naturally turned against Russian diplomats in Peking. Ch'en Po-ta, chairman of the Cultural Revolution group, provided the necessary theoretical background. On January 18 he explained that Khrushchev had led the Soviet Union along the wrong road. Ch'en observed that the October Revolution in Russia had not been enough. The October Revolution had ended private ownership of the means of production, but the economic and social revolution had not been followed by an ideological revolution. The Soviet Union had never gone through a cultural revolution. This was the cause of the Soviet Communist Party being ideologically weak. Such a thing would never happen in China, Ch'en Po-ta argued. The meaning of his argument was clear: the Chinese leaders had been wiser than their Russian colleagues and therefore could not learn anything more from Moscow. The Soviet leaders had no reason to assume a position of superiority, and should in fact recognise superior Chinese insight.

The Russians refused to follow this line of thought and would not accept the transplantation of the cult of the thoughts of Mao Tse-tung to the Red Square in Moscow, where a group of Chinese students shouted maoist slogans near the tomb of Lenin. The Russian police intervened and put them on board the train to China. This was January 25, 1967. On January 26 violent demonstrations began in front of the Soviet Embassy in Peking. For several days a visit to the Embassy was possible only through a back entrance. Visitors ran the risk of being threatened and spat upon. Everywhere in the town slogans were displayed which demanded that Brezhnev and Kosygin be subjected to the death penalty in various primitive ways. The demonstrations in front of the Embassy continued day and night and prevented the Russians from having a normal night's rest. Therefore, after a week, the Russian government decided to repatriate the wives and children of the diplomats. The organisation of their departure was a complicated and nerve-racking affair. On February 2 several Russian diplomats drove a bus to the Chinese aviation company in order to make arrangements for the arrival of special Russian planes. They were surrounded by Red Guards and were not able to leave their bus for sixteen hours. In their wall newspapers the Red Guards made fun of the Russians who were forced to relieve themselves in a corner of the bus. The Russian wives and children left under the greatest difficulties in three groups, on February 4, 5 and 6. They were spat upon and struck.

In order to reach their planes, they had to pass under an archway of portraits of Stalin and Mao Tse-tung, which were held so low that they had to bend down. It took many hours to cover the short distance between the buses and the planes.

At the same period the Yugoslav Embassy was painted with slogans such as 'Hang Tito!' and several other Eastern European embassies were involved in difficulties. There was also a serious incident in front of the French Embassy.

The question to what extent the incidents had been promoted or connived at by Ch'en Yi, the Minister of Foreign Affairs, will perhaps never receive a satisfactory answer. In early January Ch'en Yi was strongly criticised, and his wife and son were arrested. On January 24 he made a self-criticism at a meeting of Red Guards. It is a legitimate question whether the incident in Moscow on the 25th and its far-reaching consequences are related to Ch'en Yi's self-criticism. It is a fact that at this juncture Ch'en Yi could not afford to resist the attentions of the young hotheads. However, the text of the self-criticism, which was published in the unofficial press, does not touch on the problem of Soviet revisionism or foreign policy, and therefore does not provide much of a clue. Ch'en Yi confessed that during the first fifty days of the Cultural Revolution, from early June to mid-July 1966, he had followed the 'reactionary capitalist line, represented by Liu Shao-ch'i and Teng Hsiao-p'ing'. During the eleventh session of the Central Committee his eyes had been opened, but nevertheless he had again acted in contravention of the 'revolutionary proletarian line, represented by Chairman Mao'. The reason why was that he had not raised the 'red flag of the thought of Chairman Mao' high enough. He had not identified himself with the masses and often had not resisted the temptation of ordering people about. He had done his work with too much self-confidence, had relied on his long experience, and had been bureaucratic instead of democratic. In his self-criticism Ch'en Yi further said that he had failed already before the Cultural Revolution. In a speech in Canton in 1962, when defending the position of the intellectuals, he had not been guided by correct political principles and had neglected the need of political and ideological training. On other occasions also he had given a wrong idea of the relationship between political education and scientific competence. He had emphasised the latter at the cost of the former. He had demanded more experts and ignored their political colour.

What exactly the position and influence of Ch'en Yi was in January

1967, it is evident that he was not capable of stopping the Red Guards who were going too far. At this time even Chou En-lai did not warn against excesses, at least not in public.

The Chinese students who had been involved in the incident on the Red Square in Moscow arrived by train in Peking on February 1. Ch'en Yi, many other high-ranking officials, and tens of thousands of Red Guards had gone to the station to welcome them. Foreign Minister Ch'en Yi, who concurrently held the military rank of marshal, was dressed in uniform and surrounded by a bodyguard. At the same time the news spread that Mrs. Ch'en Yi, who had been held a prisoner by the Red Guard, had been released. The new anti-revisionist foreign policy seemed to pay.

Tension rose high. Eastern European diplomats, who went to the Ministry of Foreign Affairs with complaints about incidents, were told that the Chinese masses disliked revisionism and that the safety of the revisionist diplomats in Peking could not be guaranteed. Since it is generally accepted that the safety of diplomats is the responsibility of the state to which they are accredited, the persons involved were naturally worried. The tension was apparent not only from the treatment of diplomats, but also from more important areas of the foreign policy of China and the Soviet Union. There had been many rumours about delays in the transportation of Russian weapons to Vietnam. Finally, the Russian newspaper *Izvestiya* of February 3 reported that Russian planes with 'specialists' on board on their way to North Vietnam had met many difficulties during a technical landing in Peking. The unofficial Chinese press, too, gave a description of the incident mentioned in *Izvestiya*. It said that on January 31 the Red Guard staged a demonstration at the airfield, when two Russian planes landed on their way to Vietnam. The demonstrators delayed the flight by two or three hours.

On February 10 Premier Kosygin declared in a radio interview, that the Soviet Union sympathised with the opponents of the 'dictatorial régime of Mao Tse-tung'. Such pronouncements fanned the flames, yet they seemed inevitable. For Moscow feared most that during the Cultural Revolution the resistance to Chairman Mao would assume an anti-communist appearance, and that eventually, together with maoism, communism would be rejected. By his statement Kosygin tried to prevent the resistance to Mao Tse-tung from turning in an anti-communist direction. The Soviet press has consistently followed this line.

On his side Ch'en Yi helped to fan the coals of the conflict with the Soviet Union. On February 15 he said in answer to Kosygin: 'The Soviet revisionist leading clique has once again taken the lead in attacking China. Of late, they even sanguinarily suppressed our returning students and beat up our diplomatic personnel, thus pushing Sino-Soviet relations to the brink of rupture. During his visit to Britain, Kosygin, Chairman of the Council of Ministers of the Soviet Union, tried to shift on to China the responsibility for worsening Sino-Soviet relations by confounding right and wrong and openly slandering our great proletarian Cultural Revolution, crudely interfered in our internal affairs and even went so far as to make vicious attacks on our great leader Chairman Mao Tse-tung.'

The unofficial press reported a speech which Ch'en Yi made to students from Sian, capital of the North Chinese province of Shensi, on February 5. On that occasion Ch'en Yi stated: 'The problems with the Soviet Union may have consequences. It could be necessary to break off diplomatic relations with the Soviet Union. It could be necessary to . . . [*Tung-fang-hung pao* of the Peking Geological Institute of February 15, which I quote, prints several dots here; one should read 'to defend ourselves by force of arms' or some similar words]. You in Sian will then be in the front line, as well as the North-east and Inner Mongolia. If America attacks us, you will be in the rearguard.'

Never before had one of the Chinese leaders spoken so openly of the possibility of war with the Soviet Union. The same Red Guard newspaper contained reports on 'daily increasing conflicts on the Chinese-Russian border', and quoted Marshal Nieh Jung-chen as having said that the armed forces should concentrate more on military training, 'since the Soviet revisionists continue to provoke us'. By making great play with words about the possibility of a war, the Chinese leaders created the impression of foreign policy having become too important to be decided by the Red Guards. They also created an atmosphere in which internal discord appeared of secondary importance, and thus a basis on which a more or less temporary solution for the internal dissension could be worked out. Fomenting anti-Russian feelings played a role in the internal political game. One may assume that in the years of the Cultural Revolution the incidents at the border remained of moderate proportions. Before 1969 they were never reported in the official Chinese press, and rarely in the unofficial press. The most complete description which I saw in 1966 or 1967 was about an incident on the banks of the Ussuri, which forms the border between the Soviet Union and China north of Vladivostok. A battalion of the 'Soviet revisionist army' had provoked the Chinese troops on the Chinese side of the border. Eventually, the Chinese could stand the insults no longer, and assigned a company to chase the Russian battalion away. During the operation a number of Russian soldiers were captured; they were treated with great magnanimity by the Chinese and soon set free again. The report, which dated from early 1967, ended by saying that the Russians were extremely grateful when they were released. This incident, probably like most others, was not a very serious one.

Attempts towards Stabilisation

The anti-Soviet campaign was used to bring about moderation in internal politics. It was rumoured that Mao Tse-tung had requested Yeh Chien-ying, one of the vice-chairmen of the National Defence Council, to take steps to ensure that the armed forces in the border provinces were prepared for war. Notably the troops in Fukien province, in the southern province of Yunnan, and in Sinkiang, which bordered on the Soviet Union, were involved. This implied that the fighting units in these provinces were exempt from the painful process of the Cultural Revolution. In Sinkiang they were not even obliged to support the revolutionary rebels.

Chou En-lai went one step farther and ordered that in the capital too the power of the revolutionary rebels should be restricted. They were told not to enter three essential government offices, viz. the buildings of the State Council which were situated within the large Chungnanhai compound in the centre of Peking, where the 'revisionists' Liu Shao-ch'i and Teng Hsiao-p'ing resided, the Ministry of Foreign Affairs and the Ministry of Public Security. In most other ministries the revolutionary rebels (usually young civil servants assisted by students) had seized power, or were in the process of doing so. On February 11 the military restored order in the Ministry of Public Security after an interregnum of three weeks, during which different groups of revolutionary rebels had been fighting in the corridors of the ministry. The demonstrations in front of the Russian Embassy were concluded, for the time being, by a rally of a hundred thousand people in the open-air stadium. Ch'en Yi spoke, as well as Chou En-lai, but the speech of the latter, which was simultaneously transmitted by radio, was not even mentioned in the *People's Daily*. Yet it was of great importance because Chou En-lai said that the demonstrators had not entered the premises of the Russian Embassy, nor would they do so in the future. Perhaps the Cultural Revolution group did not want to give such a guarantee, and maybe this was the reason why Chou En-lai's speech did not appear in print.

Chou En-lai continued to work feverishly for stability, which does not mean that he was opposed to the Cultural Revolution. But he must have considered a minimum of stability necessary, even if one only wanted to put into effect the programme of the Cultural Revolution. In several places revolutionary students and other young people had begun to seize power from the established authorities. Revolutionary committees were being formed which took over the provincial government. In the provinces of Shansi, Kweichow and Heilungkiang such committees came into being in January. However, initially it was not clear at all what requirements a revolutionary government should meet, and the 'seizing of power' by the revolutionary rebels was usually accompanied by serious disturbances. The decrees of January 23 and 28, which stipulated that the army should side with the revolutionary rebels, had made the situation still more delicate. In some places the established authorities, who were accused of capitalist leanings, tried to arrange a fake seizing of power, which posed an enormous problem to the military. The latter could not always know *which* faction of revolutionary rebels should be supported – that is if we assume that they wanted to support the right faction. Even if they had managed to align themselves with the true maoists, it was still another question to convince Peking that this was the case.

How complicated this situation was, appears if one realises that a great number of revolutionary rebels, who in early 1967 were considered true maoists, were accused of left extremism half a year later, and many revolutionary rebels, who were called rightists in early 1967, were later accepted as genuine revolutionaries. Therefore, rules were necessary for judging the seizing of power in the various enterprises, towns and provinces. These rules were published in the *People's Daily* of February 10. The main principle was that every take-over should be the result of a co-operative effort of revolutionary rebels, the old officials of the party and the administration (*kanpu's*), and the armed forces. The co-operation of these three groups was called the 'three-way alliance'. The procedure which was followed in Heilungkiang was made a classical example. In this province the first secretary of the provincial party committee, the military commander of the province and the local revolutionary rebels had worked closely together to organise the take-over and to establish a revolutionary committee. A significant detail was that the party secretary concerned himself had a military background, which, in effect, added to the military presence in the new organ. The demand that before every take-over a 'three-way alliance' should be formed implied a compromise with the establishment, since the official press reported that 95 per cent of the old *kanpu's* were politically sound and therefore in principle were eligible for participation in a 'three-way alliance'.

Naturally the Red Guards and the other rebels, who in January had given rein to their revolutionary emotionalism, were not enthusiastic about the 'three-way alliance'. But if they resisted the new policy, they ran the risk of being accused of anarchism and cliquism.

The power of the revolutionary rebels was also restricted in other respects. It was officially announced that the rebels, who often were not themselves members of the party, were not competent to take away someone else's party membership card. Furthermore, Chou En-lai explained that in seizing power in a factory, students were bound to play a subordinate role. When the take-over was completed, they would not be allowed to interfere with production. They could remain in the factory to acquire more experience, but were not entitled to give orders. The Premier also said that the revolutionary rebels were not allowed to keep the weapons that they had captured. These weapons should be collected at a central point and sealed up. 'After the stabilisation', Chou is reported to have said, 'it will be decided what will happen to these weapons.' Moreover the Red Guards were forbidden to establish organisations on a national scale. Chou En-lai urged them to settle their internal conflicts, and to unite with other organisations and form one big local federation of Red Guards. Very slowly the mutual rivalry between the First, Second and Third Headquarters of Red Guards in Peking decreased. On February 22 a congress of Red Guards of the universities and colleges of Peking was convened, which was, however, little more than a façade. The often competing publications of about sixty different rebel organisations continued their prosperous existence without difficulty. But the appearance of unity was valuable, since without over-all organisation, even if only of a formal nature, the seizing of power in Peking would never be achieved.

Mao Tse-tung himself was worried about the quarrelling and the lack of discipline among the students and other revolutionaries. He issued a number of instructions, without exception of a vague, moralising nature. They were posted up in the centre of Peking on February 15 and copied with great devotion by large crowds of people. Chairman Mao said that one should respect one's superior and act in a disciplined way, and that one should help one another, especially if there were political difficulties, and that one should be kind to other people.

It was also decided that the Red Guards should be subjected to military training and to an ideological rectification campaign. The military training consisted mainly of drilling, which one saw in progress in the streets and parks. By the end of February the rectification campaign began which was aimed at the elimination of particularism, cliquism, ultra-democracy, liberalism, subjectivism and individualism. The campaign was stimulated by the organisation of discussion groups which relied heavily on the red book. Since the régime was trying its best to teach the Red Guards respect for order and discipline, it went without saying that the promise of four months before that in the spring the Red Guards would again be allowed to come to Peking and see Chairman Mao was not kept. The Central Committee cancelled the pilgrimage to Peking.

More decisions of the Central Committee followed. The announcement on March 7 that the peasants should start with the preparations for spring sowing was important. They must forget about the 'three-way alliance' and 'seizing power', and first of all pay attention to ploughing and sowing. The army, which seemed capable of doing everything, was ordered to assist them and to prevent the attempts of the 'class enemy' to sabotage the Cultural Revolution and production. Shortly afterwards, on March 18, the workers were instructed to get less intensively involved in the Cultural Revolution. The People's Daily published an appeal by Chairman Mao and the Central Committee to respect the eight-hour day strictly. The workers should carry on the Cultural Revolution in their spare time. With this announcement the Chinese leaders returned to the original position of the Central Committee of December 9. Depressed by three months of disorder and strikes, they seemed to be nostalgic for the situation before the January Revolution. In the meantime the January Revolution was formally concluded, when on February 24 a 'three-way alliance' of revolutionary rebels, military men and party cadres seized power from the old party committee of Shanghai.

Interlude

By early March 1967 the Cultural Revolution seemed to have burnt itself out. In Peking a relaxed atmosphere was visible similar to that prevailing at the end of September 1966, before the celebration of October the First, or in early December, when the Red Guards from outside Peking were being sent home. When, one evening in March, I walked through the shopping street Wang-fu-ching, which now was officially named *Jen-min-lu* (People's street), the neon lights were lit again, advertising 'The Fruiterer's Shop of Peking', 'Long live Chairman Mao', and 'The Department Store of Peking'. On the roof of the department store the large neon characters of the slogan 'Long live Chairman Mao' had been erected, but for some reason or another they were not illuminated. The buses, which for months had been plastered with posters and wall newspapers, had been cleaned. They looked shining and new again. Many shop-windows, which had been covered with hundreds of yards of propaganda, were scraped clean. Little boys collected the scraps of paper in large baskets, which they pushed ahead of them on small carts mounted on roller-skate wheels. Now pushing, now coasting, they swarmed like water fleas over the streets and squares. It was only slightly above freezing point, but many passers-by did not wear socks and walked bare-footed in shoes that were too large for them. The people laughed again. It was springtime and young couples dared to walk hand in hand.

That evening I was snapped at by a boy of not more than twelve years old. He sold newspapers published by the revolutionary rebels, but did not want to sell one to me. I found his unfriendly attitude out of tune with the atmosphere of the friendly spring weather, and realised at the same time that the world was still characterised by contradictions. The attitude of the by-standers was also strange. Nobody paid any attention to the heated words of the boy. Only an older girl, who was also selling newspapers, tried to convince him that he could easily sell a copy to me. 'Why don't you want to sell?' I asked him. '*Pu mai!*' ('I won't sell') was the abrupt reply, which at the same time ended the discussion between him and his older colleague. The girl immediately reconciled herself to his decision and went on selling to others.

This, in itself, unimportant occurrence may illuminate how easily the Chinese resign themselves to contradictions. They seem to be specially gifted in reconciling contrasts and opposed interests. This reconciliation is often no more than fatalistic resignation. It is not surprising that Mao Tse-tung is obsessed by the idea of contradictions. Of course, I was sufficiently used to the Chinese situation to resign myself to the boy's blunt refusal, when I noticed that my question to him remained unanswered. It often happened that vendors did not want to sell me a newspaper, but they usually informed me in a friendly way that they did not sell to foreigners.

Life seemed to be making a fresh start. In a side-street off Wang-fu-ching I saw people playing badminton. The Chinese dared again to be lazy, to laugh and to sit in the sun on their doorsteps. The army had asserted its influence and seemed committed to the solving of all problems. Soldiers were present everywhere, in the town administration, on the streets, in industry, in the villages. On a Sunday in March several friends and I went to a remote, half-completed Ming tomb, where the last emperor of the Ming dynasty, Chuang Lieh, is buried. After a car journey of nearly an hour, we walked through several small villages which were rarely visited by foreigners. The inhabitants were friendly and not even afraid of having their pictures taken. We had first politely asked whether there were any objections. Several peasants were wearing a red armband to show that they belonged to the revolutionary rebels, but nobody felt called upon to watch and follow us. In one village we met two military men, who, in conformity with the recent instructions, reminded the peasants to begin ploughing and sowing in time. They were the only ones who were somewhat nervous. The villagers discussed the question among themselves whether we were Chinese or foreigners, since we spoke Chinese. A much travelled man said that he had never seen such Chinese. Finally, one of the soldiers inquired about our nationality. The children gave us friendly waves. The loud-speakers blared in this village too. They were hanging high in the trees, but the swarms of magpies that passed over our heads drew more attention than the ever-repeated quotations from the Chairman.

Further Ideological Justification; a Parallel with the Boxer Rebellion

Appearances are deceptive, certainly in China. Of course, a certain degree of order was needed to bring production back to normal. More attention was paid to industrial production. The army protected vital enterprises against sabotage and tried to prevent strikes by arguing that industry was the backbone of national defence. In Canton and other places the military were instrumental in forming temporary 'front-line commands for grasping revolution and stimulating production'. The unofficial press emphasised the possibility of a new Great Leap Forward. However, this did not mean that the Cultural Revolution was over. The obvious problem of how the revisionist leaders, notably Liu Shao-ch'i, should be dealt with, was not yet solved. Nothing had come of the spiritual and moral reforms which were the professed aims of the Cultural Revolution. The ideological justification of the Cultural Revolution made only very slow progress.

The criticism of Chou Yang, which was published in the official press in July 1966, was elaborated on by Yao Wen-yüan in the *People's Daily* of January 3, 1967. Yao asserted that in the past Chairman Mao was repeatedly compelled to censure Chou Yang's revisionist ideas, and that the latter harboured a fierce hatred of the thought of Mao Tse-tung. The latter accusation was partly based on a speech of 1959, in which Chou Yang had complained that during the ten years of the People's Republic not enough scholarly works had been written. That was a 'dirty attack' on the works of Mao Tse-tung, which were published at just that period, Yao argued with great indignation. And to prevent any misunderstanding he added: 'Comrade Mao Tse-tung wrote many great, epoch-making marxist–leninist works covering the fields of politics, military affairs, philosophy, culture, economics and party building.'

He also held Chou Yang responsible for the publication in a literary journal in 1961 of an article on 'The Problem of Subject-Matter'. It described the aim of literature as the representation of the diversity of the world and the complex nature of life. Yao Wen-yüan regarded this view as a dirty plea for 'glorifying traitors, lackeys, hooligans, landlords, rich peasants, counter revolutionaries, bad elements and rightists'. He pointed out that in 1959 Khrushchev had expressed a similar idea, when he lauded the novelette *Fate of a Man* by Mikhail Sholokhov (who was strongly criticised in China) as a story which 'described the complex and rich spiritual world of the ordinary citizen'. According to Yao Wen-yüan, Chou Yang believed that the Chinese writers should publish similar 'renegade literature'. The questionable nature of this argument appears, if one realises that in 1960, at the Third Chinese Writers' Congress, Chou Yang had condemned this brand of 'renegade literature'. Therefore, Yao Wen-yüan could only accuse Chou Yang of playing a double game and charge him with having paid lip service to maoist cultural policy, while in reality resisting it. The critic reaches more solid ground when he asserts that Chou Yang managed to prevent large numbers of amateur writers from becoming members of the Writers' Union. It may be assumed that in this Chou Yang was prompted by the wish to assure a certain basic level of artistic quality in literature. In his defence of a description of the 'complex nature of life' he proved himself a realist. It is conceivable that, as a result of his great knowledge of marxism, he in fact was too much of a realist to be absorbed in maoist romanticism.

The Cultural Revolution had few positive contributions to offer in the cultural field. Only one novel stood the test of ideological criticism: Chin Ching-mai's Song of Ouyang Hai.[5] Red Guards who were interested in literature plunged into a discussion of whether Lo Kuang-pin, a writer living in Szechwan, had been murdered by revolutionary rebels or had committed suicide. Several pamphlets were devoted to the question. In early 1967 almost all cinemas in Peking were closed. On January 7 all television transmission was stopped; it was sporadically resumed only months later to show discussions between workers, soldiers and revolutionary students on matters which without exception could be decided by reference to the red book. Five or six modern Peking operas were shown in rotation, and at times a stage or musical performance was given by an Albanian or Rumanian military troupe. In the years 1966–7 a group of life-size clay statues was on display, known as the Rent Receiving Compound, which represented poor peasants, who were handing over rent to their landlord. However, they were continuously remodelled, with the effect that the expression on the faces gradually changed. Whereas in the autumn of 1966 there were still figures who made a tragic impression or aroused one's sympathy, one year later they were all suffused with a relentless fury.

The policy of the Ministry of Culture found no favour in the eyes of the Red Guard. In January 1967 the acting Minister of Culture, Lieutenant-General Hsiao Wang-tung, who half a year earlier had succeeded the 'revisionist' Lu Ting-i, was himself accused of counter-revolutionary revisionism. Standing on a lorry on the Square of Heavenly Peace, he was publicly humiliated and struck by the Red Guards. He was wearing a large wooden board which hung by a rope around his neck and on which his name and the accusation were written. He was maltreated in front of a large crowd, which included myself.

The resumption of teaching was hampered by all kinds of practical difficulties. A great number of teachers had been charged with revision-ism and preferred other work to instructing the young revolutionary rebels. Almost all textbooks had been rejected because of their revision-ism and bourgeois taints. Red Guards from the provinces had camped in the schools. Some furniture in the schools had been burnt during the cold winter season, and windows had been broken as a result of fighting.

An article by Ch'i Pen-yü, who, like Yao Wen-yüan, felt called upon to contribute to the ideological justification of the Cultural Revolution, shattered the hope that more relaxation was on the way. On April 1 the *People's Daily* published his vehement criticism of 'the top party person in authority who was taking the capitalist road'. Everyone knew that this phrase stood for President Liu Shao-ch'i. The latter was called a fake revolutionary, a counter-revolutionary, and 'China's Khrushchev'. Until the autumn of 1968 the official press never criticised Liu Shao-ch'i by name. Ch'i Pen-yü's article is one of the most amazing documents of the Cultural Revolution. It is largely devoted to a revaluation of the Boxer rebellion of 1900. Guided by the slogan 'rebellion is justified', Ch'i Pen-yü judged the Boxer rebellion favourably. The author described the Boxers as predecessors of the Red Guard. With apparent satisfaction he described how the masses almost seventy years earlier – dressed in red turbans and sashes, and armed with swords and spears – had marched through the streets of Peking, and had annihilated on the battlefield the European troops which came to the rescue of the foreigners. Ch'i praised the fact that the Boxers had arrested government officials who were guilty of abuse of power or had supported the imperialists. The culprits had been forced to ask forgiveness and to kow-tow to their altar. Officials who had committed serious crimes were executed. The parallel with the Red Guard action is apparent.

Ch'i Pen-yü played down the fact that the majority of the Boxers were inspired by primitive superstition and, of course, did not mention that it was precisely the most cruel and reactionary of the officials who had sided with the Boxers. He emphasised with approval the xenopho-bic element of the Boxer movement: 'The Boxers boycotted all foreign goods and, shouting "Kill the foreign devils", paraded through the streets and frightened the imperialists.'

Ch'i Pen-yü's article did not bode well for the future. At that time we wondered how it was possible that the extreme Left could make such a strong stand. Lin Piao may have had a hand in the publication of this article. There were wall newspapers indicating that in February Lin Piao had had a breakdown and, due to serious overstrain, had taken a long rest. On March 20 he appeared again among his associates and seems to have referred to his illness. We can speculate that he was hoodwinked into endorsing the article for publication in the *People's Daily* on April 1.

Activities of the Extreme Left

At the same period Chou En-lai worked steadily towards a regular take-over in the capital. On March 19 a Congress of Revolutionary Peasants was convened, on March 22 the Congress of Revolutionary Workers was founded, and again three days later the Congress of Red Guards of the secondary schools followed. Together with the earlier convened congress of revolutionary students, these congresses formed the basis of the revolutionary committee of Peking which was inaugurated on April 20. The president was the Minister of Public Security, General Hsieh Fu-chih, who had the gift of knowing how to manage the young revolutionaries. Other members of the revolutionary committee included Wu Te, secretary of the party committee of Peking and acting mayor, and Nieh Yüan-tzu, author of the first big-character poster and president of the Congress of Red Guards of the universities and colleges. The seizing of power in Peking was the result of intensive propaganda by moderate leftist factions *against* anarchism and *for* a three-way alliance of old cadres, military men and revolutionary rebels.

The way in which power was seized in Peking was subjected to sharp criticism. The objections can probably be traced back to machinations of the extreme Left, which was guided by K'ang Sheng, propaganda chief Wang Li and ideologist Ch'i Pen-yü. The extreme Left disliked the growing military influence and tried to inflame resistance to military training to which the young people were subjected. One general committed the mistake of saying in a speech to students of the 27th secondary school of Peking that the young people should devote more time and energy to military exercises and less to political campaigns. He was promptly attacked in wall newspapers, which at the same time expressed doubts about the use of subjecting students to military training as such. Most organisations of the Red Guard supported the 27th secondary school. Moreover, the unofficial press criticised the 'one-sided military approach' of the seizing of power in the various organisations and towns.

Nieh Yüan-tzu, who seems to have been on good terms with Chou En-lai, was one of the few Red Guard leaders who dissociated themselves from the quarrel between the Red Guards and the army. She held the view that it was correct to criticise the general concerned, but that it was wrong to regard the People's Liberation Army as responsible for the mistakes which individual persons had made here and there. It did not take long before slogans appeared in Peking reading 'Down with Nieh Yüan-tzu', which were answered by posters saying the opposite, such as 'Nieh Yüan-tzu is a good comrade' and 'Protect the results of the military training'.

The extreme Left further fomented criticism of Liu Shao-ch'i, for which Ch'i Pen-yü's article of April 1 had shown the way. Also the Minister of Foreign Affairs Ch'en Yi again got himself into difficulties. In April the walls in the centre of town were once more plastered with slogans which demanded the 'overthrow' or the 'burning' of Ch'en Yi. More elaborate criticism in the unofficial press, however, was still rather cautious. Of course, he was blamed again because of his attitude during the early phase of the Cultural Revolution, about which he had already made a self-criticism in January. Again his authoritarian behaviour was held against him. At a meeting with revolutionary rebels he had once even pounded the table with his fist. The Red Guards wondered whether Ch'en Yi belonged to the headquarters of Mao Tse-tung or those of Liu Shao-ch'i. They observed with suspicion that during the Sino-Japanese war the latter had been political commissar of the new fourth army of which Ch'en Yi was the commander. The Red Guard newspapers recalled that in 1963 Ch'en Yi and Liu Shao-ch'i together had visited a number of countries in South-east Asia, among them Indonesia. Alluding to the abortive coup in Indonesia of September 30, 1965, the Red Guards asserted that during that journey Ch'en Yi had plotted in a vile way and that the Chinese people had lost face through him. They recalled that, still in February 1967, Ch'en Yi had said that the conflict with President Liu Shao-ch'i belonged to the contradictions among the people and that one should not take the many wall newspapers that criticised the President too seriously. Most of all, the revolutionary rebels were annoyed by his obstinate nature. 'This year,' Ch'en Yi reportedly said at a meeting with Red Guards, 'I shall be sixty-six years of age and I do not fear difficulties. You should know that the people who, like grocers, look for small gains, do not usually come to a good end.' As a result of his refusal to give in under the pressure of groups of young people who had little understanding of either foreign policy or revolution, Ch'en Yi had manoeuvred himself into a delicate position.

By the end of April the unofficial press insinuated that Ch'en Yi, possibly through his son, had contacts with the reactionary Committee for United Action. This was a very serious accusation. The number of stories about the crimes of the Committee members was legion. A few days earlier a Red Guard newspaper had reported that a group of Red Guards of the Committee for United Action of the 47th secondary school of Peking, flying a large flag and carrying pots of black paint, had gone to the Western Hills. On their way they chanted 'Long live Red Red-red', which in Chinese rhymes with Mao Tse-tung, and painted reactionary slogans on the walls. When they arrived at a well-known peak in the Western Hills, they renamed it the 'Red Red-red mountain'. Shortly after that the culprits were discovered and arrested by the People's Liberation Army.

However, to the surprise of most observers, the Committee for United Action was officially rehabilitated a few days after Ch'en Yi (and also Marshal Yeh Chien-ying) had been charged with having illicit relations with the Committee. The arrested Committee members, totalling 139 persons, were all set free, with the exception of two young people who were under suspicion of murder.

Once again in Tientsin

Political developments in the month of April were characterised by various contradictions, which can be explained only if one takes the existence of two rival factions into account: the extreme Left and the moderate Left, both apparently full of admiration for Mao Tse-tung and, in different degrees, supporters of a Cultural Revolution. This applies not only to Peking, but also to the provinces, where, however, the moderates occasionally seemed to doubt the value and necessity of a Cultural Revolution. In Szechwan the First Secretary of the South-west Bureau Li Ching-ch'üan still managed to stand his ground. Red Guards in Peking accused him of suppressing the Red Guard in Chungking and Chengtu. Guided by the phrase 'together in battle, together in victory', they called for the 'liberation of the South-west'. Nearer home, in Tientsin, the situation was uncertain as well. In the course of February 1967 Li Hsüeh-feng, who for nine months had served as First Secretary of the Party Committee of Peking and in that function drew on himself the hatred of the Red Guards, was transferred to Tientsin 'to give guidance to the revolutionary masses'. The revolutionary masses in Tientsin, of course, were not particularly pleased to be saddled with a leader who had been discarded in Peking.

By the end of April, two months after the arrival of Li Hsüeh-feng in Tientsin, I once more visited that town, which happened that day to be celebrating the founding of a revolutionary committee in Peking. There was a noisy and disorderly parade in the centre of the town. Unlike Peking, the slowly moving crowd was equipped with fire crackers and other primitive fireworks, which were ignited preferably where the crowd and the demonstrators were packed tightly together. The intervals between the bangs were filled with the deafening roll of drums and gongs. I tried to count the slogans against and those in support of Li Hsüeh-feng. They seemed to be about even. Slogans such as 'Continue the bloody struggle against Li Hsüeh-feng to the end' and 'Smash Li Hsüeh-feng's dog's head' were balanced by exhortations that the struggle should not be directed against Li Hsüeh-feng, but against the revisionists in the old party committee of Tientsin. On April 18 a group of students of the University of Hopei had issued a statement in support of Li Hsüeh-feng. The document had been printed as a separate pamphlet and was posted up in many places. The statement ended with an appeal to protect the principle of the 'three-way alliance'. However, the opponents of Li Hsüeh-feng appeared to be powerful enough to mobilise loud-speaker vans in their campaign against the new first secretary.

The relentless activity of the rival political factions was demonstrated by a collection of posters which were pasted against the walls of the five storey department store in Tientsin. It was written on the wall at the level of the third floor that Li Hsüeh-feng should be overthrown. One floor up posters were stuck which were an appeal to support him. On the afternoon of April 20 I saw that, high above the crowds and the noise which shook the plastered and painted walls of the shops and offices, at the level of the fifth floor, revolutionary window cleaners risking their lives were busy posting the slogan 'Down with Li Hsüeh-feng'.

It was still a long time before the citizens of Tientsin were prepared to return to normality. On December 6, 1967, a revolutionary committee of Tientsin was formed. On that occasion Tientsin became an autonomous city, like Peking and Shanghai, which meant that it was

D

directly responsible to the State Council. Li Hsüeh-feng moved to Shihchiachuang, where two months later under his leadership the revolutionary committee of the province of Hopei was inaugurated.

In almost every province the founding of revolutionary committees led to serious disturbances. This appeared from reports which in the course of the summer reached the capital. Undoubtedly the central government was worried by these developments. Before relating the details of the disturbances concerned, I shall record a quiet journey to the province of Shansi.

REFERENCES

1. See the minutes of talks of the Cultural Revolution group with representatives of the All-China Red Worker Rebels General Corps in Chung Hua-min and Arthur C. Miller, *Madame Mao: A Profile of Chiang Ch'ing*, Kowloon: Union Research Institute, 1968, pp. 234–43.

2. This interpretation is supported by the criticism of P'eng Te-huai in the official press. See Li Hsin-kung's article 'Settle Accounts with Peng Teh-huai for His Heinous Crimes of Usurping Army Leadership and Opposing the Party' in *Peking Review* 10 (1967), No. 36. Reprinted in *The Case of Peng Teh-huai 1959–68*, Kowloon: Union Research Institute, 1968, pp. 209–20. See particularly pp. 216–17. The article brackets 'the counter-revolutionary revisionists P'eng Te-huai and Lo Jui-ch'ing'.

3. *The Case of Peng Teh-huai 1959–68*, Kowloon: Union Research Institute, 1968, p. 391.

4. *Ibid.*, pp. 119 and 124.

5. For details see D. W. Fokkema, 'Chinese Literature under the Cultural Revolution', *Literature East and West* 13 (1969), No. 3–4, pp. 335–59.

5

JOURNEY TO SHANSI: MAY 1967

Shortly after the celebration of the First of May the wife of an Asian ambassador confided in me that a vice-minister had told her that the Ministry of Foreign Affairs was soon going to organise an excursion for diplomats. Exactly like the year before, the excursion would begin after the Norwegian National Day and end before the Afghan Independence Day. My informant could not tell me where the journey would take us, but reported the vice-minister as having said that all preparations for the journey had been made, except that it had not yet been decided which region was to be visited.

After these disclosures, speculations about the duration and the destination of the journey soared high. Ambassadors let it be known that officials of the Ministry of Foreign Affairs had answered their probing with puzzling silence, and at times had even denied that a diplomatic trip was to be organised at all. The uncertainty was finally ended by an official communication from the ministry. During a hastily organised meeting of representatives from the various diplomatic missions, an official of the Protocol Department disclosed that we were to visit the province of Shansi.

This was perhaps a disappointment for those who had participated in the diplomatic excursions of previous years: to the North-east with its vast plains and highly developed industry, to the province of Shantung with its beautiful scenery and temples and its famous breweries, or to the distant province of Szechwan. However, it was obvious that in the spring of 1967 the journey would be to a region where the Cultural Revolution had led to the establishment of a revolutionary committee – to one of the 'liberated' areas, which apart from Shanghai and Peking, included the provinces of Shantung, Heilungkiang, Kweichow, or Shansi. Shantung and Heilungkiang had been visited on earlier occasions, Kweichow seemed a little too far, so that Shansi was left as the only possibility.

We were told, and we were to hear it again and again during the excursion, that in this province the situation was 'excellent, exactly like the rest of the country'. The struggle between bourgeois revisionism and marxism–leninism had reached a decisive stage. The victory of the ideas of the great leader Chairman Mao was inevitable. The spokesman of the Protocol Department, a man with hair that resembled a shaving-brush, and fiery eyes, seemed sure of his ground, or rather, he seemed confident that he was going to outlive the Cultural Revolution and so behaved with corresponding self-assurance. But what did he know about Shansi and the situation there? He had never visited the place and had to rely on second-hand information when lauding the phenomenon of Tachai, the production brigade which under adverse circumstances had scored many successes on the basis of self-reliance. 'One does not know what one sees. It sounds like a fairy-tale until one sees it with one's own eyes. There were many obstacles, such as unfavourable soil conditions and the climate, but the heroes of Tachai, strengthened by the thought of Chairman Mao, overcame them.' Of course, we were curious to see this fairy-tale with our own eyes.

If Shansi were new to the Protocol officer, to the vice-minister who accompanied us the provincial revolutionary committee was a surprise. The vice-minister was a taciturn but friendly man with a very intelligent face, except early in the morning when he had not yet combed his hair, which was meant to add to his revolutionary appearance. We were surprised to hear a heavy bass voice when at last, at the end of the excursion, he presided over a meeting. On arrival in the provincial capital Taiyuan, after a night's train journey through partly cultivated mountain areas, he was greeted with exuberant cordiality by Liu Kuan-i, a vice-chairman of the new provincial committee, whose revolutionary actions had been described in the Hsinhua News Agency Bulletin several days earlier. Liu invited us to take seats in shining, polished coaches and exchanged polite remarks with the vice-minister. They inquired about each other's place of birth. The vice-minister had been brought up in Shanghai and our host, who was a gay fellow and spoke clear Mandarin, had lived in Shantung for many years. Neither Liu Kuan-i, nor his boss Liu Ke-p'ing (chairman), nor Chang Jih-ch'ing (vice-chairman of the provincial committee) had lived for long in Shansi. The three principal revolutionaries of Taiyuan were puppets of the central government. This was the important lesson of the first day. Provincial manners were also alien to them. But they were proud of their new province and town. At the host's request one of the interpreters translated: 'A beautiful city, isn't it?' We looked out of the windows, remembering seeing an open square and a hotel, but we were unaware that we were still in a town. On one side (or to be specific as one is in this respect in China: on the northern side) of an extremely broad avenue we saw some farmland, resting draught animals, etc. On the southern horizon several apartment buildings, the Workers' Cultural Palace and various factories were visible. After some hesitation, an experienced ambassador interpreted the opinion of us all by replying: 'Yes, very interesting.'

Soon we passed the bridge that connects the banks of the River Fen, which contributes largely to the relative prosperity of the part of the province that we were visiting. It is a slow river (at least in May) in a broad sandy bed, which on dry windy days causes heavy dust storms. We followed the valley in a southerly direction and after about half an hour reached a workers' sanatorium, not far from the famous Chin temples that we were soon to visit. We complained about our isolation and how far we were from town, but were in fact very pleased with our lodging and would not have wanted to miss our strolls through the moonlit temples which had not suffered from Red Guard vandalism.

The Political Situation

The 'short introductions' to which we were exposed for hours on end during our stay in Shansi were more difficult to digest. Vice-chairman Chang Jih-ch'ing did most of the speaking. He was a military man with thirty years' service in the People's Liberation Army and during the war against Japan had led the guerrillas in South China together with Ch'en Yi. General Chang seemed used to taking the lead.

Shansi has 18 million inhabitants, he said, an average rainfall of 500 millimetres and an average temperature of between 4 and 14 degrees. The capital Taiyuan is a recently developed industrial town, where the population has trebled during the last twenty years. It did not take long before General Chang got on to politics. And when some days later we also had the opportunity of listening to a political explanation by Liu Ke-p'ing, the chairman of the revolutionary committee, we thought we had quite a clear picture of what had happened in this province over the past year.

The reports on the Cultural Revolution in Shansi that were read to us contained of course an official version. This official version was carefully attuned to what had happened, what had been said and what had been done in Peking. The fable of Shansi was a faithful copy of the fable of Peking. If a new faction took over in Peking, sooner or later a similar take-over, either pretended or not, would take place in Shansi. This attitude may be excused by calling it the result of party discipline. The official reports on the Cultural Revolution in Shansi were thinly disguised and it was not difficult to guess what had really happened.

According to Chang Jih-ch'ing and Liu Ke-p'ing, the beginning of the Cultural Revolution dated from June 1, 1966, the day on which the news of the first big-character poster had been broadcast. Nieh Yüan-tzu, who, together with several other revolutionaries, had written the text, was mentioned as the Number One Red Guard of Peking. In Shansi it was Liu Hao who had written the first big-character poster, so the position of Number One Red Guard of the province was bestowed on him. But in June and July 1966 the provincial and local authorities had tried to stifle the Shansi Cultural Revolution at birth. According to the official version, Wei Heng (first secretary of the provincial party committee), Wang Ch'ien (second secretary of the same committee and governor of the province) and Wang Ta-jen (a member of the provincial party committee) launched a merciless counter-revolution. They were the lackeys of Liu Shao-ch'i and played the role that in Peking was attributed to the President of the People's Republic, the General Secretary of the Communist Party Teng Hsiao-p'ing, and the former propaganda chief T'ao Chu. If in Peking the slogan 'Down with Liu, Teng and T'ao' were painted on the walls, in Shansi it would say the same, but there would also be its local version 'Down with Wei, Wang and Wang'.

Extensive but somewhat vague information was given about the 'crimes' of the counter-revolutionaries Wei, Wang and Wang. They wanted a restoration of capitalism. They obstructed the propagation of Mao Tse-tung's thought and opposed the principle of economic self-reliance symbolised in the Tachai production brigade. They disagreed with the campaign for making Tachai an example for the whole country, and gave wide publicity to another model production brigade in order to counter the idea of self-reliance. The counter-revolutionary clique in Shansi did not want to accept the maoist doctrine of putting politics first, nor did they want to believe in the possibilities of a 'people's war'. They advocated an enlargement of the acreage put aside for private use and free markets. These were the main political beliefs of Wei, Wang, Wang and their followers.

Driven by their hatred of Chairman Mao and the Cultural Revolution, the clique of Wei, Wang and Wang vehemently suppressed the revolutionary rebels and resorted to all kinds of ruses and illegalities. For example, in a certain factory they branded 180 out of 600 workers as counter-revolutionaries. Such a percentage was considered too high. They misled the people and encouraged them to write wall newspapers which attacked Chairman Mao and the masses. They even tapped telephone conversations and spied on their opponents. A considerable amount of money from provincial funds was spent on these tricks. Vacancies in the party organisation were filled with gangsters instead of followers of Chairman Mao.

At last the indignation of the people was so great that at a mass meeting on January 12, 1967, the revolutionaries decided to seize power. Liu Ke-p'ing told us that he himself, as well as Liu Kuan'-i, who was then acting governor, and Chang Jih-ch'ing, at that moment second political commissar of the armed forces in Shansi, had attended this meeting. 'The masses asked for our help', Liu Ke-p'ing explained, which, freely translated, might mean that both the old *kanpu's* and the provincial army leaders had decided to restore order. One may assume that they made skillful use of the prevailing discontent, and did not shrink from a dramatic *dénouement*. Ten thousand men occupied the offices of the provincial and town committees. Wei, Wang and Wang were put under house-arrest and at the time of our visit were said to be still living in their own homes. Several spies were arrested and murderers executed. The counter-revolutionary clique had used spies in abundance. In the office of Liu Kuan-i five or six officials spied on him, and before the take-over two armed spies used to guard his home. While searching houses the revolutionary rebels found five hundred rifles and pistols, which made them conclude that, if they had not taken action themselves, the counter-revolutionaries would have seized power instead. The victory of the revolutionary rebels was reported in the *People's Daily* of January 25, 1967.

The rest of the province soon followed Taiyuan's example. In all hundred-and-five counties of Shansi, except one, power had been seized. It is quite possible that this one exception originated in someone's imagination in order to add credibility to the fable. When asked why power had not also been seized in the hundred-and-fifth county, our hosts explained that the counter-revolutionaries still possessed great influence there, but that propaganda teams were working among the masses and that the revolutionary rebels would soon seize power. On March 12 the first meeting of deputies from the different parts of the province had been held. The deputies had been elected directly 'as in the days of the Paris Commune'.[1] They consisted of 30 or 35 per cent of the original cadres, 15 or 20 per cent of the military and 40 or 50 per cent of the revolutionary organisations. This representation met the conditions of a 'three-way alliance'. The low percentage of the military in the provincial assembly seemed to contradict a solemn statement by Liu Ke-p'ing that the army had played a decisive role in the provincial take-over. We were inclined to believe Liu Ke-p'ing, whose interpretation seemed to be borne out by the facts. The military appeared everywhere in a dominant position. This was the second important discovery during our stay in Shansi.

To what extent were we in a position to establish the facts? I must admit that my evaluation is based largely on seemingly unimportant phenomena. But other data are not at hand. Moreover, I do believe that the knowledge that we have warrants a conclusion.

In fact, there was only one representative of the revolutionaries with whom we became more or less acquainted: the twenty-year-old student Liu Hao, who in normal times would have attended the last grade of the senior high school. He was a friendly boy, always ready to laugh at a joke. When he accompanied us on our excursions, he usually fell asleep in the bus and laid his tired head on a revisionist or capitalist shoulder. Of course, more experienced revolutionaries did not approve of this. As a rule, the interpreters of the Ministry of Foreign Affairs would wake him up and suggested singing a song together, although they knew that singing was not one of the gifts of this Red Guard who was always hoarse and had no ear for music at all.

'Come on, please sing "I am a little red general of Mao Tse-tung".'

Liu Hao rejected the suggestion. A local girl with a broad, rustic face, who had assumed the role of leader, approached him with a challenging look.

'Please, Liu Hao, sing together with me "I am a little red general of Mao Tse-tung".'

But the Number One Red Guard of Shansi shook his head, as if this could stop the teasing. People made fun of him rather often, and on one occasion he completely lost face. (I in no way wish to imply that Liu Hao's behaviour was representative of the Red Guards in general.) One of the excursions led to a distillery and, as always during visits to distilleries all over the world, one had to taste the end-product. This was done at lunch, during which the words *kan-pei* (bottoms up) were heard all over the place. Our Chinese hosts made use of the opportunity too, all except Liu Hao, who did not drink, or drank too little according to the opinion of an older military man, probably an officer. After lunch, when everyone was leaving the shed where we had had our meal, we found them wrestling. With one hand the army officer held Liu Hao by his arm and with the other he tried to pour liquor into his mouth. Liu Hao defended himself laughingly and tried to make light of it, but the officer did not laugh at all and seemed to have set himself the task of breaking through the firmness of principle shown by the Red Guard. The quarrel ended when the officer grabbed Liu Hao's red armband with its proud inscription '*Chingkangshan*'. We wondered whether an army officer could play such a trick on an important Red Guard with impunity. The answer seemed to be in the affirmative, at least in Shansi, for several days later we met the same officer again, although it is possible, of course, that the case was not yet settled.

On one of the last days of our stay in Taiyuan, we visited the blast furnaces that are situated not far from the River Fen in the northern part of the town. The office walls, inside as well as outside, were completely plastered with posters. They represented a controversy among the staff. We were given first some general information, though not about production capacity or the number of workers. (Later we learned that this 'iron-and-steel-factory' employed 20,000 men.) The speaker was also unusually vague about the political situation in the factory. I asked one of the robust middle-aged army officers, who was introduced to us as a member of the management, when power had been taken over. It appeared that the process of the take-over had not yet been completed. We were somewhat surprised to learn that the revolutionary rebels in the most important industrial complex in the capital of the province, which for four months was held up as an example for the whole nation, had not yet succeeded in establishing a revolutionary committee on the basis of the required three-way alliance. But the officer seemed to acquiesce in the situation. Certainly in this factory the military were in control. Near the blast furnaces and in the workshops no wall-newspapers or slogans were seen.

Let me give one more example of the dominating position of the

D*

military in Shansi. Twice we were invited to a cultural evening in the Workers' Cultural Palace. The programme of the first evening consisted of songs and dances of the well-known kind that recalled the early days of socialist realism. As to the personality cult, the Chinese artists yield nothing to their former colleagues in the Soviet Union. The following items were represented: workers constructing high tension wires, songs and dances on themes from the works of Mao Tse-tung, veteran workers studying the works of Mao Tse-tung (choir), the young red pioneers (dance), 'grasp revolution and promote production' (a men's choir imitating a locomotive), proletarian revolutionaries forming a great alliance for seizing power (choir), the resolute girls of Tachai (dance), a ballet by negroes who, though seriously wounded, eventually triumphed with the support of the wisdom of the red book, and the heroic sisters (a Vietnam war scene that showed how an American tank was set on fire). The programme was digestible only because it was unusual. In fact, there was only one item worth looking at, a Tibetan dance dedicated to Chairman Mao. The rest of the performance was distinguished only by a deadening and deafening monotony. The singing and acting were extremely bad.

During the second evening we were convinced of military superiority in this respect; the military seemed to have more dramatic talent. (Perhaps the more gifted non-military actors were prevented from performing?) The first and last items of the second performance were performed completely by soldiers, or at least by people in military uniform. The last item, which was a combination of chorus and dance with drum accompaniment, would certainly have surprised the usual Western theatre-goer, but it was done with near perfection. The actors were very clever in juggling with their 'props' (carbines, heavy machine-guns, hand-grenades and one large artillery grenade). Other songs and dances of this second evening were not only militant but of an openly military character.

Both performances were sponsored by the revolutionary committee of Shansi and performed by the 'Alliance of Proletarian Revolutionaries'. But our impression was that, after the first evening, the revolutionary committee had ordered the glory of the People's Liberation Army to be shown more clearly, also in the domain of culture.

A Junior High School

Our hosts intended to give us an idea of heavy and light industry, the countryside, education and cultural life. During a visit to the 20th secondary school of Taiyuan, we received an impression of the way the young people were kept busy. At that time there was no question of education. The school building that was shown to us was solid but far from beautiful. As far as I recall, the walls and floors were made of plain concrete, and the door of the classroom where we listened to a 'short introduction' closed with a bolt. We were introduced to members of the revolutionary committee of the school, first a military man, second three teachers and third a student (a Red Guard of about fifteen years old in a worn-out military uniform complete with cap). The pupils of the school, which was roughly equivalent to a junior high school, were between twelve and sixteen years of age. There were a few Red Guards who listened also to the 'short introduction'. I appreciated the tea that was being continuously served, but one cannot continue drinking indefinitely. Therefore, out of boredom I could not help observing these Red Guards. They appeared to me frustrated and wild, as though every boy were at puberty. When spoken to, they often blushed.

The story that a young and pretty woman teacher told us resembled in many ways the 'short introductions' that we had listened to in a number of factories. A handful of persons in authority taking the capitalist road had judged the level of education of the 20th secondary school in such a way that it was always relegated to the lowest category. This resulted in the school having stupid students, inferior teachers, old materials and too few books. When in June 1966 the Cultural Revolution began in this school, the revisionists tried to prepare a counter-revolution by giving their lackeys positions in the party committee of the school and in the Youth League. The revolutionary rebels demanded that the town administration dismiss the revisionist teachers, but these did not accept their defeat. With the support of the army victory was eventually won. The military helped with propaganda work among the misled. On March 1, 1967, the school revolutionary committee was established according to the principles of the three-way alliance. At about the same time the Central Committee ordered the schools to be reopened (which is not the same as resuming education). Under the supervision of the army, the teachers and students of the 20th secondary school went first to the country-side for two weeks in order to acquire experience in class struggle. Back at school afterwards, extensive discussions were organised, during which 'the top party person taking the capitalist road' (the description of President Liu Shao-ch'i) was exposed and the reactionary elements that were still working in the school were criticised. In May 1967 this criticism was still the main occupation of students and teachers.

It was a relief to leave the classroom and to visit the school building. We entered the geography and physics room. Here several globes and a range of test-tubes were displayed. 'This school has always been badly treated by the handful of capitalist roaders in power,' one of the guides explained. 'Therefore, there is not much to be seen in this room'. Someone asked whether better materials would be allocated now that the revolutionary rebels had seized power. The reply referred to the concept of self-reliance, which not only applies to Vietnam, and to the production brigade Tachai, but explains backwardness as a temporary phenomenon everywhere in China. It was a sacred, revolutionary duty *not* to ask the new town administration for aid.

Outside the school, some six hundred students were practising military exercises in separate groups. Several students had been trained to command their own classes. Some military men who were enjoying the fruits of several weeks' labour were watching the parades from a distance. The exercises were combined with 'brandishing' the red book, chanting maoist slogans and revolutionary songs, and consisted of assembling, dressing by the right, marching, turning about, and doubling. It all produced enough dust and noise to make us long for the end.

It was depressing to see that the students themselves appeared to like the show. The only thing that told them of the world outside China was big-character posters about incidents in Hong Kong and oppression by British imperialism. Would it be possible to raise a new generation of Chinese in complete isolation from foreign influence and to indoctrinate them in such a way that they would not hesitate to fight an enemy, whom they considered only in caricature terms? Judging on the basis of what we saw in Taiyuan, one would be tempted to answer this question in the affirmative. But, in China as elsewhere, human nature is probably strong enough to reject complete uniformity. There were many schools in China that were slow in adjusting to the patterns of the Cultural Revolution.

A depressed mood is not always effectively countered by a logical argument, and the absence of any concrete alternative for these young students was an undeniable fact. Many members of our diplomatic group received Red Guard armbands, and did not object to them being attached to their sleeves. This, of course, strengthened the students in their belief that the panacea of maoism would indeed find world-wide application. One of our hosts, who asked about my impression of the school, had chosen the wrong moment for a conversation. I told him that I had seen nothing of any real education. He replied that the class struggle was more important, for if one understood the class struggle one would be in a position to liberate the oppressed peoples. I warned him in a friendly way that experience of the class struggle is not enough to build factories and that there must be study and work if there is to be progress. This point of view was rejected, of course, but the next day I had my revenge by showing him an editorial in the *People's Daily*, from which it appeared that the slogan 'grasp revolution, promote production' was extended with a third command, 'further other work'.

On the same day I had an interesting conversation with a member of the revolutionary town council of Taiyuan. He was a middle-aged, healthy-looking gentleman, who gave a revolutionary but not very intelligent impression. But he certainly had organisational qualities. He was in charge of the transportation of our group and had five buses under his command. If he thought that something might go wrong, he would leave his seat in the coach and stand upright in the gangway to supervise the situation and direct the driver. One excursion took us outside the immediate vicinity of Taiyuan on the road to Wenshui, a small fortified town and one of the strongholds of the once famous warlord Yen Hsi-shan. The road surface was not everywhere in good shape and at one point completely absent as the result of a flood. Road construction and poor traffic regulation caused our procession to move very slowly indeed. The town councillor rose from his seat but did not say a word. When we returned to Taiyuan we had to pass the same spot and he experienced another painful moment. The road construction workers had repaired the damage and, knowing that the distinguished foreigners were to return along the same road, they had waited for us. Arm in arm, they blocked the road and wanted to halt the coaches. Judging by their faces, the intentions of the workers were friendly – maybe they wanted to shake hands with an African ambassador or see a woman in Western dress. But their spontaneous action was not appreciated. The town councillor ordered the driver *not* to slow down, and the human obstacles seemed to be blown off the road. That no one was hurt is still a mystery to me. I was surprised at the town councillor's careless behaviour and asked an Eastern European colleague for his comment. 'These so-called revolutionary rebels do not wish to meet the people,' he said. His opinion may have been motivated either by traumatic experiences in his own youth, or by the anti-Chinese trends in Eastern European propaganda. His judgement, however, may also have been correct. With the town councillor I began a conversation on Chinese literature.

In Shansi the farmers often wear a towel on their heads, held in place by means of a knot. I told the town councillor that I had read about this head-dress in the novels by Chao Shu-li. The revolutionary town councillor enlarged upon the criminal revisionist qualities of this writer, who was allegedly a follower of the Black Clique. The town councillor inquired which works by Chao Shu-li I had read and I mentioned *Changes in the Village of the Family Li*. He commented that this novel was still 'relatively good'. However, Chao Shu-li now appeared to have close relations with party leaders taking the capitalist road. He possessed a large bank account and a luxurious house, and expressed sentiments that were incompatible with the class struggle and furthered the corruption of young people. I was on the point of saying that it was a pity that the efforts of the authorities over a period of twenty years to convince China and the world that Chao Shu-li was the greatest modern Chinese author now appeared to have been in vain, but the town councillor was interrupted by a Chinese from Peking who questioned whether it was opportune to inform a foreigner of the details of the newest political evaluation of Chao Shu-li's works and life. The town councillor was adamant. Of course, foreigners must learn about revisionism too. With an abundance of arguments and unfailing energy, he patiently silenced his Pekinese opponent. In fact, he took no risk in doing so, since Hsinhua News Agency had published extensive information on Chao Shu-li's revisionism several weeks earlier. Yet, at that particular moment, I realized that the town councillor won his argument mainly because of his energetic defence. I sensed that at that juncture of the Cultural Revolution, energy was more important than prudence.

Industry

The briefings on political and industrial affairs conveyed the same type of information that we read in the Chinese press. Figures, names, time and place differed, but the wording of the 'short introductions' was practically the same in every factory that we visited: 'Due to the Cultural Revolution the production of factory X during the first four months of this year is much bigger than during the corresponding period of last year. The capitalist policy of over-emphasising techno- logy and planning has been replaced by the proletarian propagation of the thought of Mao Tse-tung. Members of the People's Liberation Army contributed to the victory of the revolutionary rebels and promoted both revolution and production. They duly accomplished their task of propagating the thought of Mao Tse-tung.'

We were shown a thermo-electric power plant, a textile factory, a transformer factory, blast furnaces and a small chemical plant.

Our inspection of the power plant was an exercise in anti-revision- ism. The construction of the plant had begun in 1953 and the seven oldest furnaces were Russian-made. We were hurried past them but were given ample time to admire the eighth, which was built comple- tely in China and by Chinese. Four out of the six turbo-generators were produced in the Soviet Union. The two Chinese ones dated from 1960 and had been constructed in Harbin. Our guide emphasised proudly that the capacity of the Chinese generators (50,000 kwh. each) was twice as great as that of the Soviet ones.

Our tour of the plant did not last long. We were soon led into a rather small room where we were served tea and propaganda. The members of the revolutionary committee of the plant were introduced to us; no one seemed to be older than forty years of age. Of course, there was also a representative of the army. Then followed the reading of the 'highest instructions'. One of the hosts said encourag- ingly: 'Please, join us in reading!' The Chinese text drowned the English and Russian of the translators. Since there is a tradition that the *Internationale* can be sung simultaneously by different nationalities each in their own language, the Chinese thought they had found a solution to the language barrier by reciting the words of Mao Tse-tung simultaneously in different languages. The noisy recitation was ended by the announcement: 'So much for the highest instructions.' We received a mimeographed pamphlet that was subsequently read out in Chinese and translated. This was a very dull lecture. Over the open windows there was wire netting that showed the remnants of old posters. We could see two or three sub-tropical shrubs. It was very warm and everyone seemed tired. Meanwhile the speaker continued his explanation of the results of the Cultural Revolution in this factory.

There had been a fierce struggle and many workers went on strike when the proletarian revolutionaries seized power on January 18, 1967. But after the necessary political and ideological work among the strikers, *all* had returned to work. On February 15 a revolutionary committee on the basis of the three-way alliance was established. There were party members in this revolutionary committee, but they were a minority. Someone asked whether the Cultural Revolution had produced any change in wages. This was denied. The average payment of the workers and administrative staff was 57 yüan (26 U.S. dollars). There was also a question whether workers who did overtime or overfulfilled their quota received an additional allowance. The reply was evasive, not only in this factory but also on other occasions. Sometimes the answer was that the workers were not interested any more in bonuses. Sometimes, however, the system of additional allowances seemed to have been abandoned completely, although the average monthly wage had remained the same as before the Cultural Revolution.

During our visit to the 'January 26' Textile Factory in Taiyuan we were told that payment on the basis of piecework had been replaced by a fixed wage 'with additional allowances according to circumstances'. However, it was not explained *which* circumstances might influence the wages. In the textile factory the highest monthly wage was not more than 100 yüan (45 U.S. dollars), and the lowest wage not less than 40 yüan (18 U.S. dollars).

The textile factory was praised as a product of the Great Leap Forward, but construction had begun already in 1956. It started functioning in 1958. At a briefing we learned that 7,500 workers were employed in this factory, most of them women. There were 3,000 looms, which produced 75 million yards of cotton a year (that is, four yards for every inhabitant of the province). The name of the factory referred to the day when the 'Red Guard Corps' with the support of the army had taken over power. In the beginning reactionary Red Guards had been in the majority, but soon about 2,800 more young people had joined the 'Red Guard Corps'. The members of the 'Red Guard Corps' defied the reactionaries who had suppressed them and had even resorted to kidnapping. During our inspection of the factory we noticed the presence of some military men. At times they tried to help the workers, but clearly they did not feel at home in their present role. In this factory as well they had decided the outcome of the internal struggle. The vice-chairman of the revolutionary committee of the textile factory explained that, in accordance with their principle of 'looting, burning, and destroying', the reactionaries had three times invaded and destroyed the headquarters of the 'Red

Guard Corps'. The last time they had done this was on January 23 (1967). 'During the Sino-Japanese war the Japanese used the same tactics,' the vice-chairman said. 'And with the help of the Soviet armies led by Comrade Stalin we were able to liberate ourselves.' The parallel was obvious. The army was assigned the role that the Soviet forces once played in the North-east. It is not at all certain that the Chinese people will appreciate the interference of the army during the Cultural Revolution any more than it did the activities of the Soviet occupying forces in Manchuria.

In the transformer factory we did not see a single military uniform. Here the revolutionary committee consisted of *kanpu's*, revolutionary rebels and members of the militia. From a technical point of view the transformer factory was certainly inferior to the power plant and the textile factory. The four hundred workers did most of the work by hand. There was no assembly line, which must have been tiring for the workers who had to handle heavy transformers of 40, 100, 200 and more kwh.

The 'iron-and-steel-factory' mentioned earlier also made a good impression on us. As to efficiency and safety, however, it did not come up to Western standards. The complex consisted of three blast furnaces, twelve open hearth furnaces, a rolling mill and a chemical factory. The largest and most modern blast furnace was made entirely in China, and was operated automatically from a room where all the instruments seemed to have been produced in Shanghai in 1960.

Finally we visited the Huakuang shoe-polish factory, or the 'Third Chemical Co-operative' of Taiyuan. I shall enlarge somewhat on our inspection of this factory, not in order to ridicule Chinese industry – which I see no reason for doing – but in order to put forward the idea that the achievement of Chinese industry is not primarily the result of maoist ideology, but has rather been achieved in spite of maoism. The shoe-polish factory was a product of the Great Leap Forward. In 1959, inspired by the 'three red banners' (the people's communes, the Great Leap Forward, and the 'general line'), eleven housewives and four unskilled men had established the factory. At the time of our visit it employed thirty-three workers, and produced, apart from shoe-polish, camphor balls and candles. The vice-chairman of the revolutionary committee of the shoe-polish factory gave a short briefing in a nearby wooden shed. He was clearly enjoying himself and was not going to worry whether he was talking nonsense or not. 'In the past we produced nothing, but now we make three articles,' he said with a beaming face. 'This proves that the policy of the Great Leap Forward is correct.' The early history of the factory was full of obstacles, and when in 1962 the co-operative was ordered to produce shoe-polish, the immediate results were poor. Initially the product resembled cart-grease, smelled like petrol, and when used left the shoes sticky. Almost forty ambassadors and a handful of chargés d'affaires made notes or, apparently bored, looked around. Several Chinese among the audience felt embarrassed. The 'short introduction' was built on the theme of economic independence, and the speaker believed that it was a great victory of Mao Tse-tung's thought that for two years the co-operative had experimented in vain, before it was finally decided to send someone to Peking to study the process of making shoe-polish. He concluded his introduction by saying that the workers of the co-operative had decided to produce 'still another brand of shoe-polish, another brand of candles, and another brand of camphor balls to serve as bullets in the struggle against American imperialism'. We then had the opportunity of visiting the stuffy workshops. During our tour of the factory there was an explosion in the camphor workshop which caused a fire and a lot of poisonous smoke.

Yet I am sure that our visit to the 'Third Chemical Co-operative' had not been planned by some lackey of revisionism. This final part of our programme in Taiyuan was a natural consequence of the lack of understanding of the world outside China that is characteristic of the present régime.

The Production Brigade Tachai

On our way back to Peking, the train stopped in Yangchuan, where buses were waiting to take us to Tachai. Yangchuan is a small industrial mining town of relative prosperity. Here hand-carts with heavy loads are pulled not by men alone, but by a man and a donkey. I recall a park on a hill and a triumphal arch plastered with posters, and outside the town, limestone pits, burning limekilns, and endless lines of mule and donkey carts full of coal. Someone asked one of our hosts about the size of private plots. The existence of private plots was denied; there were, however, small plots which, although collectively owned, were appropriated for private use (about 2 per cent of the total arable acreage). In the model production brigade Tachai, however, there were no plots for private use.

We reached Tachai after travelling for two hours over badly paved roads that crossed dry river beds and not so dry rivers. Where communications are so poor, self-reliance is sheer necessity. The economic independence of Tachai, though, exists more in principle than in reality. This was a great disappointment, not so much for me (since I am not convinced that self-sufficiency is a solution, certainly not for small communities) as for my colleagues from Asia and Africa who had hoped that the example of Tachai might be valid for their own countries. Those who were more intelligent than credulous had lost this illusion by the end of the day.

Tachai is a small village in a mountainous area with at most 400 inhabitants. The farmers of the production brigade Tachai, which is part of a commune that is never mentioned, have experimented for years and succeeded at last in laying out terraced fields and utilising the ravines where, in the past, the rains used to wash the soil away. However, the terraced fields, that were admired by all of us, are not exceptional in Shansi, and neither is industrious labour. The only reason why Tachai became famous is that since 1953 it never asked the government for a loan or any other aid for improving soil conditions. Dynamite for blowing up stones and steel for the production of tools was purchased with funds from the production brigade. The farmers themselves experimented with the construction of dams in order to curb floods after heavy rain, and gradually learnt that the terraces in the ravines should be protected not by straight dams but by curved ones that would divert the pressure of the water over a greater area.

Ch'en Yung-kuei, secretary of the party committee of the production brigade, informed us of this. When he had finished, someone asked whether he had ever thought of asking the advice of a hydraulic engineer. Ch'en Yung-kuei answered that they had in fact consulted Taiyuan University. Strictly speaking, this was not in accordance with the principle of self-reliance.

Before we arrived in Tachai, we had met, in Taiyuan, Ch'en Yung-kuei, who by the time of our visit had become famous for his attacks on revisionism and 'China's Khrushchev'.[2] We wondered how a village of not more than eighty families, where payment per working day is 1.22 yüan, could afford to send its leader on propaganda missions inside and outside the province, to receive every week, if not every day, groups of political tourists, and to show them around and provide them with a meal. At lunch we were told that everything served had been produced in Tachai. The copious lunch consisted mainly of sweet farinaceous food and rice. We were advised to add a large amount of sugar to the all too insipid soup. Probably the sugar, and certainly the fizzy lemonade, had *not* been produced in Tachai. We assumed that the commune or the county helped to defray the expenses of the lunch, and also supported the large groups of soldiers and students whom we saw at work in the mountains around the village, marching, or reading the red book. They seemed to be a liability rather than an asset. They applied the slogan 'Learn from Tachai', but the financial or material support that enabled them to stay here seemed to violate the idea of self-reliance. Once, perhaps, Tachai was an industrious community that relied completely on its own efforts, but now it appeared to be a political monument, heavily subsidised by the state.

My admiration for the industrious farmers of Tachai is great, but it is unfair to the other people of south Shansi to hold up the long underdeveloped village of Tachai as an example for the whole of China. The fable of Tachai serves merely to illustrate an idiosyncrasy of Mao Tse-tung, which, in my opinion, stands in the way of sound and rapid economic development, and avoids a confrontation with reality. The principle of self-reliance both of small communities and of China as a whole is the logical consequence of a struggle for independence that is deeply rooted in the Chinese mind. But to the nation it means isolation, to the interior often unnecessary stagnation.

The visit to Tachai marked the end of our trip. When returning to Yangchuan by road, we passed the fertile fields of other production brigades. The Red Guard Liu Hao fell asleep and laid his head on a capitalist shoulder. It had been a tiring day.

Why had the Ministry of Foreign Affairs organised the excursion? It wanted, of course, to continue a tradition that had been welcomed by the diplomatic corps in previous years and to show that, in spite of all rumours about serious incidents in the provinces, it was quite capable of organising the trip. (No diplomatic trip was arranged in 1968 or 1969.) Moreover, a diplomatic excursion always created an opportunity for indoctrinating the participants. Perhaps another reason was that, as one African ambassador suggested, the central government had brought us to Shansi in order to encourage the provincial revolutionary committee. During our stay in Taiyuan, the 'red diplomatic fighter' Yao Teng-shan (the Chinese chargé d'affaires who some weeks earlier had been declared *persona non grata* in Djakarta) joined us. His arrival provided the provincial revolutionary committee with an opportunity to show off with a brand-new hero. During one of the evenings that we spent at the Workers' Cultural Palace, Chang Jih-ch'ing, the obvious leader of the revolutionary committee, stood up and interrupted the performance on the stage. He shouted for light and introduced Yao Teng-shan to the audience which, apart from the foreign diplomats, consisted almost exclusively of soldiers and Red Guards. He also read the latest news from the Vietnamese front and asked the audience to welcome the new North Vietnamese ambassador with a big hand. Chang Jih-ch'ing's close ties with these important figures from the international scene, of course, boosted his popularity with the local people.

The provincial revolutionary committee may have been encouraged by the almost complete acceptance of the invitation to visit Shansi by the diplomatic corps,[3] but China is not a country where things are decided by such details. When we left Yangchuan, a noisy meeting was held in the park near the railway station. The participants may not even have noticed our presence. Revolution and counter-revolution follow their own fatal road. In early June, only a few days after we had left the region, it was rumoured that in Shansi thirty people had been killed in serious incidents.

REFERENCES

1. The idea of organising elections following the model of those of the Paris Commune was popular only for a short time. The unofficial newspaper *Hung t'ieh-tao* of the Dairen Railway Institute of February 11, 1967, reported that the Central Committee had appointed Hsieh Fu-chih president of a committee in preparation of the 'Peking Commune'. The same source mentioned that since February 5, 1967, Chang Ch'un-ch'iao and Yao Wen-yüan acted as first and second secretaries of the Shanghai Commune. However, already on February 15, Chou En-lai in a speech to students from Kweichow warned against elections along the principles of the Paris Commune. He observed that in many places the revolutionary rebels were still in the minority. In such cases they should refrain from establishing communes of the type of the Paris Commune, and were advised to delay the seizing of power or to ask the army to support them.

2. His loyalty to the policies of Mao Tse-tung was rewarded by membership of the Central Committee in April 1969.

3. Due to strained relations between China and the United Kingdom, the British Chargé d'Affaires had not been invited. In Hong Kong a huge protest movement had been triggered off by a minor incident in a plastic flower factory. On May 16, 1967, half a million people demonstrated in front of the Office of the British Chargé d'Affaires. On the same day the office and residence of the acting British consul in Shanghai were invaded by the masses, who destroyed all the furniture and manhandled the consul.

6

A LONG HOT SUMMER:
SUMMER 1967

To some extent, everybody is egocentric. The foreign diplomats in Peking were no exception, and were tempted to view the internal developments in China in an international context. They wondered whether internal political changes had any consequences for Chinese foreign policy, or would affect their own status. This was a logical reaction, but it was the wrong way to understand the Cultural Revolution. To the Chinese people, foreign policy is primarily a means to strengthen their feelings of self-esteem. Chinese foreign policy is directed more towards spiritual conversion to maoism than towards pragmatic protection of interests. Chinese imperialism is ideological rather than militaristic – which does not mean that it is peaceful; it is about as peaceful as the Crusades.

The emphasis on this ideological aspect, which during the Cultural Revolution was again greatly enhanced, implies that Chinese foreign policy is an extension of internal political developments. If this holds true also for other nations, it does so even more for China. The vastness of the country plays a distinct part here. To the great majority of the Chinese people, foreign relations are a peripheral affair. This was true in the eighteenth and nineteenth centuries but is still valid in our own time. Let me mention one example. The struggle that the Chinese leaders are carrying on against Soviet revisionism is levelled not so much at Russia as at a political belief, the negative effect of which – according to Mao Tse-tung – may be observed in the Soviet Union.

This introduction must serve as an excuse for an inadequate treatment of China's relations with other countries, about which I cannot write in any detail without indiscretion. I shall, therefore, not enlarge on the difficulties that Kenya and Indonesia met in closing their embassies and repatriating their diplomatic staff, and shall not fully record the many embarrassments and instances of maltreatment that diplomats of other countries, including my own, have experienced. This does not mean that the foreigners in Peking were peacefully watching the course of the Cultural Revolution as though they were outsiders.

This chapter, like the others, will be almost exclusively devoted to the internal developments.

Disturbances in Szechwan

In early May the problems in the province of Szechwan, where Li Ching-ch'üan was still in power, reached their climax. On April 21 and May 6, in Chengtu, many people were killed and hundreds wounded in confrontations between Red Guards and armed workers, who were referred to in the press as the 'production army'. The workers, who had entrenched themselves in the 132nd factory of Chengtu, had used hand-grenades and automatic weapons. Among those killed was a Red Guard from Peking, whose portrait was published in a Red Guard newspaper of May 9.

On May 7 the Central Committee decided to dismiss Li Ching-ch'üan as First Secretary of the South-west Bureau of the Communist Party and as Political Commissar of the Chengtu military region. The military commander of Tibet, General Chang Kuo-hua, who had himself been criticised by the Red Guard and was not a genuine supporter of the Cultural Revolution, succeeded Li as Political Commissar and was concurrently appointed 'chairman of the commission in charge of the preparation of a revolutionary committee in Szechwan'. The revolutionary committee was finally established in May 1968, but even then order was not definitely restored. As I mentioned earlier, Szechwan is rightly called the first province where disorders break out, and the last to return to normal.

The decree of the Central Committee (again, in fact, a decision of an enlarged Politburo), which announced the dismissal of Li Ching-ch'üan and which was published in the unofficial press, was a courageous one. The central government seemed determined to impose its will on the provinces. But it could do so only with the support of the armed forces. The army would form a barrier between the revolutionary rebels and the moderates. The disturbances of the summer of 1967 almost always originated from such a situation. If the army was also internally divided, the incidents were more serious. This was acclaimed by the extreme Left led by K'ang Sheng and Wang Li, who for that reason aimed at increasing dissension within the army. If, however, the army was united, the conflicts were restricted to

insignificant incidents, which was the aim of Chou En-lai. Against
this background the slogan 'protect the army, love the people' which
was published in the *People's Daily* on April 28 should be interpreted.
This slogan represented the opinion of those advocating the restoration
of order.

However, the army in Szechwan did not immediately submit to
the will of Peking and the decree of May 7. The influence of Li Ching-
ch'üan was not eliminated at once. Rumour had it (but I did not read
it myself) that Li's reaction to the decree of the Central Committee
was one of proud insubordination. 'A decree of the Central Committee?' he reportedly said. 'How is that possible? I was not there, and I
know who else, besides me, were absent at the meeting of May 7.'
The workers who were ordered to lay down their arms and hand
them over to the regular army ignored the order. The Red Guards,
too, refused to hand over their arms 'because the workers did not do
so either'. Fierce fighting took place in Iping, a town in eastern
Szechwan. Here two hundred Red Guards who wanted to spread the
news of Li Ching-ch'üan's dismissal ran into 'a handful of counter-
revolutionary and revisionist elements'. An unofficial newspaper of
May 22 reported this. The same source mentioned that Chou En-lai
had requested troops to be moved to Iping. In Peking, wall newspapers disclosed that the Red Guards who had clashed in Iping with the
handful of counter-revolutionaries had been buried alive. This report
cannot be verified, but is not necessarily incorrect. Anyhow, it is
symptomatic of the hatred that was gradually being built up between
the revolutionary rebels and their opponents.

The resistance in Szechwan was not the work of one man alone.
Apart from Li Ching-ch'üan, several other officials were dismissed,
among them the mayor of Chungking who was concurrently a secretary of the South-west Bureau. In general, the opposition to the
Cultural Revolution, as it appeared in the summer of 1967, had the
following common features: it emphasised the rights of the party and
the Central Committee; it refused to abandon the marxism of Marx
and Lenin in exchange for a vague and ill-defined maoism; it defended
the interests of the working class; it advocated a rise in productivity
by modern means; and finally it was in favour of a certain degree of
local autonomy. This 'programme', which can be selected from the
criticisms levelled at the opponents of Mao Tse-tung, found enough
response in Szechwan to stiffen resistance to the policies that emanated
from Peking. In June 1967, in Chungking, posters demanded the death

penalty for several members of the 'commission in charge of the preparation of a revolutionary committee' of that town. Maoist Red Guards were forced to entrench themselves in the University of Chungking and armed themselves with daggers, sulphuric acid and crash-helmets. Their revolutionary attitude was to cause more admiration than they could ever have hoped for. Unwittingly they became the predecessors of the rebellious students in Western Europe, who sometimes seem to protest against life itself now they have discovered that the 'struggle for life' is no longer a real struggle.

In early July wall posters in Peking announced the arrest of Li Ching-ch'üan. He was supposedly taken to Peking. But this did not mean the end of the disorders in Szechwan, and in August resistance broke out again. Wall newspapers referred to the 'August Rebellion' and a (metaphorical) 'stab in the back of Chang Kuo-hua'.

Honan, Inner Mongolia, Sinkiang and other Provinces

Szechwan was far away, and has often been a dissident province in Chinese history. Still more important was what happened in Honan, a province less than two hundred miles from Peking. Here, too, Red Guards were confronted by moderate organisations. In the provincial capital Chengchow, the 'February 7 Commune', an organisation dominated by the extreme Left and supported by Red Guards from Peking, was active. Already by March 1967 the 'February 7 Commune' had run into difficulties, and students from Peking who wanted to come to the rescue, were arrested by the army at the border between Hopei and Honan. In mid-April the incident was elaborately recorded in the unofficial press.

The army did not appreciate the activities of the 'February 7 Commune', and remained strictly neutral when fighting broke out between the extremists and the moderates. During May the news spread in Peking that in Chengchow 250 maoists had disappeared. The leftist organisations in Honan sent a telegram to the central government requesting the intervention of the People's Liberation Army. In the meantime large groups of Honanese 'conservatives' arrived in the capital to plead their case with the Central Committee and the masses. The government, which was under pressure of the representatives of the 'February 7 Commune' as well, could not remain silent. On May 5, Vice-Premier Hsieh Fu-chih explained the inertia with which the Central Committee and the government were watching the incidents in Honan. He said that the Cultural Revolution group tried first to solve problems in the border provinces, and that the problem of Honan 'was in part a military issue, which would be settled in due course'. This probably meant that Peking could not rely on the army in Honan. Later, in fact, several army units in Honan distributed arms among the conservative organisations.

A revolutionary committee in Honan was not formed until January 27, 1968. From its composition it can be concluded that here, too, the revolutionary rebels had to resign themselves to a compromise.

As Hsieh Fu-chih had said, the Cultural Revolution group was pre-occupied with the border provinces. The result was that Ulanfu was dismissed as First Secretary and military commander of Inner Mongolia. On June 18, 1967, a 'commission in charge of the preparation of a revolutionary committee of the autonomous region of Inner Mongolia' was inaugurated; on November 1 the revolutionary committee itself was announced. It is quickly written down, but it was a delicate affair, partly because of the strained relations between China and the Mongolian People's Republic. The 'counter-revolutionary revisionists' in Inner Mongolia were, of course, tempted to take refuge in Outer Mongolia. This entailed the risk that Chinese troops might try to pre-vent this and would pursue the refugees on to Outer Mongolian soil. Border incidents seemed to be the inevitable result of the purge which took place in Inner Mongolia, but I have no confirmation that any such incidents did, in fact, occur. However, in August 1967, the relations between Peking and Ulan Bator were at their lowest and came close to breaking-point. In the centre of Peking, the Mongolian Ambassador's car was set on fire; Chinese demonstrators entered the Embassy, beat up Mongolian diplomats and spat on the Ambassador.

Sinkiang was an area which, because of its long border with the Soviet Union and the composition of its population, called for parti-cularly careful treatment. Here, however, the Cultural Revolution group was less successful than in Inner Mongolia. The powerful military commander and First Party Secretary Wang En-mao was initially called a counter-revolutionary revisionist, but on December 31, 1967, made it up with Mao Tse-tung during a spectacular visit to Peking. This reconciliation was rather unexpected because, during the summer of that year, Wang En-mao had been involved in a number of incidents in which he had revealed himself as an enemy of the Red Guard. This at least was the implication of reports in a newspaper of

June 17, 1967, published by Red Guards from Sinkiang who were staying in Peking. I believe that there are more reasons for accepting these reports as mainly correct than for rejecting them as sheer fantasy. I shall therefore, relate them, although with the necessary reservations.

On June 4, in a small town twenty miles north of Urumchi, units of the 'production army' attacked Red Guards of the Second Headquarters. Armed workers, numbering two or three thousand, arrived from Urumchi in lorries. The Red Guards counted eighty lorries, which were equipped with machine-guns manned by professional soldiers. Without any provocation they drove up to the Red Guards and opened fire. The unarmed Red Guards suffered three hundred casualties.

Another report from the same source did not omit the Central Asian local colour. It related how Wang En-mao had suggested to the military commander in the district of Chitai, ninety miles east of Urumchi, that he should persuade the nomads of that region to besiege the town of Chitai. The local commander obeyed, and the result was that ten thousand peasants and nomads marched on Chitai and occupied it. They had few scruples and established a 'capitalist dictatorship' of a rather crude type. Among the occupying forces were tribesmen from areas that did not understand Chinese and with whom it was difficult to argue about the Cultural Revolution. Six hundred mounted Kazakhs, who participated in the action, abducted a great number of Chinese in order to subject them to atrocious tortures at some quiet place in the desert.

The Red Guard newspapers held Wang En-mao responsible for these incidents. He was branded as a counter-revolutionary, a dictator and a henchman of President Liu Shao-ch'i, and charged with having launched a 'so-called democratic' land reform movement in Sinkiang. He had adhered to revisionist policies in the field of religion and on minority questions. He had paid too much attention to production and too little to proletarian politics. The Second Headquarters of the Red Guard did not wish to accept him as a partner in a three-way alliance, and predicted that, if Wang En-mao were included in the provincial revolutionary committee, the counter-revolution would spread all over China. In this context it is not surprising that it was a long time before a revolutionary committee was formed in Sinkiang.

There was no province or town of any significance where the Cultural Revolution did not leave its mark. In the coastal provinces, too, the workers resisted the Red Guards. The railways were repeatedly sabotaged. In Canton, General Huang Yung-sheng, commander of the Canton military region, was criticised in wall newspapers, but, although Red Guards charged him with having established a military dictatorship, Huang was fully supported by the central government in Peking. The general did not forbid the mass meetings which the Cantonese Red Guards organised in order to expose members of the Black Clique. On June 9 at such a meeting, the former First Secretary of the provincial party committee of Kwangtung, Chao Tzu-yang, was accused of having committed crimes 'against the party, socialism, the thought of Mao Tse-tung and the Cultural Revolution'. The next day a meeting was held at which the revolutionary masses promised not to resort to violence. However, as will appear from further developments, this promise did not mean very much.

In Peking the workers began to demonstrate in May to underline their demands that order be restored as soon as possible. They rejected anarchism. The *People's Daily* repeatedly emphasised the need for discipline and economy, especially under revolutionary conditions. At the same period in the small town of Changping, not far from Peking, there were armed clashes, although of no great significance. The counter-revolutionary culprits were forced to withdraw to the mountains north-west of the capital.

By early July, revolutionary committees had taken over power in the provinces of Shansi, Kweichow, Heilungkiang and Shantung, and in the cities of Shanghai and Peking. In several provinces, such as Inner Mongolia and Szechwan, commissions in charge of the preparation of a revolutionary committee were formed on the initiative of the local military commanders. However, because of the great numbers of incidents and sabotage in other provinces, and the impossibility of upholding the old administrative structures, the central government created an intermediate phase of the military take-over, which needed little preparation. The unofficial press reported in July that the People's Liberation Army had taken over in nine provinces: Tibet, Sinkiang, Tsinghai, Yunnan, Shensi, Anhwei and the coastal provinces Kiangsu, Fukien and Kwangtung. In the remaining thirteen provinces the army was preparing for a take-over, or had not even reached that phase. The latter applies to the province of Hupei in central China, the province of Kansu in the north-west and two prosperous provinces in the north-east, Liaoning and Kirin. The confusion remained considerable, but it gradually became evident that in most places the army was taking control of the administrative apparatus.

The Seaside Resort of Peitaiho

At the end of July, I took my family to the seaside resort of Peitaiho, about six hours by train from Peking. It could be described as a thoroughly reactionary place where, before 1949, many Chinese and foreigners owned villas, which have subsequently been taken over by communist and workers' organisations. The communist régime enabled meritorious workers and officials to escape from the humid summer in Peking and Tientsin and enjoy the sun and the beach here. Wu Han, the former vice-mayor of Peking, also used to spend his holidays in Peitaiho. It was here that in August 1961 he wrote the preface to his 'revisionist' play *The Dismissal of Hai Jui*. Of course, during the Cultural Revolution not many Chinese showed any interest in a visit to Peitaiho.

For us, Peitaiho meant that we were able to forget Peking for a while. We were far away from the city, where the revolutionary rebels were turning more and more openly against foreign diplomats. They did not shrink from molesting them and ignoring their diplomatic privileges. On June 12 the Indian Second Secretary, K. Raghunath, was charged with espionage, and the Ministry of Foreign Affairs put out the unusual statement that his diplomatic status was no longer recognised. The next day the diplomat was tried *in absentia* at a mass meeting presided over by the municipal higher court, and condemned to 'deportation under escort of the police and the Red Guard'. On the morning of June 14, Raghunath went to the airport, accompanied by his colleagues, who wanted to see him off, and by many members of the Indian Embassy, including the chargé d'affaires and several strong Sikhs. But nobody was able to prevent his immediate capture by a great number of Red Guards who had been waiting for him, who beat him and gave him the 'jet-treatment'. He was dragged over the airfield in order to enable every one of the several thousand Red Guards who had gathered here to strike him or to shout insults at him.

On June 14, the Ministry of Foreign Affairs issued a serious warning to all diplomatic missions in Peking. The statement, in fact, said that all 'imperialist, revisionist and reactionary' embassies were guilty of 'espionage', the meaning of which was stretched unusually far. All diplomats, and especially those who read Chinese and occasionally glanced at a wall newspaper or slogan, which was hard to avoid in the centre of Peking, could expect similar treatment to Raghunath. An editorial comment in the *People's Daily* explained that foreign diplomats 'who did not respect the Chinese revolutionary order' would be tried by Chinese courts. This was contrary to international practice, and the Chinese leaders must have been aware of it. Therefore, the attempt to deny diplomatic immunity to embassy personnel must be interpreted as 'a victory of the masses'. The police and the judiciary, who should have enforced diplomatic immunity, were no longer capable of holding out against the demands of the masses, who could not reconcile the immunity of certain foreigners with the unconditional class struggle in which no one was to be considered neutral.

The revolutionary masses were strengthened in this line of thought by Ch'i Pen-yü, the extreme leftist philosopher of the Cultural Revolution group, who, as I wrote in the previous chapter, had stressed the positive aspects of the Boxer rebellion in early April. On June 5 Ch'i Pen-yü commemorated the twenty-fifth anniversary of Mao Tse-tung's *Yenan Talks*, which are the cultural blueprint of the Chinese Communist Party. He again raised the issue of xenophobia: 'The imperialist and modern revisionist overlords slanderously accuse our great proletarian Cultural Revolution of "xenophobia". We would ask: what foreign things are we against? We always adopt a friendly attitude towards the people from any country who come to China for friendly visits, although their thinking and customs are different from ours. We give strong support to the struggle of the oppressed nations and oppressed peoples of the world for liberation. And, as for the proletarian revolutionary comrades-in-arms, we not only extend a sincere welcome to them but will fight shoulder to shoulder with them against imperialism, modern revisionism and all reaction. But if this "xenophobia" means struggle against the imperialists, revisionists and special agents who endanger the cause of the Chinese revolution, then we have swept them away and will sweep them away, lock, stock and barrel like the clearing away of the garbage heap. Such "xenophobia" is excellent! Without this "xenophobia" against the imperialists and modern revisionists, they will bully us.'

With a sigh of relief we got off the train on the small clean platform at Peitaiho. It was late afternoon. We could smell the sea, pines and shells. With various Rumanian and Yugoslav travellers, we were politely led to several cars which were waiting for us. We were given tickets and had to pay the fare to our hotel. It was a long drive through woods and dunes, along the shore and past empty villas. Peking, with its noise and dust and problems, seemed far away. We were assigned two rooms and a shower at the corner of a bungalow with a large verandah, with rattan chairs, where until late at night we used to play bridge with friends who were staying in a neighbouring apartment. The full moon was reflected in the sea. All was completely idyllic. But it was also China, and the Cultural Revolution had reached Peitaiho as well. Loudspeakers enabled those on the beach to follow the proceedings of a meeting somewhere else in the village where local revisionists were being exposed. We were annoyed, but did not feel as involved as we were in Peking. We did not need to listen, because the meeting was not directed against the Burmese, the Indians, the Russians, the British or the Indonesians. No colleagues were under attack. We became good friends with our bridge-partners – serious communists who were prepared to talk about Djilas.

The children enjoyed Peitaiho. The sea was never cold and there were often high waves on which they floated with a li-lo. There was a restaurant named 'Kiessling' after the former Swiss owner, where we could get excellent iced coffee and European dishes which we ate with forks, neatly engraved with the words *Rostfrei* and *Kiessling & Bader*. Even Anna Louise Strong, the famous American admirer of Mao Tse-tung, who was also in Peitaiho, often sent someone here to fetch her some ice cream.

Peitaiho, moreover, possessed a bookshop which was relatively well stocked. I found various novels and volumes of short stories published by the provincial press of Hopei, which were not available in the 'Hsin-hua shu-tien' in Peking. But Peitaiho did not lag behind the capital. There were many posters. Written on the pavement in large characters was the statement that the army had taken over power in Hopei province. While I was in the bookshop glancing through a booklet about an exemplary commune, a shouting mob was pushing several members of the Black Clique along the street.

After a week I returned to Peking. My wife and children followed two weeks later. A few hours before my departure from Peitaiho, I learned from a colleague who had just arrived from Peking about the Wuhan rebellion.

Rebellion in Wuhan

By the end of June a tense situation had arisen in the South Chinese

province of Yunnan which borders on Burma. This happened at just
the wrong moment, when Sino-Burmese relations were more strained
than ever before in the history of the People's Republic. There had
been incidents in Rangoon during which a Chinese expert, who
worked in Burma under the Chinese technical assistance programme,
had been killed. In response to this, huge demonstrations were organised in the diplomatic quarter of San-li-tun where the Burmese Embassy was situated. During the night of June 28, loudspeakers were
installed near the Embassy, and from that moment on, for the next two
weeks about two or three hundred thousand people marched past the
Embassy every day. They waved small paper flags on which slogans
were written that called for support to be given to the 'revolutionary
struggle of the Burmese people'. Almost every organisation or factory
in Peking sent its staff to San-li-tun in order to shout in chorus 'Down
with American imperialism, down with Soviet revisionism, down
with the Burmese reactionaries.' Although there was a cordon of
soldiers in front of the Embassy, the building was smeared with paint,
the windows were broken and the Burmese Premier was burnt in
effigy. The Burmese diplomats were not able to leave the Embassy for
several weeks. A kind-hearted colleague supplied them with fresh
bread every day over the wall between their adjoining gardens.

However, the difficulties in Yunnan had little to do with the Sino-
Burmese differences. In the provincial capital, Kunming, a conflict
between the 'Proletarian Revolutionaries of the 23rd August' and the
'Maoist Proletarian Revolutionaries' had reached proportions which
were inadmissible in a strategic border province. The armed forces in
Yunnan were as divided as the revolutionary rebels. Not only could
they not settle the dispute, but apparently there was a danger that the
extremist faction might try to act upon the slogans that were shouted
in Peking and put into effect the demand that the Burmese guerrillas
be supported. Against this background Mao Tse-tung decided to send
a delegation to Yunnan to mediate between the different factions and
to brief them on Peking's policy towards Burma. The delegation was
headed by the moderate Vice-Premier Hsieh Fu-chih, the extreme
leftist Director of the Propaganda Department of the Central Committee, Wang Li, and a number of other officials, among whom were
representatives of extreme leftist organisations of the Red Guard. The
mission was successful and the situation calmed down in Yunnan.

On their way back in the second half of July the delegation reached
Wuhan, an important industrial centre on the Yangtze and the

capital of Hupei; Wang Jen-chung, the First Secretary of the Central-South Bureau of the party, who had always been a loyal supporter of the 'revisionist' T'ao Chu, was still an influential man here. Already in December 1966, wall newspapers in Peking had branded him as a member of the Black Clique, but he had so far kept his important position. He was supported by the commander of the Wuhan military region, Ch'en Tsai-tao, to whom he concurrently served as a political commissar. The 'conservative' organisation, which in Wuhan was resisting an extreme implementation of the Cultural Revolution, was known as 'A Million Heroes' and possibly it did in fact have over a million members (some reports mention six million, spread all over Hupei and even outside this province). By definition it was impossible that so large a number of people could be resisting the policies of Mao Tse-tung, and the official press which reported extensively on the Wuhan rebellion launched the idea that 'A Million Heroes' was in essence a good organisation misled, however, by a handful of reactionaries.

On or about July 20 Hsieh Fu-chih and Wang Li, who while in Wuhan stayed near the residence of Ch'en Tsai-tao, got into trouble. 'Conservatives' entered their rooms and dragged them out on to the street. Ch'en Tsai-tao, who heard the noise, ran after them and tried to excuse himself by saying: 'Now you see for yourself what kind of hooligans I have to deal with!' Such was the rumour that circulated in Peking on the basis of reports in wall newspapers. The official Shanghai newspaper *Wen-hui pao* reported that in Wuhan Hsieh Fu-chih and Wang Li had been driven around on lorries in humiliating postures. The *People's Daily* of July 23 announced that the delegation headed by Hsieh Fu-chih had 'gloriously' returned to Peking, where the masses had given them a tremendous welcome. A film was made of their arrival, in which Wang Li figures prominently. It shows him with a black eye, while sympathetic Red Guards are handing him a pair of crutches. Oddly enough, as chief of propaganda, Wang Li was responsible for the making and showing of the film, which was bound to work against him since he was portrayed in it in a ridiculous role rather than a heroic one. Under his supervision the *People's Daily* also published the report that he and Hsieh Fu-chih had received a great many telegrams conveying expressions of sympathy.

It did not take long before the official press represented the heroic escape from Wuhan as a victory for the thought of Mao Tse-tung. The opposite was nearer to the truth as the incident in Wuhan was a turn-

E

ing-point in the Cultural Revolution. Vice-Premier Hsieh Fu-chih and
the other delegation members were able to leave Wuhan only after
either Chou En-lai or Lin Piao had interceded. The Russians said that
Lin Piao sailed to Wuhan aboard a destroyer in order to negotiate the
release of the delegation. Others believe that Chou En-lai flew to Wuhan to free the hostages. It is also possible that Chou En-lai merely
telephoned Ch'en Tsai-tao, the military commander of Wuhan, and
made the necessary concessions.

It is evident from subsequent events that the central government
was indeed forced to make concessions. Peking could not risk a confrontation with the Wuhan military region. It is true that Wang Jen-
chung and Ch'en Tsai-tao were relieved of their positions but, apart
from that, Peking officially claimed that the proletarian revolutionaries in Wuhan were capable of liberating themselves and of destroying the enemy without any outside help. Most important of all, the
Wuhan rebellion convinced Chou En-lai that the extreme Left,
which from the very beginning he himself had not supported, was
meeting fierce resistance among the people and had no political
future. The incident in Wuhan saw the decline of the power of the
extreme Left. After Wuhan, the fall of Wang Li, who had behaved
as a clown rather than as a hero, was only a matter of time.

The Extreme Left in a Tight Corner

Looking back now on the situation, it can be seen that the extreme
Left was represented, among others, by propaganda chief Wang Li,
the theoretician Ch'i Pen-yü and the journalist Lin Chieh. In varying
degrees they were supported by Chiang Ch'ing (Mrs. Mao Tse-tung),
K'ang Sheng, who was responsible for relations with communist
parties abroad, and perhaps also Ch'en Po-ta, head of the Cultural
Revolution group. Initially the acting Chief of Staff Yang Ch'eng-wu
also seemed to support the extreme Left. Chou En-lai was the most
effective opponent of leftist extremism. He was supported by a number
of generals, the administrative apparatus and a large percentage of the
common people who were politically amorphous. Although it may be
wrong to call the Premier a 'moderate', he has indeed represented
common sense among the Chinese leaders.

However, the extreme leftist factions were totally lacking in
common sense. The behaviour of Wang Li in Wuhan and later in
Peking had been injudicious. In August, moreover, he made the mis-

take of attacking the policies of Chou En-lai, and he was soon to suffer for it. In September, wall newspapers appeared, possibly inspired by Chou En-lai, which disclosed that Wang Li had committed serious mistakes in Wuhan. During the same month the rumour spread that Wang Li had been dismissed from all his functions. He was succeeded as Director of the Propaganda Department of the Central Committee by Ch'en Po-ta, who became the fourth propaganda chief in little over a year. For a long time the dismissal of Wang Li remained unconfirmed, possibly because Premier Chou En-lai did not wish to provoke unnecessary opposition to his policies.

Lin Chieh appeared to be politically unwise as well. He was one of the editors of *Red Flag* and possibly not very important. But, with Ch'i Pen-yü and Yao Wen-yüan, he was one of the small group which interpreted the ideological significance of the Cultural Revolution. This was a role through which much credit could be gained but which entailed high risks as well. In the *People's Daily* of June 16 Lin Chieh's article 'Down with slave mentality, hold proletarian revolutionary discipline aloft' appeared, which advocated the continuation of the revolution and further rebellion against the establishment. He realised that in the history of the communist party Mao Tse-tung has often been the spokesman of a minority, and he implied that now again Chairman Mao represented a minority. One should not worry about that, Lin Chieh suggested, since Mao Tse-tung at the same time represents the interests of the majority of the masses.

The reader should interpret such a statement against the background of the infallibility of Mao Tse-tung. In China, Mao has a similar position to the Pope's in Rome. By definition the Chairman represents the interests of the people, even if the people would prefer another spokesman. Like all dictators, Mao Tse-tung knows better what is good for the people than the people do themselves. Therefore the maoists believe in the People's Republic of China real democracy with proportional representation, which in maoist jargon is called 'bourgeois ultra-democracy', cannot be allowed. Lin Chieh provided a nice example of maoist dialectics by arguing that the majority which resists the policies of Chairman Mao must be called a minority: 'The "majority" which goes against the supreme interests of the broadest sections of the masses is in fact a minority, a handful.'

Although the argument was a clever one, it was injudicious to publish it in the largest newspaper in China. Lin Chieh's theory confirmed that Mao Tse-tung did not have the majority of the Central

E*

Committee behind him, which possibly had already become apparent during the eleventh plenary session in August 1966. Lin Chieh's ingenious explanations could only stiffen the opposition. In September, wall newspapers appeared which accused him of Left extremism. Since then, nothing more has been heard about him.

Relations between the Chinese leaders are greatly influenced by the position of the armed forces. In China, where one does not arrive at logical conclusions in the Western European meaning of the word, the army is far from being a single coherent body. The regional commanders are assisted by political commissars who are in close contact with the regional party organisations. Often the Political Commissar and the First Party Secretary of the area are the same man. During the Cultural Revolution the regional army commanders were placed in the dilemma of deciding whether they should give precedence to their loyalty to the local party organisation or to their obligations towards the central government. In a few instances this led to conflict, as in Wuhan. Often, after a period of clever manoeuvring, the problem was solved one way or another. It had appeared already from the criticism of the former Chief of Staff Lo Jui-ch'ing and from the conspiracy of Marshal Ho Lung that the armed forces were not completely united.

On August 1, 1967, the fortieth anniversary of the People's Liberation Army was commemorated. On the eve of that day the Ministry of Defence gave a banquet, to which a great many high-ranking military officers from all over the country as well as a few Red Guards, cadets from the military academies, diplomats and journalists were invited. All in all perhaps a thousand people. At the host's table the acting Chief of Staff Yang Ch'eng-wu was seated, together with Premier Chou En-lai, Ch'en Po-ta, Chiang Ch'ing, Foreign Minister Marshal Ch'en Yi, the old Marshal Chu Te, and several others. Yang Ch'eng-wu gave the evening's speech, in which he attacked his predecessor Lo Jui-ch'ing, whom he called a counter-revolutionary revisionist, and the former Minister of Defence P'eng Te-huai. The speech was published in the *People's Daily* of the next day, but it was interesting to hear it. The speaker was extremely severe in his criticism of Lo Jui-ch'ing and his henchmen, and it seemed that he was triggering off a new purge in the army. The applause that from time to time interrupted the speech sounded weary and obligatory. My neighbour, a colonel from Szechwan, as well as most of the other officers, listened with an expressionless face. Very few of them seemed to welcome the prospects of a new rectification campaign within the armed forces. This speech dampened the festivities of the commemorative banquet and, when Yang Ch'eng-wu sat down again the guests pounced in silence on the dishes which were brought in by military waiters.

The only one who livened things up again was Chiang Ch'ing, who rose from her seat at the main table and, together with Yeh Ch'ün (the wife of Lin Piao, who himself was absent), the ideologist Ch'i Pen-yü, and Yao Wen-yüan, walked among the representatives of the younger generation with a glass in her hand. A wave of enthusiasm stirred the part of the hall where the youthful revolutionary rebels were seated. 'Chiang Ch'ing is coming!' they shouted. The Red Guards stood up, and several went up to her and raised their glasses. Surrounded by her loyal followers, precisely as revolutionary painters have portrayed Lenin, Chiang Ch'ing walked along the tables of the Red Guards and cadets. At times she stopped for a toast. But she did not spare a glance for the colonels and generals who occupied the forty or more round tables between the host and the young rebels. On the other hand, the army officers tried to hide their curiosity as much as they could. Chiang Ch'ing, who was dressed in a neatly pressed army uniform and wore a cap on her short wavy hair, moved along quickly. In comparison with her, Yeh Ch'ün looked almost slovenly. She was naturally wearing a military uniform as well, but with an open collar, her cap on the back of her head, and with untidy hair. Both Ch'i Pen-yü and Yao Wen-yüan radiated joy. Ch'i was tall and slenderly built, bespectacled, young and passionate. Although also young, Yao Wen-yüan seemed to be his opposite; nothing betrayed his well-known intellectual faculties. He was heavily built and did not give the impression of being an ascetic or a fanatic. As suddenly as they had left their table the four returned to their seats.

But it was not long before there was another surprise. A group of Red Guards marched up to the main table to reply to the toast. They clinked their glasses with Chiang Ch'ing, Ch'en Po-ta, Premier Chou En-lai and General Yang Ch'eng-wu, but ignored Marshal Chu Te, one of the founders of the Red Army, and Marshal Ch'en Yi. When the glasses clinked behind their backs, the marshals did not move a muscle.

Yang Ch'eng-wu's plea to redouble the struggle against Lo Jui-ch'ing and his followers gained added significance from the Wuhan rebellion, which was not yet two weeks old and was scarcely under control. In response to the insubordination of General Ch'en Tsai-tao and the speech of Yang Ch'eng-wu, a slogan appeared reading 'Eliminate the handful of reactionaries in the army', which we must assume was launched, or at least backed, by Chiang Ch'ing. Yet, as we shall see below, the attempt of the extreme Left to launch a rectification campaign in the armed forces was doomed to failure.

Incidents in Shanghai, Canton and elsewhere

A campaign against the rightist elements in the army did not suit Chou En-lai, who knew that it had been possible to straighten out the Wuhan incident only on the basis of a compromise. Moreover, the problems were not limited to Wuhan. In Shanghai there were serious disturbances in which workers clashed with army units. Here the demand to eliminate the reactionary elements in the army, which sowed discord among the military and brought them into disrepute, did not succeed. The official Shanghai newspaper *Wen-hui pao* of August 7 announced a significant decree of the revolutionary committee of Shanghai. The committee called for the strengthening of the dictatorship of the proletariat and said that it would not tolerate 'the sowing of dissension between the army and the people with the aim of creating a front against the great Chinese People's Liberation Army'.

In the same month Canton was beset by serious incidents. Various organisations were active there, each exercising terror in its own way. The 'May 16 Brigade', which in early September was branded as counter-revolutionary in the official press, occupied the main station of Canton for several days. The rumour was that this organisation, which consisted predominantly of students, had branches in Manchuria, Chungking, Wuhan and Peking. During the Wuhan rebellion it had supposedly acquired weapons. Wall newspapers disclosed that the extreme leftist scapegoats Wang Li and Lin Chieh had been in touch with the 'May 16 Brigade'. In Canton an important role was also played by 'Spring-thunder' which on August 20 clashed with military units. This organisation was active in the area around Canton and for several weeks appeared to be in complete control of the region between Canton and Shumchun, where it controlled rail traffic to the Hong Kong border. The following of both organisations was so large that it was impossible to bring an action against all the members. Several leaders of the 'May 16 Brigade' were arrested, the other members were described as being misled and were requested to change their attitude. The activities of 'Spring-thunder' declined without its political aims ever having become clear. In mid-November, when the trains between Canton and Shumchun were running again more or

less normally, I saw slogans of completely opposite meaning at intermediate stations, 'Down with Spring-thunder' as well as 'Learn from
Spring-thunder'.

Apart from these two organisations, there were five or six others
which fought each other in Canton. The army did not remain neutral,
and by the end of August civil war was raging in Canton. Political
prisoners made use of the opportunity to escape from labour camps and
tried to hide in the city. The inhabitants entrenched themselves in
their houses in order not be become involved, and put up barricades in
the streets to defend themselves against banditry. They blocked the
ends of the narrow streets in the centre of the city with stone walls, in
which only a small doorway was left open for pedestrians. Finally, the
confusion in Canton was so great that Lin Piao decided to send the
47th Army on a pacification mission. This again resulted in a great
number of casualties. In late August and early September foreign
travellers in Canton heard repeatedly the sound of machine-guns. The
disturbances in Canton forced the central government to postpone the
Autumn Trade Fair for one month. It did not open until November 15.

In other places, too, there were incidents, notably in Lanchow,
Chungking and Manchuria. In September and October there was
heavy fighting in Tientsin. During these months practically no foreigner
was allowed to visit the town, which under normal conditions was
quite easy.

The incidents showed a certain similarity. In Harbin, the capital of
Heilungkiang, a delegation of the Cultural Revolution group was
beaten up, as in Wuhan, and sent back to Peking. In Manchuria for a
long time, Heilungkiang was the only province where a revolutionary
committee had been formed, and yet the Red Guards were critical of
the way the province was administered. They urged the Cultural
Revolution group to disavow the revolutionaty committee, which
dated from January 1967, and to establish a new, more revolutionary
committee. If one studies the details of the Cultural Revolution in the
north-eastern provinces, one might very well reach the conclusion that
in the second half of 1967 the leaders in Peking consistently supported the moderate old party cadres against the revolutionary rebels
in their own region.

Oddly enough, Peking even served as a safe refuge for many old
party cadres from the provinces. For instance, Sung Jen-ch'iung, First
Secretary of the North-east Bureau of the Central Committee, was
strongly criticised in his own area. But in Peking he was allowed to

review the National Day parade on October the First in the company of Mao Tse-tung and his carefully selected guests. The same applies more or less to General Huang Yung-sheng, commander of the Canton military region, who in his home town was accused of being a reactionary and dictator, but who was made much of by Mao Tse-tung in Peking. In November 1967, he returned to Canton to take control again, until he was promoted Chief of Staff of the People's Liberation Army.

The revolution appeared to make little progress. On August 12, almost four months after the revolutionary committee of Peking had been inaugurated, another revolutionary committee on the provincial level was established in the underpopulated and distant province of Tsinghai. This was one of the very few concrete successes that the central government scored.

Theory of the Revolution

Why did the revolution make such slow progress? Of course, there were many practical difficulties to solve. There was certainly the opposition of nimble bureaucrats and military men, who knew that a victory of the Cultural Revolution would not be to their advantage. But there were also theoretical difficulties. A foremost problem was to what extent the use of violence was to be allowed.

Through its vehemence, the Cultural Revolution reminded the Chinese people of the communist take-over of 1949. Even Chou En-lai pointed to the similarity between the struggle against the revisionists and that against the Kuomintang. The founding of the People's Republic was the result of what in Chinese communist jargon are called a 'people's war' and a 'liberation', in which the People's Liberation Army played a central role. It was evident that now again the army had an essential function. The question was, however, to what extent a people's war should be launched and in what form. In late July the *People's Daily* urged the end of the rebellion in Wuhan by means of a 'people's war', but the use of the word seemed to be metaphorical: the reactionaries should 'be drowned in the ocean of a people's war'. Red Guard publications advocated 'a people's war against the black line of Liu Shao-ch'i'. The *People's Daily* of August 24 called for a 'thorough people's war' against the former Chief of Staff Lo Jui-ch'ing, which, however, should be waged by means of wall newspapers and meetings.

The official press said that the people's war could be fought by discussion. The facts were different. Several towns were swept by civil war and the Chinese term for it, *nei-chan* (which, however, can also be translated as 'internal conflict'), was not avoided by the official press. On August 31, the Shanghai newspaper *Wen-hui pao* disapproved of rival organisations waging 'civil war'. Several days later the same newspaper published a decree of the Shanghai revolutionary committee to the effect that civilians were ordered to hand over all weapons in their possession to the military authorities. Furthermore, arms manufacturers were instructed not to deliver any more weapons to non-military people. In early September, a similar decision was published in Peking, which indicates that here, too, several civilian organisations had managed to acquire arms. Usually they were in the hands of Red Guards who had participated in armed struggle in Szechwan, Wuhan, or elsewhere. In Peking the walls were painted with the words: 'Oppose the armed struggle by means of verbal combat.' This was a variation of a slogan current in Shanghai: 'Attack with words, defend with arms.' In official propaganda, however, peaceful discussion predominated, and this was undoubtedly in line with the policies of Chou En-lai and Lin Piao. The latter in particular seems to have been strongly opposed to giving arms to Red Guard organisations.

In late September Premier Chou En-lai disclosed that, after the Wuhan rebellion, various hotheads had proposed to clear the country by armed force of the influence of the reactionaries and the revisionists. To that end they demanded that the Red Guards should be armed and that the People's Liberation Army should be ordered to support the purge. The Premier did not make explicit who had been propagating this policy, but probably Wang Li and Chiang Ch'ing were in favour of 'liberation' by means of arms, of those provinces where no revolutionary committee had yet been established. As regards Chiang Ch'ing this has been corroborated by a statement of Nieh Yüan-tzu, authoress of the first big-character poster in the University of Peking. Miss Nieh, who had developed into a loyal supporter of Chou En-lai, reportedly said that, if one listened to Chiang Ch'ing, civil war would be inevitable. Chiang Ch'ing was forced to change her key. On September 5 she declared: 'At the moment we do not want armed conflict.' She also realised that it would be a mistake to launch a witch-hunt in the army. The slogan 'Eliminate the handful of reactionaries in the army', which may have originated with her or one of her close friends, she now rejected. This speech of September 5 has been interpreted as a self-criticism, which Chiang Ch'ing was forced to make by Chou En-lai, Lin Piao and her husband Mao Tse-tung. However, the position of Mao himself needs further elucidation.

The Position of Mao Tse-tung and Liu Shao-ch'i

One word from the great teacher, leader, commander and helmsman, Chairman Mao, would have been sufficient to end all disorders and economic damage. But, for the time being, Mao Tse-tung remained silent. His enigmatic silence was not caused by illness, but resulted from his tragic conviction that uncertainty and conflict were bound to have a salutary effect.

Mao Tse-tung believed in uninterrupted revolution. He believed that man should be involved down to the deepest layers of his soul and that all material security had to be eliminated before he could develop into a real revolutionary. The end of the struggle could easily and quickly be reached, but that would mean either the end of the Cultural Revolution or the end of its opponents. Then, insecurity would turn into security, order would be restored, and bureaucracy rehabilitated. And so revisionism would develop again. For it is apparent that, to Mao Tse-tung, revisionism simply means *party bureaucracy plus a high standard of living*. If the revolution is left to the care of what is in principle an infallible bureaucracy and the people are freed from their own responsibility for the future of the revolution, they may be tempted to devote themselves completely to the realisation of their bourgeois and egoistic dreams. More than any other aspect of maoism, this criticism of bureaucracy and its consequences was welcomed by students in Paris, Brussels and other university cities in May 1968. Indeed, the protest of the student Left was very much directed against powerful administrative machineries and the material security provided by a high standard of living and the welfare state.

Mao Tse-tung did not want to stop the Chinese people who had started along the road of uninterrupted revolution. He was indifferent to heavy economic losses, which were partly the result of the suspension of university education. Mao Tse-tung has never shown much interest in economics. Physical and psychological suffering did not play much part in his considerations either. He refused to give guidance and abstained from action at moments when fatal errors could have been prevented, on the basis of his conviction that the people would

From the first page of a Tientsin Red Guard newspaper. The characters read: 'Whoever resists Chairman Mao – crush his dog's head!' (April 1967).

E**

shape their own destiny (although he should have known that they did not feel free to do so). He advocated 'extensive democracy' and believed that if the people would only show the *will* to commit themselves to the victory of communism, communism would almost have been realised by now. Thus, in September 1967 as well as before, maoism consisted of *uninterrupted revolution and voluntarism.*

In spite of the propaganda which clouds many of the Russian reports on the Cultural Revolution, maoism has often been better understood in the Soviet Union than in the West. The significance of the concept of 'uninterrupted revolution', which recalls Trotsky's 'permanent revolution', has been particularly well understood by the Soviets. The so-called 'troika-theory' is of Russian origin; this assumes that Mao Tse-tung constantly played the three principal powers in the People's Republic – the army, the Cultural Revolution group (with the revolutionary rebels behind them), and the administration under Chou En-lai – off against each other. As soon as one of these three became too powerful, the other two were mobilised to restore the balance. It is indeed striking that all three were forced to work together down to the lowest level, on the principle that revolutionary committees must be formed by representatives of the People's Liberation Army, the old cadres and the revolutionary rebels. The Russians saw the 'three-way alliance' as a team of three horses which represented the uninterrupted revolution.

Perhaps the troika symbolism is open to criticism, but the principle of the uninterrupted revolution has been confirmed time and again. It is the basis of Mao Tse-tung's theory that contradictions among the people can exist even under the dictatorship of the proletariat. It lends the Chinese revolution a Jekyll-and-Hyde aspect: if the opponents of the régime died, new ones would be created, since the maoists consider conflict as such a condition of social development. Against this background the question of why Liu Shao-ch'i was not relieved of all his functions as early as 1967 could be answered. The President seemed to have been preserved intentionally as a symbol of the Black Clique.

In June 1967 rumour had it that Mao Tse-tung had not wanted to give permission for Liu Shao-ch'i to be present at mass meetings where his policies were criticised. In Peking there was an office which arranged the allocation of members of the Black Clique to revolutionary rebels if they wished to convene a 'struggle meeting' with real live revisionists and counter-revolutionaries. In May or June 1967, that

From the first page of the newspaper *Chingkangshan* published by Red Guards of Tsinghua University. The banners call for criticism of Liu Shao-ch'i and Wang Kuang-mei (April 1967).

office was informed that the President of the People's Republic of China was not available. In line with his concept of uninterrupted revolution, Chairman Mao announced at the same period that one Cultural Revolution would not be enough, and that many more were to follow.

The Red Guard did not acquiesce immediately in the protection of Liu Shao-ch'i by Mao Tse-tung. In early July a great number of rebel organisations literally pitched their tents in front of the walls of the government compound Chungnanhai in the centre of Peking, where Liu Shao-ch'i had his residence. The revolutionary young people demanded the handing over of the President. They besieged the gates of Chungnanhai with sit-down strikes and made quite a carnival of it with countless slogans, wall newspapers and banners, loudspeakers blaring non-stop and spontaneous meetings. In the hurriedly built stands and army tents stood beds, bicycles and cooking stoves. The impression was that the Red Guards were there to stay. If I remember well, it was only by the end of September that the siege equipment was cleared away. But, Liu Shao-ch'i did not fall into the hands of the Red Guards.

Of course, the President must have noticed that he was being to some extent protected by no less a person than Chairman Mao himself. During the summer of 1967 Liu Shao-ch'i wrote several self-criticisms but these appear to have been influenced by the knowledge that for the time being he was not going to be put on trial by the revolutionary rebels. He was attacked by the 'New August 1 Combat Group' of the Peking Institute of Construction Engineering, and wrote an evasive defence on July 9.[1] In his letter Liu admits only the less serious mistakes. He explains that in the summer of 1966, during the so-called 'first fifty days' of the Cultural Revolution, he had indeed played a role in sending out the work teams which were to organise the Cultural Revolution in a more or less quiet way, and had tried to protect the loyal supporters of the existing party hierarchy. Liu let it be known that deploying the work teams was the result of a sort of misunderstanding. He also admitted that he had been advocating political co-operation on a broad basis without sufficiently pointing out that the proletarian revolutionaries should form the core of such co-operation. Liu said that, if the latter requirement was not met, it would be impossible to realise a revolutionary 'three-way alliance.' However, Liu Shao-ch'i said only in passing that he had acted in contravention of the thought of Mao Tse-tung. He did not speak at all of any participation in a conspiracy against the Chairman or the party.

On July 31 another statement by Liu Shao-ch'i was published, which provided the answers to eight questions which the Left extremist Ch'i Pen-yü, member of the Cultural Revolution group, had formulated. Of course, one might doubt the authenticity of the statement, which was printed as a sloppy pamphlet of the 'New August 1 Combat Group', but on the basis of internal evidence it may be concluded that the contents correspond to what Liu Shao-ch'i might have said even if he did not say it.[2] Again Liu Shao-ch'i defends his policies and tries to shelter behind the authority of the party organisation. He parries the accusation of having taken a conciliatory line towards the Kuomintang in 1946 by saying that it was not he himself but the Central Committee that was responsible for that policy. When defending his report to the Eighth Congress of the Chinese Communist Party of 1956, he hints at differences with Mao Tse-tung over the uninterrupted revolution and the contradictions among the people without explicitly referring to these concepts. 'In this report I made the mistake', Liu said, 'of stating that the contradictions between our country's bourgeoisie and the proletariat had already been resolved. But the same mistake appears in the resolution of the Eighth Congress, which reads "at the moment the socialist transformation has already won a decisive victory". This meant that the contradictions between our country's socialist proletariat and the bourgeoisie were already basically resolved.' He denies outright that in the years 1958–60 he had been opposed to the Great Leap Forward or the people's communes. He accepts, however, the responsibility for reprinting his booklet *How to Be a Good Communist* in 1962, 'although the changes in the text were made at the instigation of others or by others'. The statement, the tone of which is far from submissive, ends with what I believe is an ironical remark. Liu Shao-ch'i says he does not know why he has made mistakes: 'After the eleventh session of the Central Committee [August 1966] had criticised my mistakes, there were others who committed errors of a similar nature, but they also do not know why. I shall try my hardest to study the works of Chairman Mao and read carefully other books that Chairman Mao tells me to read, as well as the relevant articles in the press. Then it will be possible to clarify this question from the ideological viewpoint and to hold a serious self-examination among the revolutionary masses. Only then shall I be able to reply as to why I committed errors of line in this great proleta-

打倒党内头号走资本主义道路当

最高指示

在拿枪的敌人被消灭以后，不拿枪的敌人依然存在，他们必然地要和我们作拼死的斗争，我们决不可以轻视这些敌人。如果我们现在不是这样地提出问题和认识问题，我们就要犯极大的错误。

1 叫做永世不得翻身。

2 骂的是无产阶级。
刘少奇以资本家帮凶的口吻说："工人不听话（资本家）要斗争（工人）这是合法的"。

3 反的是毛泽东思想。

4 想的是资本主义。
"他所贩卖的那套人吃人的哲学，完全是为发展资本主义辩护血腥的剥削制度服务的。"

5 笑的是资本主义。
刘少奇说："资本家的剥削是有历史功绩的，这个功绩是永垂不朽的"。

6 叠的是资本主义。
刘少奇说："今天
而且有功劳。"

7 吃的是资本主义。
刘少奇说："膝多
度、花花绿绿胭脂

8 叫喊的是资本主义
刘少奇说："中国
主义太少了"。

（註：每幅漫
义还是

中央戏剧学院

Cartoons exposing President Liu Shao-ch'i as a lackey
of capitalism and revisionism.

rian Cultural Revolution and know how to correct these errors.' The statement concludes with cheers for the Cultural Revolution and Mao Tse-tung.

One can think of two explanations of the defiant and concise defence by Liu Shao-ch'i. Either he was aware of support among the Chinese people that was still considerable – and the personal protection of Mao Tse-tung –, or he refused for strictly personal reasons, such as self-respect, to humiliate himself in front of the Red Guards. These two explanations should perhaps be combined, since an honourable but tragic role is the more attractive if one can be assured of a sympathetic public.

Beginning of Normalisation under Chou En-lai

The rebellion in Wuhan was a turning-piont in the Cultural Revolution, but not everyone immediately understood it as such. Instead of moderating their pretensions, the extreme Left continued to indulge in extremism. Their disappointed fanaticism became more fanatical. The extreme Left looked for scapegoats and found them among foreign diplomats.

In August 1967 Premier Chou En-lai and Foreign Minister Ch'en Yi had neither the inclination nor the capability to stop the Red Guards from entering the Indonesian, Kenyan or Mongolian embassies, or the office of the British diplomatic mission. As I have mentioned, Chou En-lai was criticised at the instigation of Wang Li, whereas Ch'en Yi, in his own ministry, met vigorous opposition led by the former Chinese Chargé d'Affaires in Indonesia, Yao Teng-shan. At mass meetings on August 11 and 27, Ch'en Yi was accused of wanting to capitulate to the imperialists, revisionists and reactionaries and of attempting to extinguish the fire of the proletarian revolution and the liberation movements. Red Guards reported proudly that during these meetings they had kicked the backside of the Minister of Foreign Affairs. Even in the centre of Peking the latter feared kidnapping, and when he paid a visit to the Guinean Embassy he was protected by carloads of soldiers. Chou En-lai permitted the criticism of Ch'en Yi but said that he could not agree with the slogan 'Down with Ch'en Yi'. Nevertheless, in the second half of August, Yao Teng-shan, supported by his revolutionary rebels, staged a coup inside the ministry and styled himself Minister of Foreign Affairs, which position he was able to hold on to for at least four days. In his new capacity Yao ordered the burning of the office of the British Chargé d'Affaires, when

London did not comply with the ultimatum about the situation in Hong Kong that Peking had presented. On the night of August 22–23, the British Office was completely destroyed. The fire spread at a time when all the diplomatic staff were inside the building. They escaped, only to fall into the hands of the thousands of Red Guards who had surrounded the building and were waiting for them. Many were wounded and suffered from shock. The Chargé d'Affaires was wounded in the head and bleeding profusely when I met him later that night. For many months British diplomats were not allowed to leave China. Reuter's correspondent, Anthony Grey, who was put under house arrest on July 22, 1967, which lasted for more than two years, was only allowed to return to England in October 1969.

By removing Ch'en Yi and setting fire to the British Office, Yao Teng-shan and the extreme Left had gone too far. Wang Li, Ch'i Pen-yü, Kuan Feng, Mu Hsin and Lin Chieh, all members of the Cultural Revolution group, were no longer openly protected by K'ang Sheng, Ch'en Po-ta or Chiang Ch'ing. Even on August 9, the Vice-Chairman of the Communist Party, Lin Piao, had warned the members of the Cultural Revolution group that they had moved too fast and risked making serious mistakes. Now irreparable damage to their case had been done. Yao Teng-shan, who had boasted of his friendship with Mao Tse-tung, was left isolated.

Possibly supported by Mao Tse-tung and Lin Piao, Chou En-lai succeeded in bringing about official disapproval of Yao Teng-shan's coup in the Ministry of Foreign Affairs. The occupation of the ministry by revolutionary rebels was called a contradiction to the orders of the Central Committee. In spite of opposition by K'ang Sheng, Chou managed to put himself in charge of foreign affairs on August 23. In early September, Chiang Ch'ing announced that it was wrong to enter foreign embassies. As mentioned above, she also contributed to strengthening the power of the army by revoking the slogan, 'Eliminate the handful of reactionaries in the army.' She said that the belief that one could not rely on the army was wrong. More than anyone else, Chiang Ch'ing was a symbol of the Cultural Revolution. If normalisation was to be successful, her co-operation was indispensable, as well as Mao's, of course.

Probably in early September, Mao Tse-tung made a secret inspection tour of Shanghai and a number of provinces in Central and East China. Areas which were afflicted by fighting which was just short of civil war, such as Canton, Szechwan and Manchuria, were avoided.

Chou En-lai and Lin Piao should probably be given the credit for having persuaded the Chairman to see for himself the results of the Cultural Revolution. The *People's Daily* published an extremely summary report on the journey. One may conclude from the later course of events that, during his talks with the provincial administration, Mao Tse-tung was impressed by the damage done by the Cultural Revolution.

In July the official press had announced that the 'liberated' areas (those with revolutionary committees) must economise in coal, electricity, wood, paper and luxury goods. There was almost no town in China where industrial production had not suffered from demonstrations, strikes, local guerrillas or sabotage, or from a scarcity of necessary raw materials. The often repeated warning that it was forbidden to wreck the railways indicated that there were serious delays in rail transportation caused by sabotage. At a time when the central government was deluged with complaints, about the only means by which Peking's attention could be drawn to local problems was to hold up rail traffic. As can be expected in a situation of imminent civil war, there were also ordinary tactical reasons for preventing normal rail traffic. During the rebellion in Wuhan, which is situated on the strategic Peking–Canton railway, traffic along that route was, of course, impossible.

It was precisely the most vital enterprises, the coal mines, the oilfields of Taching, the blast furnaces of Anshan that were hit by the Cultural Revolution. Many left their jobs and went off to join the revolutionary rebels or the conservatives in another area or province. The more educated and skilled workmen, who knew the value of technical knowledge, were criticised or dismissed, or opposed the Cultural Revolution for as long as they could. Economic damage was a fact, and this has also been admitted by the Chinese leaders, although it was, of course, played down in the perspective of the 'great victory of the thought of Mao Tse-tung'. Wall newspapers quoted Ch'en Po-ta, chairman of the Cultural Revolution group, as having said in August 1967 that Tientsin's industry was 25 per cent behind schedule. In early October Vice-Premier Hsieh Fu-chih asserted that during the first nine months of the year the industrial plan for the year had been only 40 per cent fulfilled. In the same month Chou En-lai announced that economic damage could be repaired within six months, which possibly meant that production was several months behind schedule.

During his inspection tour, Mao Tse-tung realised that the disturbances had reached dangerous proportions. He tried to allay the disorder by a magic formula which was published in the *People's Daily* on September 14. Mao Tse-tung said: 'There is no fundamental difference of interests among the workers' class. Under the dictatorship of the proletariat, the workers' class has no reason to split into two big irreconcilable organisations.' Again Mao Tse-tung refused to face reality. He did no less than deny the fact that his country was on the brink of civil war.

Chou En-lai had to elaborate the theory that there was no difference of interests among the workers. When on September 20 he disclosed that various organisations in Peking had attempted to unleash civil war in the belief that the struggle between the two camps could be settled only by force of arms, he referred to the new instruction of Chairman Mao and rejected the view that a war would solve all problems. The propaganda machine, from which Wang Li had been removed, took note again of industrial production. An editorial in the *Red Flag* explained the new line, in genuine revolutionary jargon: 'One should realise that every extra ton of coal that is produced means that one extra train can depart, and that is a slap in the face of the class enemy.' Of course, production remained subordinate to the revolutionary goal, but it was an improvement that at least there could again be talk of a rise in production without the fear of being accused of revisionism.

As always, the central government tried to create a climate favourable to the celebration of the National Day. It was not immediately clear whether Chou En-lai's policy of restoring order and productivity was to be maintained after October the First. Would normality return, or would the revolution continue uninterrupted, with all its ups and downs?

REFERENCES

1. A translation of the letter has been printed in Liu Shao-ch'i, *Collected Works*, Kowloon: Union Research Institute, 1968, pp. 369–77.

2. The text that I have seen seems to be only slightly different from that translated in Liu Shao-ch'i, *Collected Works*, pp. 365–9.

7

STABILISATION:
AUTUMN 1967 – SPRING 1969

In the summer of 1967 the confusion had been enormous. Nobody denied this and the Chinese leaders attempted to explain the ideological significance of the confusion. Vice-Chairman Lin Piao said on August 9: 'The victory of the great Cultural Revolution is extremely great. The price that we have to pay is very, very small, and the victory is very, very great. On the surface it appears as if there is great chaos, but it concerns only the reactionary classes which are in confusion. The reactionaries have been exposed now, and the small handful who take the capitalist road have been overthrown. The confusion which we see is normal and necessary.' According to Lin Piao, who was also Minister of Defence, this confusion could be permitted because the country was backed by the great authority of Mao Tse-tung and the powerful People's Liberation Army.

For the occasion of the Chinese National Day, the Albanian Premier Mehmet Shehu visited China and let it be known that he wished to see something of the country. Mao Tse-tung arranged an excursion to Wuhan, which two months earlier had been harassed by the greatest possible confusion, and asked Chou En-lai to act as one of the hosts. The latter made use of the opportunity to give an important speech in Wuhan, which was published in the *People's Daily* of October 10.

Chou asserted that the victory of the Cultural Revolution was now a fact: 'The small handful of people, who under the guidance of China's Khrushchev took the capitalist road, have been seized, and the power they had usurped has been returned to the proletariat.' The Cultural Revolution, Chou said, has promoted the socialist construction of our country. Of course, in certain areas one has had to pay a certain price, but in the case of a revolution which leaves no stone unturned, this was inevitable and foreseeable. The Premier admitted that production had suffered from disturbances which had occurred in certain places, but excused the damage by saying that it was of a temporary nature. Chou En-lai wanted confusion only as a temporary phenomenon. Perhaps he still had certain reservations about the maoist theory of uninterrupted revolution, and in his Wuhan speech he did everything to give the impression that victory was won and the most important phase of the Cultural Revolution belonged to the past.

His view was expressed also in the propaganda media. An editorial in the *People's Daily* of January 1, 1968, launched the idea that in 1967 the Cultural Revolution had gained a 'decisive victory', and that now a beginning had to be made with 'complete victory'. Attempts to continued normalisation entailed the inauguration of revolutionary committees in the autonomous region of Inner Mongolia, the provinces Kiangsi, Kansu and Honan, as well as Tientsin, in the period between November 1967 and January 1968. This brought the number of 'liberated provinces' up to nine. If one counts the autonomous regions as provinces, there are in all twenty-six Chinese provinces.

Agriculture

In spite of severe economic damage and confusion in the field of communications and transport, food supplies, as far as I know, remained reasonable, even in the big cities. When adequate means of transportation were not available, the army came in to help. Military trucks with loads of slaughtered pigs were not an unusual sight in Peking. In the winter of 1967-8 rice was rationed, but the quantity per person each month, namely between 10 and 12 kilogrammes, seemed to be sufficient. Part of the rice coupons could be used to purchase bread. Potatoes were not rationed, but expensive for the average Chinese purse. Meat was not rationed either, but expensive as well. Vegetables and fruit were also freely available. However, cooking oil was severely rationed, less than half a litre per person a month. Well-to-do people were able to buy expensive bacon or fat. Milk was usually available at a rather high price. The reason why food supplies remained adequate during periods of great disorder was that the Cultural Revolution left the countryside practically untouched, with the exception of areas in the immediate vicinity of the big cities. The propaganda media hardly ever mentioned agricultural issues.

An exception was an article in the *People's Daily* of November 23, 1967, in which propaganda themes were announced for the winter season. By means of a long historical explanation the article revealed that Liu Shao-ch'i had consistently opposed Mao Tse-tung's collectivi-sation programme. Liu Shao-ch'i's policy, the *People's Daily* argued, involved the danger that the richer peasants might consolidate their position at the expense of the poorer ones, which could then lead to the restoration of capitalism. The newspaper warned that the peasants must abide by the original aims of the people's communes and that the existence of free markets and free commerce should not be permitted. Neither was it allowed to set certain plots of land apart for private use (as was done all over China). Furthermore, production contracts with small groups within the commune, often not larger than one household, were forbidden. Liu Shao-ch'i was charged with having spread the 'dirty wind of the three freedoms and one contract' (i.e. free markets, free commerce, private plots and production contracts according to households). However, the tone of the article seemed to indicate that the régime had no intention of taking a firm line with the peasants or of restoring the commune system in its original glory. The *People's Daily* was only firing a warning shot and in that way hoped to prevent the peasants from further descent down the capitalist road.

The Seamy Side of the Revolution

Crime used to be dealt with behind closed doors: the press scarcely ever mentioned a lawsuit. The Cultural Revolution changed this, and a number of criminal cases were reported in the official press. As a matter of fact, crime had grown as a result of the great confusion and the corrosion of lawful authority. The big Chinese cities were again as unsafe as New York or Amsterdam, and hold-ups and thefts were often organised by young people who were members of the Red Guard or pretended to be. This was, of course, an undesirable situation and the régime decided to deal with it in the open. It was inevitable for the image of the Red Guard to be hurt by the publicity.

The *Peking Daily* of September 28, 1967, reported extensively on a mass meeting of the day before, where the municipal court pronounced the verdicts in a number of 'counter-revolutionary and criminal' cases. In maoist jargon all criminals are *per se* counter-revolutionaries. At this meeting five people were sentenced to death, and the other defendants received long prison sentences.

Several of the defendants had been involved in the murder of a Red Guard in the First Machine Tool Factory of Peking. The murderer, Ku Wen-chung, had fallen foul of the law earlier. As a boy of fifteen he had been accused of rape and sent to a reform school. Since 1964 he had worked at the First Machine Tool Factory. In September 1966 Red Guards sent him back to his home town in the province Liaoning, but Ku returned to Peking in October and became a member of the organisation of revolutionary rebels in the same factory – with a view to 'revenging himself and his class', according to the *Peking Daily*. One evening in May 1967, he reportedly provoked a fight near the factory entrance and fatally wounded a Red Guard of the Technical School of the Town Housing Bureau. The defendant was sentenced to death and executed immediately after the meeting. One of his accomplices was the worker Li Hsi-sheng, who had a bourgeois background and nursed 'a deep hatred against the communist party and the socialist system, because several of his relatives had been punished or suppressed'. During the Cultural Revolution he had become a member of a rebel organisation. Taking advantage of his position as a revolutionary rebel, he tried to rehabilitate his 'capitalist' father, opposed the People's Liberation Army and had a private prison in order to intimidate his opponents. In the factory he organised fighting gangs equipped with daggers. After Ku Wen-chung had killed his Red Guard victim, Li Hsi-sheng tried his hardest to obstruct the judicial investigation. He was sentenced to eight years in jail.

Also, three students at the Drama Institute, who had been accomplices in several cases of rape, were heavily punished. Over a period of three years, one of them had supposedly raped more than ten women. Moreover they had stolen two watches, some money and several sweaters. One evening in June 1967, they had passed themselves off as members of the 'Congress of Red Guards of the Capital' and, under the pretence of providing her with a train ticket, had escorted a girl to a park where she had been robbed and raped. The next evening they had posed as guides offering to find accommodation for the night. Again a young woman was their victim, who was robbed of her possessions and her honour. The principal culprit was given a suspended death sentence, with a two-year probationary period. As for the two others, one was sentenced to life imprisonment and the other to twenty years.

The *Peking Daily* reported a number of other cases, but those mentioned exemplify various important trends. The concept of 'class revenge', i.e. the attempt to revenge the unjust treatment inflicted upon parents or other relatives for political reasons, apparently played an important part. Furthermore, it appeared that opponents of the

Cultural Revolution sometimes passed themselves off as Red Guards in order to reach a privileged position from which they could gain their own political ends. From the facts that have been published, one cannot, of course, conclude that during the Cultural Revolution there was more or less crime than, for instance, in Western Europe. However, one may conclude that the Cultural Revolution has furthered criminal behaviour, since during a period of disrespect for law and order it was very hard to fight crime. Moreover, it is possible that criminal elements were attracted by Red Guard activities, because the revolution required a certain degree of unscrupulousness.

Education and Culture

In the autumn of 1967 the Red Guards had outlived their political function. However, most Red Guards did not wish to give up their unrestrained and sometimes dissolute way of life. The régime tried to discipline them, and assigned the army a crucial role in this. The authorities gradually attempted to revive the educational system. This was no simple affair. One of the greatest difficulties was that the teachers and professors, who had suffered under the criticisms of their students, were not inclined to resume teaching – without text-books, following a 'revolutionary programme', and in co-operation with the sergeant-majors of the People's Liberation Army or the Red Guards who had subjected them to physical torture.

The resumption of education, however, was an important part of the normalisation drive of Chou En-lai, and in the autumn of 1967 serious preparations were made. On October 14, the Central Committee published a decree that education should begin again in the primary and secondary schools as well as the universities. However, the decree was largely ignored and there are reasons for assuming that K'ang Sheng was opposed to it.

The *People's Daily* of October 22 reported that a large number of primary schools in Shanghai and Wuhan had opened their doors, and a secondary school in Peking where teaching had started again was held up as an example to the nation. Apart from the usual subjects, the teaching programme consisted of the study of Chairman Mao's quotations, revolutionary songs, military training and practical work. The resumption of education took place under the aegis of the three-fold movement of promoting class struggle, production and scientific experiments. Due to a shortage of teaching staff, furniture, books and equipment, the schools as a rule opened only for half a day.

On October 24 Vice-Premier Hsieh Fu-chih gave an important speech to an audience mainly composed of Red Guards. He explained that education was necessary since China was a poor and culturally backward country. He ordered all the 360 secondary schools of Peking to resume teaching at once and announced that the Peking institutions of higher education were making preparations for doing the same. 'Teaching *must* be resumed,' the Vice-Premier said. 'If it starts again, you can still continue your quarrels: please, study in the morning, and quarrel during the afternoon!' (laughter among the audience). The Vice-Premier also said that the members of the revolutionary committees who were students should take up their studies again.

On November 3 the *People's Daily* devoted the entire front page to higher education. It suggested that the examination system be abolished, as well as the system of repeating classes, and that proletarian children should have priority in being admitted to higher education. These discussions on education led to serious incidents in Peking. K'ang Sheng and other opponents of normalisation probably feared the political consequences of a resumption of university courses. If these began again, the principal shock troops of the Cultural Revolution, i.e. the revolutionary students, would be neutralised, and the old cadres and the military would monopolise the political stage.

The arts and humanities did not flourish, although one might expect the opposite in a Cultural Revolution. The revolution, however, should have been called an *ideological* one, and was rightly described as, in effect, a *political* revolution by Mao Tse-tung himself. When the revolutionaries did turn their attention to art and culture, their interest was mainly negative. The once highly acclaimed painter Ch'i Pai-shih was now called a revisionist. In Shanghai Lin Feng-mien, a pupil and admirer of Vlaminck and Matisse, who was famous for his paintings of cranes (birds) in the modern Chinese style, was under heavy pressure from the revolutionary rebels. The well-known writers Liang Pin and Wu Ch'iang, whose novels have been translated into English, were accused of counter-revolutionary activities. In the autumn of 1967, the official newspapers devoted entire pages to criticism of Sholokhov. Also Yevtushenko, Voznesensky, Rozhdestvensky and other representatives of the younger generation of Russian authors were heavily criticised. In cultural affairs it was still Chiang Ch'ing who called the tune. It sometimes appeared as if she was the only one who dared pronounce her views on the arts and the other Chinese leaders feared to burn their fingers on this delicate matter.

On November 12, 1967, Chiang Ch'ing, Ch'en Po-ta and K'ang Sheng addressed a meeting of the revolutionary representatives of the cultural organisations, which was attended also by Chang Ch'un-ch'iao, Ch'i Pen-yü, Yao Wen-yüan, acting Chief of Staff Yang Ch'eng-wu and General Wu Fa-hsien. According to a Red Guard publication of November 16, Chiang Ch'ing made a speech which may be summarised as follows: 'For a long time I did not receive any suggestions from the comrades. Perhaps the comrades are dissatisfied with us, because they do not understand our position. Although I was partly disabled (as a result of war injuries), I gave all my energy to the reform of the stage and music. That was work which could not be completed overnight. You can see that clearly in the field of the cinema. There one sees the contradiction between form and content. The cinema must also be artistically renewed; otherwise one will fall back into the old patterns. From the beginning of the Cultural Revolution I have had very little time to bother about the stage, films and music. I have done other things and inspected many organisations for their vigilance. I have come to the conclusion that work has come to a standstill in many places and that the people must be woken up again. Various organisations, such as those of the ballet, do not yet have a decent revolutionary 'three-way alliance'. There the enemy must be destroyed! Destroy the enemy! Drive out the enemy! You should fight the enemy and not bother about internal conflicts! If one is not going to fight the enemy, creative thinking will be confused.'

Chiang Ch'ing went on to say that there were eight models: five modern Peking operas, two ballets and one symphony. But she also remarked that the oldest and most famous of these, the ballet *The White-Haired Girl*, which had been performed and revised innumerable times, had now been revised in too crude a manner. She called herself responsible, but added that she had had too little time to spend on it.

Finally Chiang Ch'ing said: 'I am tired and was not able to be well prepared for this speech. Do not consider my remarks as final. I wish to come to an exchange of ideas with you, and, if I have been incomplete or incorrect, please criticise me.'

One may draw several conclusions from Chiang Ch'ing's address. In the first place Mrs. Mao Tse-tung throws a glaring light on the cultural poverty during the great proletarian Cultural Revolution. She cannot mention more than eight revolutionary works, produced by a people of 750 million. She could have added at most *one* novel which had not been rejected by the cultural authorities on ideological grounds.

In the second place, her remark about *The White-Haired Girl* is interesting. By advocating a new revision of the already often revised ballet, she seemed, in fact, to strive after a sort of uninterrupted revolution in the field of art. In her view, the text is never final. There have been writers who were of that opinion in Europe also, but in China the theory that creative works have to be continuously revised, i.e. adjusted to the political conditions of the day, if possible in an artistic way, has been applied more consistently and meticulously than anywhere else. The adjustment of the repertoire to new political developments means an enormous amount of work, unless there is a considerable reduction of the repertoire. So far, the last solution has been chosen.

Finally, I must comment on the remark that she was tired and had not prepared her speech. These words may have been motivated in part by conventional Chinese modesty. The traditional poets wrote 'Please, correct me' when they dedicated a poem to a friend. But in Chiang Ch'ing's address the recognition of her own inability seems too emphatic for a mere concession to convention. The whole tone of the speech is tired. Again and again she says that she is short of time. A good work is not yet good enough. She seems to be in the grip of a perfectionism which reveals a fanatic extremism or overstrain, or both.

Chiang Ch'ing's speech was not without consequences. Although, when she had finished, Ch'en Po-ta immediately praised her address as the highest wisdom and urged the whole nation to study it, several Red Guard newspapers who published a summary of the text were reprehended. They should not have printed the speech in that form. Allegedly, important passages had been left out. But if one pieces all the evidence together, one must conclude that Chiang Ch'ing had in fact not said much more than the unofficial press had published, and that the leaders of the Cultural Revolution probably were ashamed of the poor content of her address.

Chiang Ch'ing had overstrained herself and disappeared temporarily from the political stage. Vice-Premier Hsieh Fu-chih was appointed to make an official announcement to that effect. He said that, after much strenuous work for the Cultural Revolution, Chiang Ch'ing needed a period of rest. Later there was a rumour that Mrs. Mao Tse-tung had been admitted to hospital, but this is not necessarily true. But it is a fact that for several months she made no speeches or public appearances.

Tourist in Hangchow

In early 1968 I was given permission to visit Hangchow and Shanghai. Travelling in January is not always pleasant, anyway not in China. For reasons of economy, the temperature in the cabin of the old Viscount, which, apart from a great number of mailbags and myself, was occupied exclusively by military men and revolutionary rebels, was kept just above zero. According to a Chinese saying, in the winter one may find three loyal friends in the bamboo, the pine-tree and the plum blossom. I admired them in Hangchow. But I should have appreciated them less and moreover have died from cold in the airplane or the unheated hotel in Hangchow, had I not been accompanied by my most loyal friend in the Chinese winter: a heavy fur-lined overcoat.

Hangchow is undoubtedly worth a tourist's pilgrimage, but sunshine is necessary. On the day of my arrival the weather was good enough to take a boat trip on the Western Lake. My guide, a young man who had studied English at the University of Amoy and had worked for three years in Hangchow, explained that the town was famous for silk, tea and scenery. He pointed to the dry, brown stalks that rose out of the water and told me that they were lotus plants. The lotus was cultivated not only for aesthetic reasons, he explained, but also because the roots and seeds were edible. The Western Lake served not only for recreation, but also for production.

We left the pier in front of the 'Hangchow' Hotel, where I was staying, and rowed to an island in the middle of the lake. In five minutes the red book was placed on the table and the guide began to read the quotations. I had to interrupt him to take a picture of the hills behind us or of the Pao-shu Pagoda which contrasted grey against the white clouds.

What is so special about Hangchow? The hills around the lake are, in fact, not very impressive, and are no challenge to mountaineers. But they seem to arise from the lake spontaneously, with gentle slopes suffused in light. The lake is the heart of this enchanted region, and, when seen, it immediately charms the viewer. There is no need to take long walks along its shores. The pavilions built in earlier times – such as the famous 'Reflection of the Autumn moon in a Peaceful

Lake', which was erected by order of the Emperor Ch'ien Lung – only emphasise the feeling that one must stand and gaze. When one is tired of silently observing, one moves slowly onward. A quick pace is impossible here, and therefore the loudspeakers, which here, too, blared out the need for revolutionary action, were an unwanted imposition.

In only one aspect does maoism seems to be correct here. In beauty Hangchow does not fall short of San Francisco or Istanbul. When one looks over the lake from the well-kept boulevard on the island of Kushan and recalls the magnificent history of this town of Po Chü-i and Su Tung-p'o, the fame of which has spread far beyond China's borders, it is tempting to imagine that one is in the centre of the world. When Chairman Mao stays here, he can be justly proud of his country, which in the course of history has accomplished so much through her own efforts.

In his explanations my guide was strongly influenced by the Cultural Revolution. During our visit to the Ling-yin Temple he explained that sinister henchmen of China's Khrushchev had wanted to destroy the buddhist statues that are carved out of the rocks, but that alarmed Red Guards had prevented this. I saw several statues that had been damaged in an amateurish way. I asked my guide to take me to the three nearby Indian temples, but, after having pretended for a while that he had never heard of these temples, he finally admitted that one was not allowed to visit them. I asked him to show me the mosque, of which I could give him the address thanks to my *Guide Nagel*. He answered that he had never heard of a mosque in Hangchow and refused to take me to the address I gave him. While we were boating on the lake, I asked him to point out the temple and the tomb of General Yüeh Fei, who died in the twelfth century.

'There has never been a temple of Yüeh Fei,' was the answer, 'and the tomb has been destroyed. In August 1966, the Red Guards studied the history of the Sung dynasty and came to the conclusion that Yüeh Fei was not a hero of the people. He suppressed several peasant uprisings. There is no reason whatsoever to commemorate him. He wanted to protect himself and the propertied classes.'

'Why was the tomb not removed immediately after the Liberation?' I asked.

'That was due to the sinister hand of China's Khrushchev who, precisely like Yüeh Fei, wanted to protect himself.'

'Are you a member of the Red Guard?'

He nodded and told me that in the summer of 1966 the revisionists had cruelly suppressed him, that he had lost his job with the China Travel Service and had only got it back in December 1966. He said that the Red Guards in the schools and institutes of Hangchow had formed a great alliance and that in January 1967, together with other revolutionary people, they had seized power from the old town administration. On December 20, 1967, a revolutionary committee had been inaugurated in Hangchow and the situation for the establishment of a revolutionary committee of the province of Chekiang was almost ripe. (By the end of March 1968 the committee was formed.) From the beginning of January, my guide and his friends had been studying the speeches of Chairman Mao on party organisation and party reform. Every morning they rose at six o'clock, ran for half an hour, washed and studied the works of Chairman Mao for two hours. (Anna Louise Strong said in her *Letter from China* of September 23, 1967, that in China about 200 million people spend four to six hours a day on political activities. The study of the Chairman's works should be placed among these political activities.)

'If you are so interested in the reform of the party, you are perhaps a party member?' I inquired.

'No, but I want to prepare myself for possible membership.' He added that he was a member of the Communist Youth League, but it had been inactive over the past two years. Characteristic of both himself and the Red Guard species in general was the emphasis with which he presented everything. He repeated: 'We rise at six and run for half an hour. That is sometimes difficult, but very healthy. Then we study for two hours. Yes, we want to prepare ourselves. I want to improve myself, but I do not think that I have much chance of becoming a member of the party.' The latter was said with the same shy smile that is characteristic of professional evangelists.

During a visit to a tea-house, where we were served a bowl of lotus root compote with acacia sugar – a sickeningly sweet delicacy – my guide inquired what I wanted to see the next day. I could not escape a visit to a factory and in order to avoid needless discussions I left the choice up to him. He knew my interest in the production of raw silk, but took me instead to the weaving-mill 'Tung-fang-hung' on the Pao-chien road. The factory dated from 1922 and by then employed 1,700 workers. There were 330 electric looms. It produced mainly silk fabrics with colourful traditional designs for export. However, comrade Cheng, the representative of the revolutionary rebels, explained that the production of silk portraits of Mao Tse-tung was the principal work of the factory. First the revisionists had been opposed to the production of the portraits. But the workers had been in favour of it, and the people wanted them. The mill also produced portraits of Lin Piao and Chou En-lai, pictures of the famous spots in the history of the revolution, such as Yenan and Chingkang-shan, as well as reproductions of the poems of Chairman Mao in his own calligraphy. The mill produced twenty different portraits in all of the Chairman. Extremely well done was a portrait of the Albanian party leader Enver Hoxha in eighteen colours; (this reminds me of the menu in my hotel, which was available in only two languages, Chinese and Albanian). There was also a romantic silken picture of Lenin and Stalin saying farewell to each other near a rowing boat. Stalin on his own was also produced in large quantities.

During the introduction before the conducted tour through the mill, the artistic ideas of Mao Tse-tung were quoted, whereupon I inquired whether these silk portraits of the communist leaders could be called socialist-realist. The question embarrassed both comrade Cheng and my guide. I recalled then that in 1942 Mao Tse-tung in his *Yenan Talks* had said that he was in favour of socialist realism (but did not add that the term had fallen into disuse in 1958). The rebel representative declared that the production of the portraits was a revolutionary act requested by the revolutionary masses. My guide added that admiration for Chairman Mao was real. They did not decide that the silk portraits were an expression of revolutionary realism. They did not want to pin a label on these curious creations in silk, partly because of political caution, and perhaps partly because of the belief that uninterrupted revolution requires that the terminology used for interpreting cultural phenomena always remains open and variable. If this is true, a dialogue with China will become more complicated.

Visit to Shanghai

The temperature in the 'Hangchow' Hotel being just above zero, I always ate my meals in an overcoat. Since I was the only guest, the hotel management made use of this opportunity to economise on heating, with the result that I did not want to prolong my stay in Hangchow unnecessarily. The Peace Hotel in Shanghai, where I stayed next, was better heated. But there were also other guests: overseas Chinese, Vietnamese, Albanians and a few despondent Euro-

pean businessmen. I made the journey from Hangchow to Shanghai
by train – alas, during the night. The night train had the advantage of
beginning in Hangchow and, therefore, of leaving more or less on
time. My guide advised me not to take the morning train, which came
from Szechwan and would probably be delayed.

In Shanghai a guide was waiting for me who introduced himself
as Ch'en and who left me almost completely free. He tried to book me
a place on the train to Peking, but this appeared to be impossible due
to crowding caused by the approaching Chinese New Year. I had to
return by air. Ch'en also tried to arrange a visit to the Lu Hsün museum,
to several temples and to the old Chinese part of the town. After
various consultations with a colleague, he told me that the museum
and the temples were closed 'since several problems in connection
with the Cultural Revolution had to be solved first'. Neither did he
encourage me to go to the old Chinese town, known in Shanghai as
Nan-tao. 'It is not much more than a bazaar; there is nothing to see!'
he said. I asked Ch'en, who had a cold, to show me something of the
city by taxi, which gave him a chance of showing me the house where
the Chinese Communist Party was founded. During the afternoon
I walked alone through the town.

The slums of Shanghai have partly disappeared. The notorious
Ziccawei district has been rebuilt, but the slum dwellings along the
embankment of the River Wusung are mostly still there. Everything
cannot be done at once, but the inhabitants of Shanghai may have
expected more. The slowly flowing Wusung has accumulated so
much silt that the bottom of the river is about as high as the surrounding land. In Shanghai high stone walls have been constructed along the
river, which serve as dams. Along these, relatively high quays have
been built in order to ease loading and unloading across the walls.
The houses along the quays are built on lower ground. When it rains,
the water runs from the quays into the houses.

When I walked along the Wusung (which I could see only when
crossing a bridge because of the high retaining walls), it was raining.
The road consisted mainly of mud and cinders. It was mostly women
who were doing the heavy work. Some children were playing with a
simple kite, others with paper marbles. Another group possessed a
shaky little cart which resembled the undercarriage of an old perambu-
lator. With bursts of cheering it was pulled forward until its passenger
lay in the mud, whereupon one of the children shouted 'Long live
Mao Tse-tung' and the others joined in with a big laugh.

Shanghai is different from Peking and always has been; it has a much richer intellectual tradition and has always had more contacts abroad. The Shanghai Chinese appears more business-like and faster-moving. Shanghai is a city in the grand manner. Its inhabitants are more self-assured and seem miles away from the countryside. Shanghai is to China what New York is to the United States.

Something of this grand character of the town is reflected in the humour and tricks of the children, in the self-confident and undisciplined behaviour of the young people, and in the arrogance of the older generation. The unruliness of the young revolutionaries was obvious. Here I witnessed one of the few fights that I saw in China. It was a clash between 'conservatives' in a high office building and 'revolutionary rebels' who arrived in a small lorry and ran quickly into the building in order to free a colleague, to give someone a beating or perform some other revolutionary act. I believe I saw arrogance in the old men who played cards all day on the street, or chatted in the crowded tea-houses of the old Chinese town. Fatalism, or the pertinent refusal to let themselves be intimidated by the Red Guard, or the knowledge that the Cultural Revolution had passed its peak helped to preserve the old bourgeois habits. They probably knew that the Red Guard organisations preferred to fight each other, because each of them wanted to have a larger influence in the new administrative committees. They probably also knew that the noise in the streets, of lorries loaded with workers, who with drums beating drove to the town committee in order to announce the inauguration of a revolutionary committee in this or that factory, did not mean very much. The town committee had set a deadline for establishing revolutionary committees in the factories and organisations. Therefore the requested revolutionary committees were formed. In some cases this was a serious matter, but especially in the smaller enterprises it was done with a laugh and a joke.

Final Stage of the Cultural Revolution

Our arrival in China coincided with the beginning of the Cultural Revolution. When we returned to the Netherlands, it was fairly evident how the revolution would end. On February 16, 1968, I left for Canton together with my family and went on the next day to Hong Kong. At that moment Canton was in a festive mood because the inauguration of the revolutionary committee of the province

Kwangtung was expected at any moment. The taxi that brought us from the hotel to the train needed more time than usual because of the huge crowds which had assembled around the station. For the last bit we had to push ourselves through the crowds, which enlivened the scene with fire-crackers. Our guide reassured us that the noise indicated a celebration. On the walls one could read that the founding of a revolutionary committee in Kwangtung was a good thing.

Thus we took our leave of China. It was a departure that, on the one hand, we disliked, because we had to leave many good friends behind – some of them in official or unofficial captivity – but that, on the other hand, we had been looking forward to. The Shanghai newspaper *Wen-hui pao* wrote in a report on the political situation that 'the trees wish rest, but the storm has not yet subsided'. The restoration of law and order coincided with disorder and unrest. In February 1968, in Peking, there were still arrests, with the victims being forced to wear dunce's caps. We assumed that the 'action of the masses' was now directed against leftist extremists, who had in their turn subjected many innocent people to similar treatment.

The leaders in Peking found it necessary to curtail the extreme left wing. The theoretician Ch'i Pen-yü, who had aired dangerous ideas about xenophobia, was removed from the political scene. Open criticism of his policies and ideas began in mid-February 1968. By the end of March the acting Chief of Staff Yang Ch'eng-wu was dismissed who at first was probably closely associated with the extreme Left, but since August 1967 had tried to disentangle himself and to forge an independent political role for the army. He was succeeded by Huang Yung-sheng, commander of the Canton region, who was supposedly a moderate. The change was generally interpreted as an important step towards normalisation.

Normalisation continued, but so did confusion. In some provinces it was still many months before a revolutionary committee could be formed under the protection of the army. At other places the revolutionary committees which had been established were subjected to severe criticism. In several provinces, after the exposure of 'counter-revolutionary traitors' who had 'wormed' their way into the revolutionary committees, the composition of the committees was changed. In the summer of 1968 the founding of a revolutionary committee in the autonomous region Kwangsi-Chuang in South China was preceded by heavy fighting during which arms consigned for the war in Vietnam were used. The fighting spread to the adjacent province

Kwangtung and resulted in a great many casulties. Many mutilated bodies drifted down the river to come ashore in Hong Kong.

Finally, on September 5, 1968, revolutionary committees were established in Tibet and Sinkiang. In spite of the Red Guard demand that Wang En-mao, the powerful party secretary and military commander of Sinkiang, should not participate in a 'three-way alliance' of old cadres, the army and revolutionary rebels, he was made one of the vice-chairmen of the Sinkiang revolutionary committee. It was a standard example of the political compromise which was one of the indispensable conditions of a return to law and order. When the revolutionary committees in Tibet and Sinkiang were formed, Chou En-lai formally announced that all provinces and autonomous regions, 'with the exception of Taiwan', possessed a revolutionary committee.

In my opinion, the Cultural Revolution was a disaster to China. It was the army which finally contained that disaster; no wonder the military were dominant in the revolutionary committees. About half the chairmen of the provincial revolutionary committees were military men.[1] This, too, seemed to be one of the conditions for restoring law and order.

In 1968 and 1969 the young people were still the greatest problem of Peking. Several organisations of Red Guards fanatically opposed the resumption of higher education, and they knew that in this they were supported by the small extreme leftist group among the Chinese leaders, who wished to preserve the Red Guard as a political force. This extreme left wing under the leadership of K'ang Sheng was tolerated by Mao Tse-tung, because he considered revolutionary impetuosity and political confusion a necessary condition for continuing the revolution. How much revolutionary impetuosity and political unrest were necessary to Mao's aims was, however, a debatable question. It appears that Chou En-lai and Lin Piao looked for ways to curtail the extremist leanings of the Red Guard.

In the autumn of 1968 a large-scale campaign was organised to transfer students to the countryside. If order was to be restored, teaching must be resumed. And if one wanted to resume teaching and avoid overcrowding, a solution had to be found for the students who in the summer of 1966, 1967 or 1968 had not taken any examinations. They had to make room for the new generation. Mao Tse-tung insisted that these students should go to the countryside in order to learn from the peasants. The announcement of a directive to that effect on December 21, 1968, resulted in an enormous exodus from the big cities. In January

F

1969, the official press reported that since the beginning of the Cultural Revolution about 200,000 Red Guards and other young people had departed for the countryside from Peking alone. Undoubtedly the régime aimed at achieving the integration of intellectual and physical work, which was one of its dearest ideals, by means of such an enormous migration, which was of course not limited to Peking.

The reorganisation of education also contributed to the old marxist ideal of the integration of intellectual and physical work. In 1968 Mao Tse-tung ordered that workers and poor peasants should run the schools and universities in order to prevent the return of bourgeois influence. In administration as well as in teaching and the enrolment policy, political reliability took precedence over competence. In admitting students to schools, political criteria were decisive, which defeated the object of equal opportunities for everyone. These political criteria were applied in such a way that an egalitarian enrolment policy was impossible. Under the new regulations students with a 'bourgeois' background had, at least in theory, no chance to continue their studies.

It appeared as if the régime wanted to prevent large numbers of students from following higher education. As in many developing countries, the Chinese leaders feared that many students after completing their studies would not succeed in finding a suitable job. This fear deepened as a result of the adverse consequences of the Cultural Revolution in the field of industrial development. In the years 1966-8 expansion of the industrial potential and thus the number of highly qualified jobs had not been possible. On the contrary, economic dislocation resulted in fewer opportunities for graduates. The régime feared the creation of an intellectual proletariat without work and without a future, and jobless academics can make a dangerous opposition.

The Twelth Session of the Central Committee and the Ninth Party Congress

The rehabilitation of the party was an indispensable part of the normalisation process. Already during the eleventh session of the Central Committee in August 1966, Mao Tse-tung suggested that the next party congress be convened in 1967. On October 24, 1967, Vice-Premier Hsieh Fu-chih announced the Ninth Party Congress, which, he said, would be held during 1968. He raised the possibility that a number of Red Guard leaders would be admitted as party members, but left no room for speculation about their ever reaching a dominating position within the party.

The expectation that the party congress would be held in 1968 was too optimistic. Between October 13 and 31, 1968, a plenary session of the Central Committee took place, where preparations were made for the coming congress. This twelfth session discussed a revised draft constitution of the Chinese Communist Party written in the spirit of maoism, decided on the method of selection for the deputies to the Ninth Congress and accepted a report on the 'renegade, traitor and scab' Liu Shao-ch'i.

The text of the party constitution[2] placed the thought of Mao Tse-tung on a par with marxism and leninism. This equality entailed a change in the spelling of Mao's name in the English translation of the constitution done in Peking. The hyphen between *Tse* and *tung* was dropped, and so the text in the *Peking Review* mentions 'Marxism–Leninism–Mao Tsetung Thought', from which it appears that the years of political upheaval and economic disintegration have not destroyed the age-old Chinese philological acumen. The constitution confirmed the split in the communist world by describing 'proletarian internationalism' as co-operation with 'the genuine marxist–leninist parties' in other countries, which excludes the Communist Party of the Soviet Union. Lin Piao was called Mao Tse-tung's close comrade-in-arms and successor. In contradiction to Soviet sources, the text contains a paragraph on democratic centralism: 'The organisational principle of the Party is democratic centralism. The leading bodies of the Party at all levels are elected through democratic consultation.' It is not completely clear what this election through consultation means in practice. There are indications that the deputies to the Ninth Congress, after some consultation of the regional administration, were in fact appointed by the party leaders in Peking and were neither directly nor indirectly elected. The only congress of the Chinese Communist Party that consisted of more or less democratically elected deputies was the Eighth Congress (1956). The activities of many Central Committee members, who were elected at that very congress, did not find favour in Mao Tse-tung's eyes. This may be one of the reasons why the idea of democratic elections was dropped.

It is not certain whether the twelfth session, apart from the formal repudiation of Liu Shao-ch'i, discussed the reputation of other 'revisionists'. But when the Ninth Congress was finally held between

April 1 and 24, 1969, it appointed a new Central Committee (170 members) from which many people who had played crucial roles in the history of the Chinese Communist Party were missing: the President of the People's Republic of China Liu Shao-ch'i, the General Secretary of the Chinese Communist Party Teng Hsiao-p'ing, the former Director of the Central Committee Propaganda Department T'ao Chu, Marshals Ho Lung and P'eng Te-huai, the Minister of Agriculture T'an Chen-lin, former Mayor and First Secretary of Peking P'eng Chen, the alternate members of the Politburo Ulanfu, Po I-po and Lu Ting-i, and furthermore four out of the five first secretaries of the regional party bureaux and all six provincial party secretaries who had been members of the preceding Central Committee.[3] Among the latter was also Wang En-mao, the once-powerful ruler of Sinkiang, who was, however, elected as an alternate member of the new Central Committee.

Others were only partly demoted. Marshal Chu Te did not belong any more to the standing committee of the Politburo (five members), but remained in the Politburo (twenty-one members). Ch'en Yün, Li Fu-ch'un and Ch'en Yi were degraded to common members of the Central Committee. This was a defeat for the faction that represented a well-run administration. Their place in the Politburo was taken by military men, who held the real power, and under whose protection the administration was functioning. Only one-third of the members of the Politburo of 1965 stood the test of the Cultural Revolution and were still on the 1969 Politburo elected from the ninth Central Committee.

It seemed as if Mao Tse-tung wanted as much as possible to keep the factional quarrelling away from the standing committee of the Politburo, and therefore had it limited to five people. Before the Ninth Congress, the standing committee had ten members. Now it consisted of Mao Tse-tung, Lin Piao (crown prince and Minister of Defence), Chou En-lai (representing the administration), Ch'en Po-ta (former private secretary to Mao Tse-tung, propaganda chief and chairman of the Cultural Revolution group), and K'ang Sheng (in charge of relations with communist parties abroad). There were not representatives of either the moderate military leaders (Liu Po-ch'eng, Yeh Chien-ying, Wu Fa-hsien or Hsü Shih-yu) or of one of the extremist members of the Cultural Revolution group (Chiang Ch'ing, Chang Ch'un-ch'iao, Yao Wen-yüan, Yeh Ch'ün) included in the standing committee. They were all common members of the Politburo, and in its meetings they were probably balanced against each other, precisely as in the standing committee Mao Tse-tung may have attempted to play off Ch'en Po-ta and K'ang Sheng against Lin Piao and Chou En-lai. So the composition of the highest governing bodies of China provided a basis for continuing the revolution.

The Ninth Party Congress signalled the end of the Cultural Revolution which undoubtedly involved the greatest purge that the Chinese Communist Party has ever had to endure. Precisely because the Cultural Revolution was not only a power struggle, but also a battle of ideas, the scapegoats were not limited to the higher regions of the party. The total number of victims among the less important party members or non-party people, the descendants of land-owners and shop-keepers, the children of professors and officials, the pedlars and all others whose parents or grandparents had had an occupation that provided them with a minimum of independence, may never be known for certain.

REFERENCES

1. Richard Baum, 'China: Year of the Mangoes', *Asian Survey*, 9 (1969), No. 1, pp. 1–18; see p. 7.
2. The draft constitution was published in English translation in *The China Quarterly*, 10 (1969), No. 37, pp. 169–73. The final text, which was passed at the Ninth Congress, appeared in *Peking Review* 1969, No. 18, pp. 36–40, and differs only in minor points from the draft.
3. The four missing first secretaries of the regional bureaux are: Li Ching-ch'üan, Liu Lan-t'ao, Sung Jen-ch'iung and Wang Jen-chung. The six missing first secretaries of the provincial party committees are: Hu Yao-pang, Li Pao-hua, Lin T'ieh, Ouyang Ch'in, Ulanfu and Wang En-mao. Li Pao-hua is a son of Li Ta-chao (1888–1927), one of the foremost leaders of the Communist Party in the 1920s.

8

BALANCE SHEET OF THE
CULTURAL REVOLUTION

So far I have confined myself mainly to describing the facts of the Cultural Revolution. It is too early for a sound interpretation of those facts. First, it is not always possible to evaluate the reports appearing in both the official and unofficial press, particularly if they concern political developments in distant provinces, and, secondly, we know that some of the facts are unknown to us.

The reasons behind the dismissal of the acting Chief of Staff Yang Ch'eng-wu, in early 1968, remain as hypothetical as those behind the eclipse of Hsiao Hua, head of the Political Department of the People's Liberation Army, in August 1967. In general, the effect of the Cultural Revolution on the army is, of course, shrouded in secrecy.

Also in the economic field, our knowledge is far from complete. We know that, particularly in 1967, many factories were idle as a result of strikes and local conflict. The transportation system was dislocated because of overcrowding. Moreover, the people living near the railways used to wreck them in order to force the attention of the central government on to their local problems. Furthermore, the local authorities tried to assemble as much rolling-stock as possible within their own region. By the end of 1967 there were complaints that in Manchuria large numbers of locomotives and carriages had been accumulated which did not belong there. Many lorries were taken away from their intended tasks in order to carry people to demonstrations and other political activities. The result of all this was that, in many factories, production suffered from a deficiency of the raw materials and spare parts which were produced elsewhere. Sales, too, went down due to the chaos in the transport system. In Peking several products which before the Cultural Revolution were normally available were temporarily out of stock or scarce. However, precise data on the economic consequences of the dislocation of the transport system are not known. Neither is there any clear picture of the finances of the People's Republic of China. It is not known what happened to the savings that were confiscated, the looted works of art and precious metals, the distributed funds, the tax system and the collective possessions of the communes. To a certain extent the booty of the Red Guards must have balanced their expenses.

One must conclude that economic production in 1967 was less than that of the year before.[1] Exports went down in 1967 but, in view of the modest volume of Chinese foreign trade (which comprises, for example, only about 25 per cent of Dutch foreign trade), this hardly provides a clue to the size of the gross national product. It is evident that, because of the lack of concrete data, the economic damage of the Cultural Revolution cannot be calculated for the time being. In such a calculation must be included the effect of changes in the management structure, the liquidation of a large number of experts and cadres, the interference by revolutionary rebels and the military with industry, the disruption of technical and higher education, and the possible consequences of the Cultural Revolution for the growth of the population.

Also the facts of the Cultural Revolution in the cultural and educational field cannot be easily interpreted. It looks highly improbable that all the well-known writers, with the exception of Hu Wan-ch'un, could have been silenced over a period of about two years or more, and yet this has been the case. It sounds unbelievable that in the years of the Cultural Revolution, apart from Chin Ching-mai's *Song of Ouyang Hai*, no novel appeared which was favourably received by the national press, and yet this is a fact. A few years ago the sharp criticism of Chou Yang, the organiser of the literary inquisition between 1949 and 1966, would have been as unimaginable as the present vilification of the show piece of recent Chinese literature Chao Shu-li.

During the Cultural Revolution the impossible and unbelievable happened. It goes without saying that the interpretation of what is, in our view, an illogical development is a precarious affair. But I realise that, without an attempt at evaluation, this book would not be complete, and so I shall make some suggestions which, I hope, may help the reader to arrive at his own assessment.

Why was the Cultural Revolution necessary?

The Cultural Revolution was more than a power struggle and was largely determined by ideological issues. The conflict between Mao Tse-tung and his opponents was dramatised by his criticism of President Liu Shao-ch'i – or China's Khrushchev, as he was called in the official press before November 1968. Already in August 1966 the Defence Minister Lin Piao, instead of Liu Shao-ch'i, was earmarked as the future successor of Mao Tse-tung. Liu Shao-ch'i and Lin Piao personify different mentalities and political convictions.

Lin Piao is a born military man. At the age of twenty-five he was already a well-known commander. In 1937 he was severely wounded in a battle with Japanese troops, after which he went to the Soviet Union for medical treatment. He stayed there four years and served as a representative of the Chinese Communist Party during that period. During the years 1948–9 he commanded about a million men and played an important role in the struggle against the Kuomintang. He assimilated the guerrilla tactics of Mao Tse-tung. In his speeches, which are hard to understand because of his central Chinese dialect, Lin Piao has proved himself a real demagogue. He has an inspiring, hypnotic look and his calligraphy seems to show that he is an intemperate man. He appears to believe in will-power, the word of Chairman Mao and violence. His inclination towards deeds of personal courage has been contained by the determination to engage only in matters of primary importance. Like Mao Tse-tung, Lin Piao succeeded surprisingly well in not exposing himself unduly during the Cultural Revolution.

Liu Shao-ch'i owes his career in the party to his close contacts with the trade unions, which have a hierarchy which is completely different from that of the army. Liu played a central role in the organisation of the party and provided his loyal supporters with essential jobs in the propaganda machine. Unlike Lin Piao or Mao Tse-tung he placed little confidence in subjective will-power, which in the army has been counter-balanced by all kinds of regulations and a rigid command structure. In the organisations President Liu had to work with there were no means of restraining outbursts of self-reliance. Although the party, the National People's Congress, and the regional and national administrative institutions are not organised on democratic principles as these are understood in the West, their structures contain more democratic elements than that of the People's Liberation Army. In Liu Shao-ch'i's organisation, selection by means of competition, election and nomination played a crucial role. Unlike Lin Piao, President Liu had to deal with a great variety of jobs and people. Liu believed that the many facets of society, science and art needed experts. In the grip of their guerrilla psychosis, Lin Piao and Mao Tse-tung were strangers to complex social structures. They feared any liberalisation and its accompanying social competition and complicated control methods, and did not understand the demands of a modern economy. They did not understand the many-sidedness of society and the needs of a bureaucracy. Their distaste expresses itself in a preoccupation with the common man, the one that can help himself, the eternal amateur, the worker who is also an intellectual and the intellectual who does the work of a labourer, the farmer who writes or at least recites poetry; in a word, the all-round, self-reliant guerrilla. Mao Tse-tung considered the Cultural Revolution necessary in order to restore the ideal of the common, proletarian man to its original glory.

The ideological implications of the conflict between Mao Tse-tung and Liu Shao-ch'i are clear. The ideological element provides the Cultural Revolution with more than national significance. The Chinese problems have a deceptive resemblance to those of the present period of crisis in the West. Mao Tse-tung has said: 'To put things in order organisationally requires our first doing so ideologically.' But in practice his followers undermined the social order before they knew what the new ideological order was going to be. The process of maoist thinking can be compared with the attitude of a poet who sits before a blank sheet of paper and creates a new world out of nothing. However, Liu Shao-ch'i seemed to attribute more importance to organisation than to ideology. More than Mao Tse-tung, he seemed to be aware of the demands of reality. He knew that a prosperous socialist society was not going to arise from nothingness, nor could it be created by a simple act of will. He could not agree with the anarchism inherent in Mao Tse-tung's programme of destruction first and construction in the course of this destruction. If Mao Tse-tung can be characterised as a romantic, Liu Shao-ch'i must be called a realist.

The great difference between the Cultural Revolution and the stalinist purges of the 1930s lies in the ideological aspect which in China played a principal role and in the Soviet Union a secondary one. Thus, in China, the active participation of the masses was made possible, whereas in the Soviet Union the purges were carried out by the secret police. The similarity between the Chinese and Russian purges is that both Mao Tse-tung and Stalin were striving for absolute power at the cost of an unimaginable amount of human suffering and economic disruption.

F*

Nationalism or Communism?

We have described the Cultural Revolution mainly as an internal Chinese affair. But one is justified in inquiring whether in that way the Cultural Revolution is not being underestimated. There has been much speculation as to whether Mao Tse-tung in 1965–6 believed that China was entering a period of *peace* and that the coming years could be best used by subjecting the Chinese people to an ideological and political rectification campaign; or that he wanted to use the Cultural Revolution as a means of preparing his people for an inevitable *war*. If one is to believe Chinese propaganda, the latter alternative seems more probable. The slogan 'Grasp revolution, promote production and other work' has been extended with a third exhortation: 'Be prepared for war.' The Ninth Party Congress of April 1969 took place under the aegis of the appeal to 'be prepared against war, be prepared against natural disasters, and do everything for the people'.

However, there is some reason to doubt whether these pronouncements should be taken literally. A Japanese communist source reported that in March 1966 Mao Tse-tung had predicted that within two years China would be involved in a war with the United States and the Soviet Union.[2] From a Chinese source we know that early in 1967 Foreign Minister Ch'en Yi spoke of the danger of a war with Russia or America. There is no reason to doubt that Mao Tse-tung or Ch'en Yi expressed themselves thus, but in interpreting these alarming predictions we should take account of the Chinese inclination towards dramatisation and metaphorical language; the danger of an American invasion implies the menace of a restoration of capitalism, and the possibility of war with the Soviet Union is a warning against revisionism. It is clear that an ideology which has made of the people's war one of its most precious ideals will not reject the settling of disputes by force of arms. According to Mao Tse-tung, the threat of war may serve to liberate the people from apathy. He admires the mentality of the guerrilla, but probably his admiration is for the guerrilla *attitude* rather than guerrilla *warfare*.

China is a country which in modern times has never been completely occupied by a foreign power and which, because of its size and inaccessibility, is to a certain extent militarily invulnerable. The prospect of war with a foreign power therefore contains no great deterrent effect. The Chinese may believe that there will always be a chance to withdraw into the interior. For the great majority of the people, the front will be countless miles away, and few will be in a position to form an adequate idea of what the enemy is really like. Against this background the threat of a Russian or American invasion can be employed in a figurative way.

The danger of war was probably not the most important theme of the Cultural Revolution. In general, the relations with foreign countries do not claim a large share in the motivation of Chinese politics. There is more reason to see the Cultural Revolution as a logical continuation of the Chinese revolution, as a sequel to land reform and the movement for the suppression of counter-revolutionaries, the anti-rightist campaign and the introduction of the people's communes. The commune system suffered a series of setbacks. Too high expectations gave rise to exaggerated production figures, which later had to be corrected. In 1961, it was officially recognised that the agricultural production plan for the previous year had not been achieved. In present-day Chinese historiography the years 1960–2 are called a period of 'temporary economic difficulties resulting from the betrayal by the revisionist clique of Khrushchev and serious natural disasters'. These were the years during which Mao Tse-tung planned to eliminate the factors that prevented the success of the people's communes. He pondered means to make the Chinese people ideologically prepared and weary enough politically to accept total collectivisation. The Cultural Revolution was the result of that reflection; one might call it a correction of the commune-system. The Cultural Revolution displays the untiring perseverance of Mao Tse-tung and is in line with the principle of the uninterrupted or continuous revolution, which is the core of maoism. The relationship with uninterrupted revolution has been confirmed by the official announcement that the process of the Cultural Revolution will be repeated in the future. Whether this will in fact happen is, of course, open to doubt.

China tends to be self-centred, and therefore we should hesitate to seek external causes for such an important internal phenomenon as the Cultural Revolution. The country is so big and varied that it may have good reason to consider itself the centre of the world. On November 6, 1967, Lin Piao said in a speech that was published the next day in the *People's Daily*: 'We must build our great motherland into a still more powerful base for world revolution; we must intensify our efforts in studying and mastering Mao Tse-tung's thought and disseminate it still more widely throughout the world; these are the glorious tasks entrusted to the people of our country by history. . . .' Undoubtedly we are dealing here with an example of chauvinism, or sinocentrism, but also with the ambition to contribute to world revolution. It appears that we can equate maoism neither with nationalism nor with international communism. Mao Tse-tung hopes to turn China into a stronghold of the international communism of the maoist brand. Maoism is national communism with international ambitions.

Export of the Revolution and the Border Conflict with the Soviet Union

If one assumes that relations with foreign countries do not count heavily in the considerations of the Chinese leaders, the question remains how the political and material support given to 'liberation movements' and the border conflict with the Soviet Union should be explained. An analysis of Chinese support for the Vietcong, the Palestine Liberation Organisation, the Liberation Front of Thailand, the Angolan resistance, or the Burmese and Indonesian communists falls outside the scope of this book, and I shall therefore confine myself to a few general observations. The idea of self-reliance is not only a basic principle of the Chinese economy – in particular the economy of inaccessible regions – but also the foundation of the people's war. Rather than concealing Chinese political objectives, it fulfills an objective necessity. The extent to which China may in fact support the liberation movements militarily and economically is limited. By disseminating economic and military self-reliance a virtue is being made of necessity. In his speech of September 1965 on the people's war and the encirclement of the industrial nations, Lin Piao elaborated on the principle of self-reliance. And precisely because of his emphasis on this principle, which was used also by the Chinese Communist Party in its struggle for power, that speech has been interpreted as an attempt to temporise over the question of foreign aspirations. That does not alter the fact that Lin Piao's address drafted, in greater detail than ever before, a programme for maoist world domination. But the Chinese leaders do not seem to be in a hurry to act on the programme. The fact that the model of the Chinese revolution was held up as an example to other developing countries was in itself already a partial realisation of chauvinistic expectations. Lin Piao's speech was also heavily coloured by sinocentrism.

Peking does provide the liberation movements with weapons, but the Chinese characters with which these are marked betray the chauvinism behind this military aid. It is no secret that many African and Palestinian guerrillas have been trained in China. At the end of their training they were sometimes received by Mao Tse-tung, and the highest possible honour they could give him on such occasions was singing a maoist song *in Chinese*. One should ask the question: what is more important to Mao Tse-tung, liberation from the colonialist or neo-colonialist yoke, or the fact that the liberation struggle may enable the Chinese press to publish pictures of Angolans, Palestinians or Thais brandishing the red book. Just because the export of the revolution has a function in the glorification of Mao Tse-tung and can provide material for the Chinese press, Peking is tempted to co-operate only with parties and movements which adhere unconditionally to Mao Tse-tung's thought. If some African or Asian country deviates from the maoist blueprint, it may evoke a hatred similar to that felt towards the Soviet Union, Yugoslavia, or the United States. When in August 1967, relations between Kenya and China were at their lowest and Red Guards tried to storm the Kenyan Embassy, a negro was hanged in effigy on the embassy gate. The straw figure with its blackened face stayed there for many months. It served as a visual reminder that the Chinese leaders expect as much loyalty from their foreign pupils as from the Chinese people. This intransigent attitude leaves little room for political compromise, which restricts China's possibilities of increasing her foreign influence.

The border conflict with the Soviet Union also has an ideological aspect. The incidents had been largely verbal until March 1969, when a clash on Chenpao Island (Damanskij) in the Ussuri River resulted in many casualties. Both Moscow and Peking were interested in publicising the event. By playing on feelings of nationalism, the Soviet leaders hoped to make the Russian liberals more tractable. They also appealed to the feelings of solidarity among their Eastern-European allies and tried to arouse sympathy in the West for their role of defenders against Chinese 'aggression'. It was considered a sensation that Moscow ordered its ambassadors to inform the Western governments about the incident. Perhaps the Russian hope of finding sympathy for the role of the Soviet army in the conflict around Chenpao was illusory, but they were also intending to divert attention from the occupation of Czechoslovakia. Anyway, in spite of the many reports and pictures published by the Soviets, the Chenpao incident has not proved Chinese military aggression.

There was a political reason behind the persistent defence of the island by the People's Liberation Army. Peking, too, was interested in the incident for internal reasons, since it could be used as an example of the depravity of the revisionists. A few weeks before the Ninth Party Congress, reports of the heroic struggle of the People's Liberation Army against the Soviet revisionists were welcome indeed. Again the indignation about Soviet revisionism appeared to be aimed at revisionism rather than the Soviet Union. If the Chinese initiated the Chenpao incident, the Soviets probably took the initiative in the summer of 1969 on a confrontation along the Sinkiang border. One may assume that Peking feared that the Soviet forces might be tempted to act against the Chinese nuclear installations. On October 20, 1969, negotiations to settle the dispute began in Peking at vice-minister level.

During the Cultural Revolution, China was too much involved in her own internal problems to be in a position to launch an aggressive foreign policy, and was also not prepared militarily to back such a policy. But the episode of national self-criticism – which the Cultural Revolution really was – has ended now, and one can hardly predict in what direction the Chinese leaders will move. The future foreign policy of China will be largely determined by the answer to the question of whether the Cultural Revolution has realised its original aims. Since it appears to have produced only a partial victory for maoism, Chinese foreign policy will probably be characterised by half-heartedness: it will display the same discrepancy between verbal propaganda and actual deeds that was distinctive in the situation before the Cultural Revolution.

Was the Cultural Revolution a Success?

If my interpretation is correct that Mao Tse-tung wanted to use the Cultural Revolution in order to settle an ideological dispute, one must conclude that he did not completely succeed. The Cultural Revolution did not usher in the mass production of the new proletarian man, who would be prepared to forgo material possessions, position and glory in order to devote himself in complete anonymity to the construction of communism. Material incentives do still play an important role. As a result of the Cultural Revolution, corruption and crime have increased instead of decreasing. Heavy political stress and the risks of the revolution led to insincerity and indifference. The distance between appearance and reality has become wider. Now that every household possesses a set of the Chairman's *Selected Works*, the principles of maoist ethics are certainly more widely known, but this does not imply that they are unequivocally put into practice.

If from the beginning Mao Tse-tung and Lin Piao intended to get rid of their rival Liu Shao-ch'i, this aim has been achieved. Also the principal followers of the President were dismissed and they have disappeared from the political stage. Although their liquidation could have been accomplished much more simply, it was the ideological aspect of the Cultural Revolution that forced Mao to attempt to create the impression that the dismissal of the Chinese revisionists was demanded by the people. Considering the dimensions and the consequences of the Cultural Revolution, which far exceeded Mao's original estimates, one cannot conclude that he fully succeeded in creating that impression.

If it was a secondary aim to purge the party apparatus of bureaucratic elements, the maoists succeeded only partly in this. In the revolutionary committees that were formed in the years 1967 and 1968 a majority of military men and old party cadres are sitting side by side with a small number of inexperienced revolutionary rebels.

If Mao Tse-tung ever wanted to bolster China's military strength by means of the Cultural Revolution, this purpose can hardly be said to have materialised. Perhaps the People's Liberation Army is now better prepared for defensive guerrilla warfare than before the Cultural Revolution. But, as a result of an increasing defence of particularist interests, discord within the armed forces has grown and the total strength of the army has been weakened thereby.

If, finally, Mao Tse-tung intended to procure a basis from which to launch a second Great Leap Forward and a new collectivisation programme, one cannot but observe that this basis has not been attained. The people have no sympathy for a new movement for frugality. The moral courage and will are lacking for deeds of self-sacrifice and for extraordinary efforts of labour. In industry there may still be unrepaired damage. The transport system has suffered from sabotage and the inexpert use of rolling stock. And in the provinces there is less interest in the propaganda activities of the central government than there was twelve years ago.

In this summing-up the balance of the Cultural Revolution turns out to be negative. But one would be mistaken if one believed that the Chinese leaders evaluate the result of the Cultural Revolution in the same way we do. If the Cultural Revolution was originally an ideological revolution, it goes without saying that the intentions of the revolutionary rebels are as important as the results of their deeds. The Cultural Revolution created, if only temporarily, a wave of semi-spontaneous enthusiasm for the maoist, self-denying man. A great many bourgeois illusions were destroyed, which left a void which was not filled by new expectations. There was destruction, but no construction. The genuine maoist does not view this as a negative phenomenon, but as characteristic of a transitional period. Indeed, maoism as such is hardly constructive and places a change of mental attitude higher than concrete results. The maoist believes that the present indifference of the Chinese people will change for the better.

There are more phenomena which we disapprove of, but which are highly valued by the maoists. Where China is concerned our values are not always valid and many of our concepts have a completely different meaning.

We believe that in China the discussions and demonstrations are consuming too much time and delaying social progress. Although this complaint may be heard in China as well, the maoists have given it a different connotation. The Chinese are in less of a hurry than the Western-Europeans. The genuine maoist believes less in social progress, especially if this means raising the standard of living. Moreover, it takes time to convince a people of 750 million.

In our opinion the Cultural Revolution has produced an unnecessarily large amount of violence and cruelty. But Mao Tse-tung was willing to pay that price. He believed that he should stir up the people in this way, for fear that his ideal of continuous revolution and world revolution should fall into oblivion.

In our view the net profit of the Cultural Revolution is division: there is bitterness in many and a revolutionary mentality among a militant minority. But on the road to a communist future, Mao considers this revolutionary mentality indispensable. The embittered and frustrated, who as a result of the Cultural Revolution have lost all faith in communism, are no liability. On the contrary – the maoist would reason – the conflict between conservatives and revolutionaries, which must be regarded as part of the class struggle, will thus be intensified. The more intense the class struggle, the earlier will communism triumph.

China is not only self-reliant, she is also self-centred. She has rejected the Russian example and is trying to find her own way. In collision with other views, in severing old bonds of friendship, in the conflict with foreign powers China is again and again being confronted with herself, and in this confrontation she gets to know herself and her own role in the world. The role of the humiliated and semi-colonised, nineteenth-century empire appears to have been abandoned long ago. But the humiliation has not been forgotten and has repeatedly been called to mind in the twentieth century. The humiliations that have been inflicted on China may provide an explanation of the confusion and self-investigation of which the Cultural Revolution was composed.

In my opinion the policy of confrontation can be avoided. Self-identification and respect for others can also be achieved in peaceful encounters and the exchange of ideas. In this contact with one another we do not need to abandon our own familiar concepts, but we must learn their relationships to those of another country by means of an unbiased study of its views, culture and history. This is an absolute necessity. Only in that way will a dialogue between China and the West become possible.

REFERENCES

1. More precise estimates in Robert Michael Field, 'Industrial Production in Communist China: 1957–68', *The China Quarterly*, 11 (1970), No. 42, pp. 46–65.

2. Kikuzo Ito and Minoru Shibata, 'The Dilemma of Mao Tse-tung', *The China Quarterly*, 9 (1968), No. 35, pp. 58–78; see p. 67.

THE POLITBURO OF THE
CHINESE COMMUNIST PARTY

(The names of newly elected members and those added in the periods between two Party Congresses have been italicised.)

1945 SEVENTH PARTY CONGRESS	1956 EIGHTH PARTY CONGRESS	1969 NINTH PARTY CONGRESS
1. Mao Tse-tung	1. Mao Tse-tung	*Standing Committee:*
2. Liu Shao-ch'i	2. Liu Shao-ch'i	1. Mao Tse-tung
3. Chou En-lai	3. Chou En-lai	2. Lin Piao
4. Chu Te	4. Chu Te	*further in alphabetical*
5. Ch'en Yün	5. Ch'en Yün	*order:*
6. Chang Wen-t'ien	6. Lin Piao	Ch'en Po-ta
7. K'ang Sheng	7. Teng Hsiao-p'ing	Chou En-lai
8. Lin Po-ch'ü	8. Lin Po-ch'ü *(d. 1960)*	K'ang Sheng
9. Tung Pi-wu	9. Tung Pi-wu	*Other members of the*
10. *Lin Piao (1950–)*	10. *P'eng Chen*	*Politburo (in alphabetical*
11. *P'eng Te-huai (1954–)*	11. *Lo Jung-huan*	*order):*
12. *P'eng Chen (1951–)*	*(d. 1963)*	*Chang Ch'un-ch'iao*
13. *Teng Hsiao-p'ing*	12. *Ch'en Yi*	*Ch'en Hsi-lien*
(1955–)	13. *Li Fu-ch'un*	*Chiang Ch'ing*
	14. P'eng Te-huai	*Ch'iu Hui-tso*
	15. *Liu Po-ch'eng*	Chu Te
	16. *Ho Lung*	*Hsieh Fu-chih*
	17. *Li Hsien-nien*	*Hsü Shih-yu*
	18. *K'o Ch'ing-shih*	*Huang Yung-sheng*
	(1958– d. 1965)	Li Hsien-nien
	19. *Li Ching-ch'üan*	*Li Tso-p'eng*
	(1958–67)	Liu Po-ch'eng
	20. *T'an Chen-lin*	Tung Pi-wu
	(1958–68)	*Wu Fa-hsien*
	T'ao Chu (1966–8)	*Yao Wen-yüan*
	Ch'en Po-ta (1966–)	Yeh Chien-ying
	K'ang Sheng (1966–)	*Yeh Ch'ün*
	Hsü Hsiang-ch'ien	
	(1966–9)	
	Nieh Jung-chen (1966–9)	
	Yeh Chien-ying (1967–)	

CHRONOLOGY

1949
October 1   Founding of the People's Republic of China.
1949–50   Land reform.
1950–53   Korean war.
1955   Movement for the Supression of Counter-revolutionaries.

1956
February 25   Khrushchev criticises Stalin in a 'secret speech'.
May 2   Mao Tse-tung launches the slogan 'Let the hundred flowers
                     bloom, let the hundred schools contend'.
September 15–25   Eighth Congress of the Chinese Communist Party.
November   Hungarian uprising.

1957
February 27   Mao Tse-tung's address on contradictions among the
                     people.
May   Climax of liberalisation.
June   Beginning of the Anti-Rightist Campaign.

1958
April   Founding of the first people's commune.
August 29   Resolution of the Central Committee on the establishment
                     of people's communes.
December 10   Second resolution of the Central Committee on the people's
                     communes; the Central Committee accepts Mao Tse-tung's
                     proposal to resign as President of the People's Republic of
                     China.

1959
September   Because of his criticism of the commune system and the
                     Great Leap Forward P'eng Te-huai is dismissed as Minister
                     of Defence and succeeded by Lin Piao.

1961
January 14–18   Ninth session of the Central Committee and announcement
                     that in 1960 the agricultural production plan was not
                     fulfilled.

1962
September 24–27   Tenth session of the Central Committee.
1963–66   The Four Clean-ups Campaign (Szu-ch'ing).
1964   Shao Ch'üan-lin accused of 'bourgeois humanism'.

1965

January	Shen Yen-ping (Mao Tun) dismissed as Minister of Culture and succeeded by Lu Ting-i.
November 10	Yao Wen-yüan criticises Wu Han's play *The Dismissal of Hai Jui.*

1966

April 19	Editorial in *People's Daily* about the Cultural Revolution.
June 3	Announcement of the dismissal of P'eng Chen as First Secretary of the Party Committee of Peking.
June 13	Decision of the Central Committee to suspend university teaching.
June–July	Lu Ting-i dismissed as Director of the Propaganda Department of the Central Committee and Minister of Culture, and succeeded by respectively T'ao Chu and Hsiao Wang-tung; Lo Jui-ch'ing dismissed as Chief of Staff and succeeded by Yang Ch'eng-wu.
August 1–12	Eleventh session of the Central Committee; degradation of Liu Shao-ch'i; Lin Piao is appointed as the future successor of Mao Tse-tung.
August 18	First parade of the Red Guard.
November 8	Nieh Yüan-tzu criticises Liu Shao-ch'i and Teng Hsiao-p'ing.
December 9	Decision of the Central Committee to involve the workers in the Cultural Revolution.
December 26	The official press urges the workers to carry through the Cultural Revolution in industry.

1967

January	Strikes and fighting in Shanghai; the 'January Revolution'; T'ao Chu dismissed as Director of the Propaganda Department of the Central Committee and succeeded by Wang Li.
January 4–5	Mass meetings in Peking, where P'eng Chen, Lu Ting-i and Lo Jui-ch'ing are being accused of revisionism.
January 14	Revolutionary committee established in Shansi province.
January 23	Decision of the Central Committee authorising the army to support the revolutionary rebels.
January 24	Self-criticism of Ch'en Yi.
January 25	Revolutionary committee established in Kweichow province.
January 26	Beginning of demonstrations against the Soviet Embassy in Peking.
January 31	Revolutionary committee established in Heilungkiang province.
February 4–6	Departure of Russian women and children from Peking.
February 10	Kosygin declares that the Soviet Union sympathises with the opponents of the 'dictatorial régime of Mao Tse-tung'.

February 24	Revolutionary committee established in Shanghai.
March 2	*Idem* in Shantung province.
March 7	Decision of the Central Committee to suspend the Cultural Revolution in the countryside.
April 1	Article by Ch'i Pen-yü on the Boxer rebellion, criticising 'China's Khrushchev'.
April 20	Revolutionary committee established in Peking.
April 21 and May 6	Serious fighting in Szechwan.
May 7	Dismissal of Li Ching-ch'üan as First Secretary of the South-west Bureau.
June 17	First Chinese test of a hydrogen bomb.
July	Self-criticisms of Liu Shao-ch'i; rebellion in Wuhan.
August 12	Revolutionary committee established in Tsinghai province.
August 22	Office of the British Chargé d'Affaires set on fire.
Late August	Serious fighting in Canton.
September	Inspection tour by Mao Tse-tung; Wang Li dismissed as Director of the Propaganda Department of the Central Committee and succeeded by Ch'en Po-ta; the extreme Left loses influence.
October 14	Kenyan Embassy closes down.
October 24	Hsieh Fu-chih orders schools to open again and announces that the Ninth Party Congress will be held soon.
October 30	Suspension of diplomatic relations between China and Indonesia.
November 1	Revolutionary committee established in the Inner Mongolian Autonomous Region.
December 6	*Idem* in Tientsin.
1968	
January 5	*Idem* in Kiangsi province.
January 25	*Idem* in Kansu province.
January 27	*Idem* in Honan province.
February 3	*Idem* in Hopei province.
February 5	*Idem* in Hupei province.
Mid-February	Wall posters criticise Ch'i Pen-yü.
February 21	Revolutionary committee established in Kwangtung province.
March 6	*Idem* in Kirin province.
March 23	*Idem* in Kiangsu province.
March 24	*Idem* in Chekiang province.
Late March	Yang Ch'eng-wu dismissed as acting Chief of Staff and Huang Yung-sheng appointed Chief of Staff.
April 8	Revolutionary committee established in Hunan province.
April 10	*Idem* in Ninghsia Hui Autonomous Region.
April 18	*Idem* in Anhwei province.
May 1	*Idem* in Shensi province.
May 10	*Idem* in Liaoning province.

May 31	*Idem* in Szechwan province.
June–July	Serious fighting in Kwangsi and Kwangtung provinces.
August 13	Revolutionary committee established in Yunnan province.
August 19	*Idem* in Fukien province.
August 26	*Idem* in Kwangsi Chuang Autonomous Region.
September 5	*Idem* in Tibet and Sinkiang Uighur.
October 13–31	Twelfth session of the Central Committee which decides to dismiss Liu Shao-ch'i from all his functions.

1969

April 1–24	Ninth Congress of the Chinese Communist Party.
October 20	Beginning of negotiations between China and the Soviet Union on their border conflict and other problems.

1970

August 23– September 6	Second session of the Ninth Central Committee.

REFERENCE MATERIAL

Barnett, A. Doak, *Cadres, Bureaucracy, and Political Power in Communist China*, New York: Columbia U.P., 1967.

Baum, Richard, 'China: Year of the Mangoes', *Asian Survey*, 9 (1969), No. 1, pp. 1–18.

Baum, Richard and Frederick C. Teiwes, *Ssu-ch'ing: The Socialist Education Movement of 1962–66*, Berkeley, Calif.: Center for Chinese Studies, 1968.

The Case of Peng Teh-huai 1959–1968, Hong Kong: Union Research Institute, 1968.

Ch'en, Jerome (Ed.), *Mao Papers, Anthology and Bibliography*, London: Oxford U.P., 1970.

Chen Nai-ruenn, *Chinese Economic Statistics, a Handbook for Mainland China*, Chicago: Aldine, 1967.

Chung Hua-min and Arthur C. Miller, *Madame Mao, a Profile of Chiang Ch'ing*, Hong Kong: Union Research Institute, 1968.

Esmein, Jean, *La Révolution Culturelle chinoise*, Paris: Le Seuil, 1970.

Fairbank, John K., Edwin O. Reischauer and Albert M. Craig, *East Asia: The Modern Transformation*, Boston: Houghton Mifflin, 1965 (*A History of East Asian Civilisation*, Vol. 2).

Field, Robert Michael, 'Industrial Production in Communist China 1957–1968', *The China Quarterly*, 11 (1970), No. 42, pp. 46–65.

Fokkema, D. W., 'Chinese Criticism of Humanism: Campaigns Against the Intellectuals 1964–1965', *The China Quarterly*, 7 (1966), No. 26, pp. 68–81.

Fokkema, D. W., 'Chinese Literature Under the Cultural Revolution', *Literature East and West*, 13 (1969), No. 3–4, pp. 335–58.

Fokkema, D. W., *Literary Doctrine in China and Soviet Influence 1956–60*, with a Foreword by S. H. Chen, The Hague: Mouton, 1965.

Geoffroy-Dechaume, François, *China Looks at the World, Reflections for a Dialogue: Eight Letters to T'ang-lin*, translated from the French by Jean Stewart, London: Faber and Faber, 1967.

Gittings, John, *The Role of the Chinese Army*, London: Oxford U.P., 1967.

Glaubitz, Joachim, *Opposition gegen Mao, Abendgespräche am Yenshan und andere politische Dokumente*, Olten und Freiburg i.B: Walter-Verlag, 1969.

Goldman, Merle, *Literary Dissent in Communist China*, Cambridge, Mass.: Harvard U.P., 1967.

Goldman, Merle, 'The Unique "Blooming and Contending" of 1961–2', *The China Quarterly*, 10 (1969), No. 37, pp. 54–84.

The Great Cultural Revolution in China, compiled and edited by the Asia Research Centre, Rutland, Vt., and Tokyo: Charles E. Tuttle, 1968.

Ho Ping-ti and Tsou Tang (Ed.), *China's Heritage and the Communist Political System*, with a Foreword by Charles U. Daly, 2 vols., Chicago: Univ. of Chicago Press, 1968.

Hunter, Neale, *Shanghai Journal: an Eyewitness Account of the Cultural Revolution*, New York: Praeger, 1969.

Ito Kikuzo and Minoru Shibata, 'The Dilemma of Mao Tse-tung', *The China Quarterly*, 9 (1968), No. 35, pp. 58–78.

Levenson, Joseph R., *Confucian China and its Modern Fate*, 2nd ed., Berkeley and Los Angeles: Univ. of Calif. Press, 1968.

Liu Shao-ch'i, *Collected Works 1958–1967*, Hong Kong: Union Research Institute, 1968.

Lowenthal, Richard, 'Unreason and Revolution', *Encounter*, 33 (1969), No. 5, pp. 22–35.

Mao Tse-tung, *Selected Works*, 4 vols., Peking: Foreign Languages Press, 1967.

Nee, Victor and Don Layman, *The Cultural Revolution at Peking University*, New York and London: Monthly Review Press, 1969.

Powell, Ralph, 'The Party, the Government and the Gun', *Asian Survey*, 10 (1970), No. 6, pp. 441–72.

Schelochowzew, A., *Chinesische Kulturrevolution aus der Nähe, Augenzeugenbericht eines sowjetischen Beobachters*, aus dem Russischen übertragen von Joachim Glaubitz, Stuttgart: Deutsche Verlags-Anstalt, 1969.

Schram, Stuart R., 'La "révolution permanente" en Chine, Idéologie et réalité', *Revue française de science politique*, 10 (1960), No. 3, pp. 635–58.

Schram, Stuart, *Mao Tse-tung*, 2nd ed., Harmondsworth: Penguin, 1967.

Who's Who in Communist China, 2 vols., Hong Kong: Union Research Institute, 1969–70.

INDEX

(Functions before 1945 have in general not been included among the biographical data.)

182

Liu Ke-p'ing, member of the Central
Committee (1956–), chairman of the
revolutionary committee of Shansi
province (1967–), first political
commissar of the Shansi military
district and political commissar of
the Peking military region (1967–),
90–4
Liu Kuan-i, vice-chairman of the
revolutionary committee of Shansi
province (1967–8[?]), 90, 93
Liu Lan-t'ao, b. 1904, member of the
Central Committee (1956–69), first
secretary of the North-west Bureau
of the Chinese Communist Party
(1963–7), 66, 159
Liu Po ch'eng, b. 1892, marshal (1955),
member of the Central Committee
(1945–), member of the Politburo
(1956–), 158
Liu Shao-ch'i, b. 1898, member of
the Central Committee and the
Politburo (1945–68), vice-chairman
of the Chinese Communist Party
(1945–66), President of the People's
Republic of China (1959–), 7, 14,
23, 26, 32–5, 47, 50–2, 55, 58–63,
65–70, 72, 75, 81, 83, 85, 92, 98,
105, 113, 126, 128, 130, 132–3, 136,
139–40, 142, 149, 157–8, 162–3,
169
Liu T'ao, daughter of Liu Shao-ch'i,
59, 60, 67
Liu Tzu-hou, alternate member of the
Central Committee (1958–69), first
secretary of the party committee of
Hopei province (1966–7), member of
the Central Committee (1969–), 42
Liu Yün-jo, son of Liu Shao-ch'i, 68
Lo Jui-ch'ing, b. 1906, general (1955),
member of the Central Committee
(1956–69), chief of staff of the
People's Liberation Army (1959–66),
16, 58, 61–5, 122–3, 126
Lo Kuang-pin, writer, 82
Lu Hsün (1881–1936), writer, 36–7, 152
Lu P'ing, vice-minister of railways
(1954–7), vice-president of Peking

University (1957–60), president of
Peking University (1960–6), 7
Lu Ting-i, b. 1904, member of
the Central Committee (1945–69),
director of the Propaganda Department of the Central Committee
(1949–66), alternate member of the
Politburo (1956–68), minister of
culture (1965–6), 16, 58–9, 82, 158

MAO TSE-TUNG, b. 1893, one of the
founders of the Chinese Communist
Party (1921), principal leader of the
party since 1935, chairman of the
Chinese Communist Party (1945–),
President of the People's Republic
of China (1949–59), passim
Mao Tun, pseudonym of Shen Yen-
ping, b. 1896, writer, minister of
culture (1949–64), 30, 36
Marx, Karl, 28, 35, 49, 110
Matisse, H., 145
Mihajlov, Mihajlo, 38
Miyamoto Kenji, 69
Mu Hsin, journalist, member of the
Cultural Revolution group (1966–7),
137

NIEH JUNG-CHEN, b. 1899, marshal
(1955), member of the Central
Committee (1945–), chairman of the
National Scientific-Technical Commission of the State Council (1958–),
member of the Politburo (1966–9),
74
Nieh Yüan-tzu, lecturer in philosophy
at Peking University, member of the
Peking revolutionary committee
(1967–), alternate member of the
Central Committee (1969–), 7, 34–5,
84–5, 92, 127

OUYANG CH'IN, b. 1899, first secretary
of the party committee of Heilungkiang province (1956–67), member
of the Central Committee (1956–69),
159
Ouyang Shan, b. 1908, writer, 29

1967, for four days 'minister of foreign affairs' (August 1967), 106–7, 136–7

Yao Wen-yüan, b. *circa* 1925, literary critic, editor of the *Liberation Daily* (Chieh-fang jih-pao) (1966–), member of the Cultural Revolution group (1966–), member of the Central Committee and the Politburo (1969–), 5, 81, 83, 107, 121, 123, 146, 158

Yeh Chien-ying, b. 1897, marshal (1955), member of the Central Committee (1945–), chief of staff of the People's Liberation Army (1945–7), member of the Politburo (1967–), 75, 86, 158

Yeh Ch'ün, wife of Lin Piao, member of the Cultural Revolution group (1967–), member of the Central Committee and the Politburo (1969–), 59, 123, 158

Yevtushenko, Ye A., 145

Yüeh Fei (12th century), general under the Sung dynasty, 149

ZHDANOV, A. A., 15, 49